To: Helene and Henry in appreciation of your kindness during my stay in Philadelphia April 94

Regards Keith

TREASURES ON EARTH

A good housekeeping
guide to churches
and their contents

TREASURES ON EARTH

A good housekeeping guide to churches and their contents

❀

EDITED BY

Peter Burman

DONHEAD

© 1994 Donhead Publishing Ltd

Individual chapters are the copyright of
their authors. Copyright of the photographs
resides with the photographer or owner
acknowledged in the photograph's caption.

First published in the United Kingdom
in 1994 by
Donhead Publishing Ltd
28 Southdean Gardens
Wimbledon
London SW19 6NU
Tel. 081-789 0138

ISBN 1 873394 10 1

A CIP catalogue record for this book is available from the
British Library.

Typeset by Keyboard Services, Luton
Printed in Great Britain at the Alden Press,
Osney Mead, Oxford

CONTENTS

✳

vi   *Contents*

FOREWORD

�֎

The Archbishop of York,
Dr John Habgood

Philip Larkin could hardly be called an avid churchgoer. Yet his poem *Church Going*, in which he described surreptitious visits to empty country churches, has struck a chord with many Christians, and can help to underline the importance of the practical matters discussed in this book. He described how it pleased him to stand in what he called 'a frowsty barn', 'a serious house on serious earth', a place which, however hard to comprehend now, spoke of destiny.

Church buildings tell of that which lies beyond themselves, even to those for whom the language of faith seems no longer to bear a significant meaning. They are reminders of faith, and points of access to it for tens of thousands of people who are not themselves regular worshippers. The care of them by active church members is thus a responsibility held in trust for the whole nation.

A well-kept church building, which is clearly loved and prayed in, speaks of God more loudly than one of Larkin's 'frowsty barns'. I hope, therefore, that the good advice given in this book will be widely studied and followed by all those who have the care of churches. We are indeed the inheritors of many treasures on earth. But they are not only architectural treasures. They are part of our spiritual inheritance too.

JOHN EBOR:

PREFACE

✻

During the time I was Secretary of the Church of England's *Council for the Care of Churches* and the *Cathedrals Advisory Commission for England* (as it was then called) I was blessed by a remarkable team of really able and enthusiastic colleagues, especially Donald Findlay, Richard Gem, Bill Martin and David Williams, and one of the things we tried to do together was to forge a really effective publications policy so that clergy, church wardens, keen PCC members, and just about anyone with an interest in churches, chapels and cathedrals could find the information they needed – whether it was about bats and belfries, the conservation of mural paintings or church monuments, or the care of parochial records, or how to approach the care of the church building as a whole – in an attractive series of publications. One bigger idea that didn't get off the ground, for various reasons, and which Bill Martin (now with English Heritage) and I were particularly keen on was a sort of 'Good Housekeeping Guide' in which much of what was needed as a *vade mecum* for the 'care of all the churches' (as St Paul so beautifully and aptly put it) would be within the covers of one handsome book. We had to wait, as it turned out, for a supportive and imaginative publisher in the form of Jill Pearce who had faith in the idea and who has encouraged the bringing together of this volume which we hope will appeal to and be found useful by anyone of goodwill who is interested in the preservation of our ecclesiastical heritage.

It is our hope that it will be found helpful by the guardians of churches or chapels of every denomination in the United Kingdom. The various forms of rot, woodworm, and so forth are not greatly interested in varieties of religious dogma, and the problems which beset our buildings – sacred and secular – will generally be found to have their origins in a failure of basic maintenance, or an inability to see the building and its surroundings as a whole. These two factors cannot be too strongly stressed.

The chapters have been commissioned from a group of colleagues who have also become friends. All of them care passionately about the conservation of churches in the widest sense, while having their own area of special expertise. Everyone has found something fresh and stimulating to say, while emphasizing the basic truths of conservation in a way which is accessible and persuasive.

We offer the book to our readers in the confident hope that it will encourage and inspire them; and, above all, that a reading of it will lead to skilful actions and wise policies so that our sacred places may survive and continue to fulfil their vital purpose.

PETER BURMAN

There is something in a country church for everyone. They are easily accessible and, a few cathedrals apart, admission is free. There are flints and English limestones, carstone, and ironbound conglomerate for the geologist, and sandstone and granite erratics brought down from Scotland and Scandinavia in the ice. There are orchids, lichens and rare flowers and mosses for the botanist; kestrels, jackdaws, swallows and owls for the ornithologist and, for the archaeologist, the still largely undisturbed remains of early English Christianity under the soil. Churches are the home of bats, bees, mice, snakes, frogs and toads; sheep grazing in the churchyard, elusive moles, dogs, cats, the occasional cow and goat. There are organs to play, bells to ring, stained glass to photograph, inscriptions to decipher, brasses to rub, baptismal registers to study, battered cornets and tubas tucked away in vestry cupboards to dust down and blow.

Whatever your beliefs (or lack of them) learn to love churches: they are magical, mysterious places which owe their origin to powerful myths, strange houses of unseen gods and spirits, built by men of a long gone age, the product, in many cases, of a thousand years of craftsmanship and devotion, the setting (whatever you think of regular Sunday worship) for the centuries-old rituals surrounding birth, marriage and death. Country churches are living reminders of England's gripping past.

ANDREW ANDERSON

~ 1 ~

CARE OF THE CHURCH FABRIC: AN INTRODUCTION

✳

Peter Burman

Our churches are our history shown
in wood and glass and iron and stone
Churchyards, from *Poems in the Porch*,
John Betjeman, 1954

A visit to the Church of St Andrew, Pickworth, in Lincolnshire, on an early summer evening was instructive. Barbed wire fencing around the churchyard perimeter suggested that it was being grazed by sheep, an effective means of keeping the grass short in a country churchyard. The headstones are, in many cases, of slate – blueish-grey Swithland slate for the Georgian graves, up to about 1830, later ones in purplish-blue Welsh slate. But all, alike, with good lettering. There are some earlier, and a good many later, grave-markers of various kinds of natural stone. But there is a merciful absence of recent black polished granite headstones, or other mass-imported stones.

At the south porch, rebuilt in 1659, there was a sudden halt: the outer gates were padlocked. However, a large and beautifully lettered notice inside proclaimed 'Welcome to Pickworth Church' (good calligraphy is

---

1.1 Church of St Andrew, Pickworth, Lincolnshire. (Photograph by Christopher Dalton.)

a great joy when encountered in a church porch, as is fine letter-cutting and carving in churchyards); a smaller, but clearly readable, notice gave the names and addresses of the two key-holders (both churchwardens and, as it turned out, mother and daughter). So the key was readily obtained, and access gained.

Even before entering the church it was possible to notice a number of points for wider consideration. The outer gates of the porch were, as has been noticed, locked; but, happily, the celebrated south door with its magnificent early fourteenth century decorative ironwork stood wide open. Elsewhere in the building, which dates chiefly from the same period but with twelfth century Norman work in the lower part of the west tower, windows stood open, with the open casements protected by wire mesh to prevent birds from flying in and becoming trapped. So the first great lesson in conserving an old church (or any other substantial old building) had been acted upon: good through ventilation, which prevents condensation and reduces the danger of fungal decay.

A walk round the outside of the church showed that vegetation was being kept clear of the walls, that the lead roof covering of the nave had a considerable overhang so that rain might drip down clear of the clerestorey walls, that the weathering surfaces on top of the buttresses had been covered with lead to protect them from water penetration, that the pointing (though varied) had mostly – over the years – been carried out using soft lime mortar, and that there was a general unobtrusive air of well-being.

Inside, a similar story was evident. The first pleasure was to encounter the warm stone steps leading down into the church, and the many attractive floor textures and surfaces throughout the building which were allowed to speak for themselves instead of being drowned, as is often the case, in suburban carpeting. There are areas of tiles (including good nineteenth century tiles, and some earlier ones), areas of stone paving, ledger stones, and so forth.

In addition to the welcoming notice there was both a guide leaflet, *A Walk Round the Church*, and, most enterprisingly, for a modest 50 pence you could buy a visually attractive and informative broadsheet which, using excellent drawings and good calligraphy, explained the iconography of the well-known mural paintings (a *Doom*, a *St Christopher*, a *Weighing of Souls*, the *Three Living and the Three Dead*). The broadsheet also drew attention to the outstanding fourteenth century Decorated window tracery in the chancel, the headless but handsome and richly polychromed figure sculpture of a female

1.2 Church of St Andrew, Pickworth, Lincolnshire. (Photograph by Christopher Dalton.)

saint in the south aisle, and the decorative wrought ironwork on the south door. A positive note was struck in the message at the foot of the broadsheet explaining how:

> The continuity of Christian worship, spanning almost a third of the Christian era, enriches our worship in Pickworth today. We have inherited St Andrew's as our forefathers built it and enriched it. We are inheritors, with them, of faith, and similarly plagued by fear and superstition... We have been greatly honoured and supported by the interest of HRH Charles, Prince of Wales, who visited St Andrew's especially to see the mural conservation on 23rd November 1988.

A particular pleasure of churches is that, by using one's powers of observation, it is possible to learn or deduce much about their history and development. At Pickworth, for example, the two-decker pulpit is dated 1693 — no argument about that; while the altar rails, which look seventeenth century, are dated 1767 and signed 'Jos. Dabell fecit'. A modest exhibition (which is within the powers of any parish to organize) in the north aisle tells of the rediscovery of the mural paintings, under layers of limewash, in 1947, and relates something also of the conservation programme begun by Dr Clive Rouse and continued, and recently completed, by Ann Ballantyne. A notice by the entrance door explains how, in 1966, an award was made to the master craftsman John Herbert Palin who, under the direction of the church's then inspecting architect, Lawrence Bond of Grantham, expertly repaired the outstanding finely carved wooden chancel screen.

Many aspects of the care of churches are invisible (or should be), others readily discernible, but taking Pickworth as our prompt and gathering together the threads of experience the following broad principles are suggested for our care of the church fabric.

1. Adopt a simple strategy for regular maintenance, the simpler (and therefore the more easily understood) the better. Write it down, discuss it in the Parochial Church Council (or other local church or chapel committee), and see that a copy is posted up in the vestry or church porch.

2. Appoint someone to be responsible for the maintenance strategy, perhaps with the title of 'Fabric Officer'. It might be a churchwarden, the clergyman, or other existing office holder; or it might be someone

1.3 Church of St Catherine, Little Bardfield, Essex. An oil drum is employed as a substitute for a proper drainage system. (Photograph by Donald E. Smith.)

else in the community who feels able and willing to make this particular contribution toward the care of their local church or chapel. Whoever it is, he or she must know what they are looking for and patient study of the Council for the Care of Churches' two key publications *How to Look After Your Church* and *A Guide to Church Inspection and Repair* will be found invaluable in this respect, as in others.

3. The most fundamental part of a maintenance strategy is regular visual inspection linked with good record-keeping. For example, it is a good idea to walk slowly round the outside of the church, and then to examine the inside, once a month – say on the first Sunday or Saturday of the month, so that it becomes as regular as clockwork and part of normal routine. It is a useful practice to keep a diary of such inspections, and also (since many of us can handle a camera) to take photographs.

Outside the church the vigilant eye will notice if gutters are cracked or leaking, or blocked (it is a good idea, from time to time, to carry out such inspections while it is actually raining); if soakaways and drains seem not to be functioning properly; if vegetation is encroaching too closely to the walls; if vegetation is growing in the gutters; if windows are cracked or broken; if there are signs of vandalism, or attempted intrusion; if unexpected cracks have appeared, or widened; if there are open joints in masonry or brickwork, suggesting a need for local areas of repointing; and if there are any other signs of water penetration, damage to rainwater goods, or any other changes since the last inspection.

Inside the church the equally vigilant eye will take a general look at standards of good housekeeping as regards the wooden furniture, carpets and other textiles, the metalwork, the floor surfaces, and so forth. But perhaps the most helpful action will be to keep a sharp look-out for any hint of water penetration as this could lead to wet or dry rot or other damage, and to possible expensive repairs if not dealt with quickly and sensibly, for, as Sir Christopher Wren remarked in the late seventeenth century, 'Drips come suddenly, and do great mischief'. It is also a good idea to look out for signs of furniture beetles (for example, cream-coloured dust), or death-watch beetle, or bat droppings. It is necessary to be especially vigilant during the months of April and May.

4. All that has hitherto been suggested can be achieved by any

observant person who is prepared to give a modest amount of time to adopting a regular monthly routine, and to make clear and accurate notes in an ordinary exercise book. The next challenge is to make effective use of good professional help. In an Anglican context (but readily adaptable to other churches and circumstances) this centres on making a good choice of an inspecting architect (so-called because the primary duty is to make a quinquennial inspection of the church, concluding with recommendations for action based on an order of priorities), and then making good use of the relationship. Two excellent Anglican publications (already mentioned), *A Guide to Church Inspection and Repair*, and *How to Look After Your Church*, give the gist of what is required and what is desirable in this area; and the advice they contain should be interpreted in the light of recent Church of England *Care of Churches* legislation. A *Care of Cathedrals Measure* similarly provides a framework of legislation and good practice for cathedrals. Some other churches, notably the Church of Scotland and the Church in Wales and the Methodist Church, have produced their own publications of guidance.

But it is perhaps worth saying here that the effective use of professional skills (which, inevitably, costs money) depends upon having a truly effective working relationship between the church authorities and the architect. If an inspecting architect visits once every five years to produce a report, and nothing is seen or heard of him or her between visits, then the relationship can scarcely be said to be working. First, therefore, trouble should be taken over the selection of an architect (or, for that matter, of other professional advisers when needed). In the Church of England context the Diocesan Advisory Committee (DAC) will give advice on suitable architects (and indeed must give its approval to the choice). Advice may also be sought from the local authority Conservation Officer, and from the national amenity societies (chosen according to the date of the church), namely the Society for the Protection of Ancient Buildings (37 Spital Square, London E1 6DY), the Ancient Monuments Society (St Andrews-by-the-Wardrobe, Queen Victoria Street, London EC4V 5DE), the Georgian Group (37 Spital Square, London E1 6DY), the Victorian Society (1 Priory Gardens, Bedford Park, London W4 1TT), or the Twentieth Century Society (58 Crescent Lane, London SW4 9PU). In Scotland, recourse should be had to the Architectural Heritage Society of Scotland and, in Northern Ireland, to the Ulster Architectural Heritage Society. It is worth remembering that, while there are many architects who are good 'all-rounders', others make a special career in the repair and care of old buildings. Nineteenth or twentieth century churches (and other buildings of these periods) require particular skills and knowledge, so it is worth seeking out architects who really know these specialist fields.

A list of names and addresses is one thing, even if it comes with authoritative advice; but it is good practice for the Fabric Officer or parish committee to interview two or more potential architects if the relationship is to become a real one. Points to register when selecting include whether the architect has attended courses on the care of old buildings (such as those run by the Centre for Conservation Studies, Institute of Advanced Architectural Studies, at the University of York, or the Society for the Protection of Ancient Buildings); whether he or she seems familiar with the publications of the SPAB, English Heritage, or other literature concerned with conservation; whether he or she is prepared, at no extra charge, to come and explain the inspection report to the relevant church committee; what evidence they can give of their track record, enthusiasm, and so forth.

It is worth bearing in mind that some church work (for example, liturgical re-ordering, lighting schemes, additions and extensions) requires particular design skills. The primary emphasis for the church architect should be in the field of care and repair of the existing building; if new design work is needed and falls also within their scope, then well and good. But, otherwise, special design skills can be brought in later as required; and after appropriate consultation with the church's architect.

The continuity of a relationship is important, so it is best if great care is taken over the choice of an architect and that both sides then take proper care to ensure that their relationship really works. If the relationship breaks down, the fact should be openly and honestly acknowledged; a fresh selection of a new advisor may then be made, otherwise, the building will suffer. A further point worth making is that a church architect should never be chosen on the basis of competitive tendering; this is no basis for a proper professional relationship and should be resisted. Good professional advice is worth a great deal, bad advice less than nothing.

5. All other specialists should be chosen on a similar basis, taking into account the advice of the architect and (where appropriate and available) the relevant church authority. All advice given conscientiously, and without self-interest, is worth attending to; but the relationship with the church architect will suffer if decisions are

taken without offering him (or her) the opportunity to make suggestions, give advice and to talk through the possibilities. Advice from the
local jobbing builder (or other such) should never be taken as deter-
minative. Although the best possible church care will be provided
by the faithful vigilance of local people, examples of the kinds of
specialist advice which may, from time to time, be needed include the
following:

- The archaeologist, usually the county or diocesan archaeologist;
  in Scotland the voluntary archaeology service is organized by
  the Council for Scottish Archaeology, which has a network of
  advisors. The Council for Scottish Archaeology is also compil-
  ing a country-wide inventory of church buildings and sites,
  which will clearly be extremely useful.
- The architectural or art-historian (if such are needed, the
  national amenity societies can advise).
- The archivist, generally the county archivist (or, in Scotland,
  the archivist to the Regional Council).
- The structural engineer, who will normally be suggested by the
  architect.
- The conservator (for example, the conservator of woodwork,
  whether painted or plain; the conservator of mural paintings or
  other decorative painting; the conservator of monuments,
  or other sculpture; of textiles; of books and archives; and
  so forth). The conservator will usually be suggested by the
  architect, or by bodies such as the Council for the Care of
  Churches and English Heritage. In Scotland a helpful source of
  advice about conservation and conservators is the Conservation
  Bureau operated by Historic Scotland at 3 Stenhouse Mill Lane,
  Edinburgh EH11 3LR.
- The organ builder.
- The arboriculturalist and tree surgeon.
- People knowledgeable about grasses, wild flowers, birds and
  bats.
- The skilled craftsmen working in stone, brick, lime mortars and
  plasters, wood, and so forth.
- Heating and lighting engineers (whose technical competence
  may be beyond reproach, yet who may not be aware – or much
  aware – of the special factors which apply in relation to old
  buildings generally, or to churches in particular, or to archaeological, historic or aesthetic factors).

6. At this point it may be worth noting that, just as almost everything in life may be viewed either positively or negatively, so virtually everything to do with the care of churches may be regarded either as an opportunity or a nuisance. If regarded as an opportunity, then many creative actions will follow. For example, all over Britain excellent letter-cutters and carvers are to be found and a wise church council will have a firm policy for the introduction of new grave markers, insisting on good local materials (or at least appropriate materials) and the employment of good lettering. Even the simplest church notice is an opportunity for good lettering, whether professional or amateur.

The commissioning of new furniture, new stained glass, new vestments, or whatever, should be treated as an opportunity for adding something special to the church, for the growing and development of the church community. As with churchyard memorials, a specially commissioned work from an artist-craftsman is by no means prohibitively expensive or necessarily more expensive than a mass-produced machine-made object, designed without thought of context or significance. Advice may be sought from the regional Arts Councils, and from the various national bodies in London, Edinburgh, Glasgow and Cardiff whose details are given in Chapter 17, Conclusion and Sources of Advice. Commissioning grants may sometimes be available.

7. Grants for the repair (but not maintenance) of churches in use are available, on conditions carefully evolved and regularly evaluated, from the relevant national bodies. In England the Historic Churches Preservation Trust gives grants in appropriate cases to churches of all denominations. In Scotland, the Historic Buildings Council is the channel for state funding of church repair, and the equivalent of the Historic Churches Preservation Trust is the Scottish Churches Architectural Heritage Trust. In Wales, the Historic Buildings Council is again the channel for state funding for church repairs, though the Historic Churches Preservation Trust covers Wales as well as England.

8. It ought to go without saying that every intervention (whether of repair or new work) in a church or chapel should be an exemplar, setting an example to the whole local community. A neglected and apparently unloved building, in uncared-for surroundings, must be a discouragement and disincentive – whether to a regular or a potential church-goer, or to a visitor. By contrast, a building which is open (or, anyway,

accessible by means of obtaining the key), welcoming, visibly cherished and cared for, will spark off interest and enthusiasm in all who visit or encounter it. A single positive or negative experience can change lives, so churches have a special responsibility for setting a good example in the following areas:

(a) Ecological soundness (for example, bats deserve cherishing as well as mural paintings, though it has to be confessed that there is sometimes a conflict of interest here).

(b) Responsiveness to local distinctiveness in materials, craft techniques, style, textures, and so forth.

(c) Use of traditional materials and techniques which will invariably be found to be best when it comes to the care and repair of a building of, say, pre-1840. For later buildings, innovative materials and techniques may be used, though a thorough understanding of nineteenth and twentieth century building materials and methods will be the surest guide.

(d) In all older (i.e. pre-1840) buildings, and indeed many later ones, it is essential, in repair work, to use materials which are less rigid than the original ones and especially to insist on the use of lime mortars for repointing and replastering.

(e) Work should not be undertaken (in either church or churchyard) without proper authorization, as appropriate. This may be planning permission (for example, for any 'development', which includes changes in material for a roof covering), listed building consent (dependent upon decisions relating to the 'ecclesiastical exemption'), or the Church of England's system of faculty control (for churches) and the network of Fabric Advisory Committees and the national Cathedrals Fabric Commission for England (for cathedrals).

(f) All work should be properly recorded, and the whereabouts of the documentation clearly identified in a log book (which is obligatory for Anglican churches, and sensible for all other churches). Depositing the documentation in a county record office is one way to ensure its survival for future generations.

(g) All furnishings and works of art should be properly recorded in an inventory, with descriptions and photographs. It is preferable for there to be at least two copies of an inventory, one kept locally and the other in a record office and it is prudent for the contents to be kept reasonably confidential so that the inventory does not become a thieves' guide.

CONCLUSION

To sum up, it may be said that, properly and positively understood, the care of churches is a pleasure on the one hand, and on the other an opportunity to combine both conservation and creativity in a way which is enriching to a spiritual community and an encouraging example to the wider community. To be effective, care of a church building, in a particular place needs only one person willing to commit a certain amount of time and energy to motivate others and to be a channel of good communication for both volunteer help and good professional advice and skills.

A regular maintenance strategy will prevent damage getting out of hand, and lay a secure foundation for further action. The carrying out of quinquennial inspections of churches, by suitably qualified architects and building surveyors, makes a fundamental contribution to the care of churches and chapels within the Church of England and wherever else it has become part of established practice. However, the usefulness of such reports is only fully realized if there is committed local vigilance, and a pattern of regular action, following the recommendations laid down in the report.

Let us give the last word in this chapter to John Ruskin, from *The Seven Lamps of Architecture*, first published in 1849:

> Take proper care of your monuments, and you will not need to restore them. A few sheets of lead put in time upon the roof, a few dead leaves and sticks swept in time out of a water-course, will save both roof and walls from ruin. Watch an old building with an anxious care; guard it as best you may, and at *any* cost, from every influence of dilapidation. Count its stones as you would jewels of a crown; set watches about it as if at the gates of a besieged city; bind it together with iron where it loosens; stay it with timber where it declines; do not care about the unsightliness of the aid: better a crutch than a lost limb; and do this tenderly, and reverently, and continually, and many a generation will still be born and pass away beneath its shadow.

PETER BURMAN

Peter Burman was born in Warwickshire and, from an early age, became absorbed in studying the architecture and history of the parish churches of his native county. After reading History of Art at Cambridge he became successively Assistant Secretary, Deputy Secretary, and (from 1977–1989) Secretary of the Council for the Care of Churches and the Cathedrals Advisory Commission for England and, during this time, he and Marcus Binney researched and mounted a major exhibition at the Victoria and Albert Museum in London entitled *Change and Decay: The Future of our Churches*. Since 1989 he has been Director of the Centre for Conservation Studies at the University of York which, as he says, 'provides a unique platform for disseminating the practical skills of building conservation and for following in the footsteps, however humbly, of John Ruskin, William Morris, W.R. Lethaby and A.R. Powys'. He is Chairman of the Fabric Advisory Committee of St Paul's Cathedral, London, a member of the Fabric Advisory Committees of Durham and Lincoln Cathedrals, Vice-Chairman of the Society for the Protection of Ancient Buildings, and lives on the edge of the North Yorkshire Moors.

~ 2 ~

HEATING AND VENTILATION

Colin Bemrose

Until about 150 years ago, churches were essentially unheated and the fact that so many mediaeval and earlier buildings have survived in a good state of repair indicates the soundness of their design and construction. A well-heated church is a Victorian invention and a late twentieth century expectation. Over the past 40 years most people have come to expect buildings to be warmer largely because of the rapid growth of domestic central heating and warm cars. For most churches with large volumes, massive and poorly insulated construction and relatively low intensity of use, heating to the standards demanded in the home would be prohibitively expensive, apart from the danger of causing undesirable effects on the structure and fabric of the church itself. The problem is aggravated by the low efficiency of many existing church heating systems and the financial problems of trying to use those systems to maximum advantage. The spiral of reducing congregations resulting from uncomfortable conditions, resulting in reduced funds for heating, has led many churches to change to new systems which claim improved comfort and lower running costs. However, when making such changes the effect on the building itself and its contents is often given inadequate consideration. A more efficient system may mean that less heat is put into the building and this will usually result in the building becoming damper. Thus it is important to consider church heating as part of the total building operation.

Heating and ventilation have two main purposes. Firstly there is a need to provide comfortable internal conditions for worshippers and visitors. Secondly, the fabric of the building must be maintained and preserved effectively as part of the nation's heritage. These two purposes are often difficult to reconcile and when overlaid with financial constraints on installation and running costs, the solutions are by no means obvious.

HEATING

Heating and comfort

Air temperature is often used as a measure of comfort conditions. However, surface temperatures, air movement and thermal radiation are almost equally as important in determining comfort. Comfort is also markedly affected by mode of dress and when physiological factors are ignored, erroneous decisions are easily made. In order to achieve the desired comfort conditions for an hour or so, vast quantities of heat may be pumped into the building for a very short time. This may give comfortable conditions for the occupants, but is equally likely to result in substantial air movement (thermally or mechanically generated) and the loss of much of the heat from the higher parts of the building. Such heating regimes may also cause rapid changes of humidity so that the building fabric is subjected to serious stress from the changes of both temperature and humidity. The attainment of comfort conditions cannot be divorced from consideration of the building fabric.

Heating and protection/preservation

Provided a building is weatherproof there should be little deterioration even if it is unheated and unvisited. The problems arise when people visit the building and bring in moisture by respiration and possibly on wet clothing. The problems become worse when those visitors require some measure of physiological comfort. Moisture levels are not readily sensed by humans, but their magnitude can have dramatic effects on the building's fabric and its contents. As temperature is to comfort, relative humidity is to preservation and there is a major potential conflict between the needs of the church and its contents, and the desire to reduce heating costs by the use of quickly responding heating systems. Moderate conditions are best; excessive dryness can cause organic materials to crack and crumble; dampness leads to rot and corrosion; and fluctuations cause condensation and dimensional changes. It is often assumed that drying automatically accompanies heating. However, this is only certain when there is continuous heating and plentiful ventilation. Heating alone may not solve the growing problem of dampness, which results from a combination of three effects:

+ The prevalence of intermittent heating.
+ The increasing use of heating appliances which do not require combustion air drawn from within the church.
+ Efforts to seal the building and reduce draughts.

Heating and aesthetics

When planning a new heating (or environmental control) system in a historic building the question of aesthetics needs careful consideration. Not only does the appearance matter but also other impacts on the environment and its users. It is quite possible to install a system which provides the desired physical conditions but is noisy or may in the long term cause thermophoretic deposition of dust particles in sensitive areas. These potential problems need to be evaluated carefully before installation. Likewise the possibilities of fire, leakage, explosion and fumes must also be considered.

Ventilation

Ventilation can be the major source of heat loss and therefore needs to be examined carefully. Ventilation includes natural air movement through doors, windows, the roof structure and through cracks and interstices in the building itself. The amount of natural ventilation varies markedly according to wind speed and direction, the state of the building fabric and the temperature gradients which exist inside, and between the inside and outside of the building. Air change rates in churches tend to be very low, but the total volume of air moving through the building can be very large. At least some of this ventilation air movement is necessary to carry away excess moisture which may be generated within the building. Control of the ventilation rate may be desirable as a means of controlling the heat losses, but adequate ventilation must be ensured to maintain the desired humidity levels.

Draughts

At room temperature air movement exceeding 0.15 metres per second becomes noticeable and at twice this speed it becomes unpleasant. Colder air is perceptible at lower speeds. Draughts may arise from openings (lobbies, windows etc.) or may result from strong convection currents, appearing as downdraughts. Isolating towers can significantly reduce draughts. Turning up the heating may aggravate convection generated draughts. Local heating may ameliorate the problem; operating the heating for longer at reduced output may also help.

Humidity and condensation

Water vapour is always present in the atmosphere, and the amount of vapour which can be carried by the air (the saturation humidity) depends on the temperature. At 20°C each cubic metre can contain about 20 grams of water vapour. In the temperature range of interest, saturation humidity roughly doubles for every 5°C rise in temperature. Likewise most building materials contain water vapour and an equilibrium is established between the solid and the air. This equilibrium depends not on absolute humidity but on the relative humidity, which varies with temperature for a given value of absolute moisture content. Thus without any change of the amount of water vapour present in the building, the equilibrium between solid and air is disturbed by a change of temperature.

When air comes into contact with a cooler surface, the relative humidity rises and if the surface is cold enough for the air to reach saturation humidity (the dew point), condensation will occur. Condensed moisture may run off the cold surface, or it may collect there, or it may be absorbed into the solid. Windows, window sills, and plaster are, respectively, examples of these three phenomena. When the dew point is reached at the surface of, say, a stone wall, condensation will be obvious. However, since there will be a temperature gradient across the wall of a heated building, the dew point may be reached somewhere inside the wall and give rise to interstitial condensation. This damaging situation may persist for a long time before its effects are noticed. It is particularly prevalent where insulation has been applied internally or foam backed carpets fitted to floors.

Buildings which are only intermittently heated are especially prone to condensation problems due to the temperature (and hence relative humidity) cycling which occurs. Ideally relative humidities should be maintained in the range 45–65 per cent, although 40–70 per cent is probably acceptable in many cases. Sustained higher relative humidities give rise to high moisture levels in, for example, timber which is then subject to increased risk of rot.

A further condensation problem can occur if the outside temperature exceeds the inside temperature as sometimes happens in the spring and autumn. Cooling of the air entering the building by infiltration can result in warm weather condensation, which can be overcome by heating or by using a dehumidifier. Under more usual conditions, when the inside is warmer than the outside, ventilation can result in the replacement of air with a high absolute humidity by air with a lower absolute humidity. In order to maintain a sufficient constancy of the moisture equilibrium it may be necessary to provide ventilation in excess of the natural infiltration, either by passive means (such as opening windows) or mechanically.

The question of condensation and dampness is considered further in Chapter 5, Mural Painting and the Fabric.

Stratification

Since warm air rises, temperatures at the top of a lofty building will be significantly higher than those near the floor. Heating bills can be reduced if this warm air is returned to floor level by a fan system. Unfortunately research has shown that heat reaching an uninsulated roof is rapidly lost through the structure so that destratification fans are often of very limited value. It is vital to check temperatures at high level before committing expenditure on this type of equipment.

HEATING MECHANISMS – PRACTICAL SYSTEMS

Fuels and heat generation

The choice of fuel may be extensive or may be limited by local availability. Almost all locations have electricity available, but since this is principally generated from fossil fuels at a maximum of about 34 per cent efficiency, it is expensive to use for direct heating purposes. Some forms of direct electric heating can be very rapid in their results and this may give economic justification. Under-pew heaters can fall into this category, possibly as a supplement to some other form of background heating. Commercial considerations have led the electricity companies to offer off-peak electricity at very favourable rates for use with storage heaters but this advantage is financially driven and could change at any time. Many different tariffs are available and should be reassessed periodically. Not all electricity companies will take the initiative in suggesting a more advantageous tariff, but they usually respond helpfully when requested. Electricity has the advantage of not requiring any on-site storage facility.

Natural gas is a common choice where it is available, and often represents the cheapest fuel. It also does not require local storage. Natural gas mains are being extended further into rural areas so that an increasing number of churches have this option. Modern gas-burning appliances can have combustion efficiencies up to 90 per cent or more.

Solid fuels, oil, and liquefied petroleum gas (LPG) are available anywhere but must be stored locally. This needs space, but also means that the supply is assured when stocks are held. However, most heating systems also require an electricity supply for the control and pumping system, so that the advantage of local storage is lost unless the cost of a portable generator can be justified by extreme unreliability of the electricity supply. Storage needs careful consideration. For solid fuels it can become unsightly, or if left against an outside wall can ultimately damage the wall. Overground oil tanks can also be unsightly. Underground tanks can be used with suitable precautions but then require pumping of the oil to the boiler.

Electricity (or other fuels) can be used in heat pumps which essentially use a refrigeration cycle in reverse. Heat is extracted from outside air, or a water source such as a lake, and transferred into the building by means of warm water or warm air. The heat output is greater than the (electrical) energy consumed and the ratio of the two is the 'Coefficient of Performance'. However, they are expensive to install and not very suitable for intermittent heating applications in historic buildings.

Mention must be made of solar heating. Much of the incoming solar energy is stored in the structure of heavyweight historic buildings and smooths the internal temperature. Old churches tend to be cool inside in the summer and warmer than the outside in winter. Solar gain through windows can be beneficial, but the same windows cause much heat loss overnight unless they are suitably shaded. This passive solar heating is a small but important element in the total heating. Active solar heating using fashionable solar collectors is unlikely to be cost effective for old buildings in the UK.

Whatever fuel is used, it must be converted into heat. This can be done centrally and the heat itself distributed around the building (usually as hot water or warm air), or the fuel can be distributed and converted into heat at the point of need. Solid fuels nowadays are almost always used centrally (although in the early days of church heating individual coke burners were common). Electricity is usually converted into heat in individual appliances. Natural gas can be used in either way, as can oil, although the latter is more commonly used in central plant. LPG may be used centrally or can be used in free standing 'Calor' gas heaters.

Whenever fossil fuels are burnt consideration must be given to the supply of combustion air and removal of the products of combustion. Modern appliances can have considerable freedom for the siting of the flues but do still require access to the outside within a few metres. The only exceptions are some large natural gas fired air heaters and free standing LPG heaters where the products of combustion are allowed into the heated space. Flue requirements may limit the type of equipment which can be installed.

Many smaller gas fired heaters are now available in room sealed versions. In these the combustion air is drawn directly from outside the heated space and the products of combustion are flued back outside. These appliances can reduce heat losses by ventilation and draughts associated with the ingress of combustion air near the appliance, but care must be taken that reduced ventilation does not upset the humidity balance. Electric heaters have no need of flues.

Heat emitters

Whatever source of fuel is used, the heat generated has to be emitted into the space to be heated, whether the emission is of radiant energy or of warm air. The emitters are the elements of any system which will be seen within the building and they are therefore subject to aesthetic as well as technical constraints. Some techniques, such as underfloor heating, can be made almost totally invisible by using existing parts of the structure; others, such as some forms of overhead radiant heating, may be very intrusive visually. Not all the products offered by manufacturers have a satisfactory appearance, but there is a wide choice and no client should feel pressurized into buying products which are deemed unacceptable in the particular setting.

Radiant heaters

All bodies emit electromagnetic radiation, the total quantity of which increases very rapidly as the temperature rises. The average wave-length of the radiation falls as the temperature rises so that four categories can be described:

1. Short wave (white heat).
2. Medium wave (red heat).
3. Long wave (black heat).
4. Low temperature thermal (normal hot water radiators).

The hotter sources are more intense, so that the areas required for a given heat output are approximately in the ratios 1:20:300:4000. Air is relatively transparent to short wave radiation, but water vapour absorbs some longer wavelengths strongly. The main advantage of radiant heating is that the heat can be directed to those parts or those people who need to be heated and is not expended heating up the air and the building structure unnecessarily. However, the radiant source needs to be reasonably close to the people being heated since radiation intensity decreases in proportion to the square of the distance. Short wave radiation contributes to a greater feeling of well-being since it can penetrate clothing and skin more effectively than long wave radiation.

Short wave radiant heaters Short wave radiant heaters are always electric, usually electric lamps, and often with integral reflectors. The visible light can be filtered out if this is a problem. Rapid response makes these heaters good for improving local comfort quickly, but some form of background heating may be needed for building preser-vation. For sustained heating, the running costs may be unacceptable.

Medium wave radiant heaters Medium wave radiant heaters may be either electric or gas fired and usually emit a red to yellow glow. The electric units are often heating coils encased in a silica tube and mounted on a wall or suspended from a ceiling. Gas fired units are more powerful than their electric counterparts but can be slightly noisy. Portable versions are available but for safety reasons should only be considered for temporary use. Most of these gas heaters are flueless and care must be taken over their installation and main-tenance, while also recognizing that for every 7 kilowatts of power output about 1 litre per hour of water vapour will be added to the atmosphere in the building.

Long wave radiant heaters Long wave radiant heaters, using either gas or electricity, operate at about 300°C and produce what is often referred to as 'black heat'. They are usually long and tubular, and mounted at high level. The gas fired units often have fan-assisted flues, and a reflector behind the tube. Electric versions may be either strip heaters or the less efficient panel heaters, which have no reflector. These heaters are less suitable for occasional heating than the other radiant types.

Low temperature thermal heaters Many of these heaters are on the borderline between radiant and convective heating. Water heated panel radiators operating at 45–80°C emit about 50 per cent radiant energy and can permit personal comfort at slightly reduced air temperatures. Wall, floor and ceiling heating, operating only a few degrees Celsius above ambient can improve comfort conditions, but are usually slow acting and are most suitable for continuously heated buildings or for background heating. The large area panels or embedded pipes or electric elements can be expensive to install, and even more expensive to repair if damage or breakdown occurs. Effective insulation is most important behind the elements.

Convector heaters
Most heaters are predominantly convective, including many units commonly referred to as 'radiators'. There are two main types: natural convectors which use the buoyancy of warm air to provide circulation and promote heat transfer, and forced convectors which use a fan to assist the circulation.

Radiators Many different patterns of radiator are in use, ranging from the traditional cast iron types to the common pressed steel units (with or without convector fins on the rear), to units made from assemblies of aluminium castings. In the early days of circulated water heating, the aim was simply to provide a sufficient surface area of water pipe to give the required thermal characteristics. This gave rise to the use of large bore pipes and large water content with the corresponding slow warm-up and response. In some cases 'radiators' were made by providing additional lengths of pipe in a self-contained unit. Some of these have been particularly well maintained for example in the parish church of St Mary the Virgin at Great Brickhill.

Natural convection heaters In these devices, some form of secondary surface is usually included so that the area in contact with the air is larger than that in contact with the heat source. A common type includes a water-containing tube with gills or fins attached to the outside by welding, or mechanical pressure, or extrusion. They are often encased in some form of enclosure so that air enters at the base and exits near the top. The heaters may be long and thin, placed near the skirting board or under windows, or they may be individual units located on walls. In churches they are also commonly placed within floor trenches and covered with metal grilles. Those convectors where the heating element is enclosed can suffer considerable degradation of performance due to dust and dirt. They are often inaccessible but efforts should nevertheless be made to provide regular cleaning.

Natural convectors inevitably cause the heated air to rise so that heat and air distribution are often not good. Suitably placed units can, however, counteract downdraughts from windows, clerestories and the like. In high buildings much of the heat can be dissipated ineffectively above the congregation's head. There can be a tendency for thermophoretic deposition of fine dust on surfaces just above the heaters.

Forced convection heaters Greatly increased heat output can be obtained by using a fan to force air through a heat exchanger. The air outlets may also be directional to ensure that the heated air is discharged where it will heat appropriate parts of the building and its occupants rather than just rising to roof level. Rapid warm-up is a further beneficial feature of this type of heat emitter. Fan speed can be varied according to heat output requirements and to give control over noise. Many units are very quiet, but air movement inevitably produces a certain amount of noise which may be unacceptable in particularly sensitive environments. The rapid temperature changes associated with forced air convection heating can also cause rapid changes of relative humidity and give rise to building stress brought on by moisture movement into and out of walls and woodwork. Pipe organs may be particularly prone to problems of this sort, and may also change their tuning as the temperature varies.

Forced convection heaters may be supplied with hot water from a boiler system (when they are known as fan convectors) or they may be oil or gas fired. Fired convectors often blow air across a heat exchanger which contains the products of the burning fuel. A flue is used to remove the products of combustion, and this may be either a natural draught flue (or chimney) or a balanced flue, or a fan powered flue. Some types of gas fired heater simply pass fresh air over a burning flame and blow the heated air together with the products of combustion (and its associated moisture) into the heated space. Often a single large heater is used for the entire building which is effectively pressurized to a slight extent so that air leaves the building through all crevices. This system gives rapid warm-up and the best possible thermal efficiency. It is economical on internal space requirements but can suffer from noise, and moisture problems as well as stratification under some conditions.

Central heating

When the fuel source is converted to heat in a central location the heat generated must be distributed throughout the building. The medium most commonly used is water at low pressure, although high pressure hot water systems were often used at the end of the last century because of the higher temperatures thus achieved. Air circulation systems can be used to distribute the heat but these are not often appropriate in old churches. Steam is a further heat transfer medium but is rarely used for space heating outside industry. Special thermal oils can provide higher temperature operation without the pressure penalty, but these are little used.

When solid fuels were universal, central heating gave advantages of:

+ Cleanliness.
+ Space utilization (because combustion was removed from the church).
+ Improved thermal efficiency.
+ Controllability.
+ Lower capital and maintenance costs.
+ Reduced fire risk.

Nowadays a central system is not necessarily the most cost effective or practical solution. Points which need to be evaluated include:

+ Convenience (for operation and maintenance).
+ Flexibility (ability to modify the system and adapt to different fuels).
+ Thermal efficiency (central plant is not necessarily more efficient).
+ Controls (modern controls offer more design freedom).

• Benefits of using standard mass produced units.
• Expected life.

Many old wet central heating systems still exist, often with so-called gravity circulation, although usually now fitted with a booster or accelerator pump. Modern systems always use pumped circulation which permits smaller pipe sizes, lower installation cost, less water content and faster response. Most water systems require a feed and expansion tank at high level. This can give rise to potential problems due to freezing, leaking, and increased humidity levels near to roof timbers. Some systems dispense with this tank and use a separate pressurization unit.

For premises which are extensively used, the installation of a condensing boiler, especially in a multi-boiler system, should be considered.

Efficiency

Efficiency values are commonly quoted for all types of equipment, though they are not all compatible with each other, and can be misleading. Electric heaters are often rated at 98–100 per cent efficiency, which is correct at the point of use but does not take account of the efficiency of generation of the electricity from a fossil fuel. Many gas fired appliances quote efficiencies in the range 70–90 per cent (or even 100 per cent for direct fired equipment) but fail to note that this does not take account of part load performance or intermittent use. So-called seasonal efficiencies are a better guide but may still not be appropriate for the type of heating schedule usually employed in churches. There is still sometimes confusion over the efficiency of gas fired appliances. In the United Kingdom gross calorific value is used whereas in continental Europe it is common to use the nett calorific value. For natural gas this can give efficiencies up to 15 percentage points higher.

Monitoring of system performance should be undertaken. The regular checking of meter readings can indicate unexpected changes. This is more reliable than simple scrutiny of quarterly energy bills.

Calculations

When designing a system, standard methods are available for conventional buildings. These are often based on the use of 'U'-values for elements of the structure and a design outside temperature (usually $-1°C$). However, for a church building with massive walls and especially one which is only intermittently heated, the steady state conditions implied by 'U'-value calculations are rarely achieved. Although heat losses may typically be 1 watt per cubic metre of church volume per degree Celsius between inside and outside temperature, the thermal capacity of the walls may be the most important factor in determining the rate of heating achieved.

CONTROLS

An environmental regime which is satisfactory for both fabric and users can, in principle, be designed. However, practical maintenance of that regime needs to be assured. Occasionally there may be an appropriate person who can control the installed system and maintain temperature, humidity and ventilation, efficiency and running cost as desired, but normally some measure of automatic control is vital. While it may be thought desirable to allow or encourage individuals to make adjustments or turn heaters on and off when it is felt necessary, this may not give either the best environmental conditions, or the highest efficiency of use, or the most economical heating. Because people's comfort perceptions differ, it is necessary to control the environment to a mutually acceptable level and to limit individual control, otherwise the premises may be overheated or not heated at all for the next users. This is especially true for systems and buildings with slow response times. The use of individual portable heaters, whether they are electric or gas, is therefore recommended only as a last and temporary resort.

Types of control

For all the different types of heating system employed, effectiveness depends largely on the method of control. Very sophisticated systems are available (at a price) but for most church applications comparatively simple and effective products are on the market at reasonable cost. Improvements to a control system can often bring quick benefits.

The first and obvious essential is to ensure that an adequate 7-day timer is fitted and is used. In many, or even in most, situations heating requirements differ from week to week and the time control chosen must be simple to operate, must be understood by the appropriate person and must be sited where it can be used easily. There must be a responsible person charged with this task. Too often an elderly, malfunctioning mechanical clock is hidden in an inaccessible space and is therefore rarely adjusted.

The next essential is some form of thermostatic control, which must be tamperproof. An old heating system may sometimes struggle to achieve a tolerably comfortable temperature on a cold day, but in spring and autumn there may be occasions when the thermostat is necessary. Some forms of thermostat give only very coarse temperature control which can cause user dissatisfaction and these should be avoided or replaced. Highly sensitive electronic thermostats may be justified in some circumstances.

In many cases a simple form of optimum start control can be justified. This ensures that heating is switched on earlier on cold days and later on warm ones, with consequent savings.

Where a building has particular problems or contains precious artefacts, automatic control of humidity, either simply by ventilation or by humidification/dehumidification, should be considered. Humidity control has become much more reliable over recent years.

Any new system will be provided with comprehensive safety controls but it may be prudent to check that existing systems are adequately protected.

The above controls apply to any form of heating. For hot water systems and for gas fired systems it may be appropriate to add controls to modulate the generation or the output of heat to match the load.

SYSTEM SELECTION

It is all too easy to make a poor choice when installing or replacing a heating system because the requirements appear obvious. However, the problems are often much more complex than is initially apparent. It is important to make a careful and thorough assessment, including requirements for the preservation of artefacts, and ventilation and humidity control in addition to heating. As with the other areas of caring for inherited treasures, it is advisable to retain the services of a consultant for design and contract supervision of new heating systems. Clients may be tempted to save cost in this area, but it is often the case that installers and suppliers put forward different speculative schemes which cannot be properly compared with each other. Thus a carefully prepared brief covering performance standards is needed and the consultant will be able to ensure that all aspects are considered. Effort expended at this stage is likely to be amply repaid.

Intermittent use

Intermittent occupancy represents one of the most difficult requirements for any environmental control system. The balance between comfort, cost and building preservation gives rise to a series of incompatible requirements which necessitate compromises. It is as a result of this that care is needed so that the compromises are recognized before great expense is incurred. A composite system combining a low level of continuous heating with localized intermittent heating is one type of compromise which can be envisaged.

Cost

In many building matters, not least for heating/ventilation systems, there is a tendency to consider only the initial capital cost. Most church systems can be expected to have a basic life of at least 20 years during which time their running and maintenance costs will exceed the capital cost several times over. In fact in many situations, heating costs are probably the largest item of expenditure after provision for clergy stipends. Thus the overall lifetime cost of any improvements should be assessed rather than the simple capital cost. It may be possible to anticipate later changes and improvements at the design stage if it is essential to limit the initial capital expenditure. Cheap solutions to the 'obvious' problem may turn out to be very expensive for succeeding generations.

INSTALLATION, OPERATION AND MAINTENANCE

It is important to appoint installers who are used to working with historic buildings. These can include such diverse matters as the making of holes in walls and the need for sensitivity when the premises are being used concurrently by others.

Commissioning of a new system is normally done by the installer. However, experience during the first few weeks of operation will lead to slight adjustments of various controls to arrive at the best settings.

Ongoing operation normally requires one person who takes responsibility for becoming fully conversant with all parts of the system and is prepared to undertake the continuing work of looking after the weekly control. Such a person will need initial instruction about the system and this aspect must be firmly handled with the designers and installers. It must be supported by good documentation from the installers.

Maintenance requirements are of two sorts. Firstly, there are items such as filter cleaning which can often be achieved effectively by voluntary labour. Secondly, there are items more closely associated with safety and performance requirements. These should be entrusted to a reliable professional firm. In both cases it is important that the work is done. Too often churches are cold simply because regular maintenance has not been carried out.

THE GREEN ISSUE

Much concern has been expressed over recent years about environmental issues. As custodians of the earth and as inheritors of architectural treasures, we have a moral duty, if nothing more, to use the earth's resources wisely and prudently. The late twentieth century has become profligate in its use of energy, which is still comparatively cheap. In their early years our inherited treasures were operated with considerable economy, albeit providing very limited levels of comfort. However, we must beware the danger of simply throwing more and more energy at the problems of church heating. At the very least we should ensure that the energy which we must necessarily expend is used as efficiently as possible.

GLOSSARY

Flue   A pipe or passage for conveying the products of combustion of a fuel from the inside to the outside of a building.

Heating   A means of providing comfort conditions for building occupants when the ambient temperature is too low for comfort. It also refers to the addition of energy to maintain fabric or artefact temperatures at satisfactory levels for preservation.

Humidity – absolute   The quantity of water vapour contained within a mass of air usually measured in kilograms per kilogram (kg/kg).

Humidity – relative   The proportion of water vapour present in a mass of air compared with the maximum amount of moisture which can be contained in that air at a particular temperature.

Infiltration   The air which naturally leaks into a building through all available orifices such as around doors and windows, through stonework, floors, roofs and any other gaps or porous regions.

Radiator   A device containing hot water which is used to provide heat at a particular location. It is usually made of metal and does not contain any moving parts.

Thermophoretic deposition   The deposition of very fine dust particles (less than 5 μm) in a slight temperature gradient, often causing staining above hot pipes or ducts.

Thermostat   A device for controlling a temperature to a fixed level.

Ventilation   The provision of fresh air from outside a building either by the presence of open areas (such as windows) or by the use of positive means (such as fans), *see* Infiltration.

COLIN BEMROSE

Colin Bemrose is a physicist and Chartered Engineer with 30 years' experience in industrial and University research, largely associated with heat exchangers, heat transfer and energy problems. He now works as an independent energy consultant and is increasingly involved in church heating projects.

~ 3 ~

PAINTED CEILINGS AND SCREENS

❋

Anna Hulbert

Church ceilings, screens, pulpits and font covers often carry some of the most important mediaeval paintwork that survives in England. Before planning any restoration, it is essential to understand their original function, and if they are to play a meaningful part in the setting of modern worship, we should consider also the various changes in liturgical arrangements since the Middle Ages. There are also a few post-Reformation examples, equally deserving of understanding and care. Let us, therefore, look first at the historical background of our subject before we turn to the environment of the building and the care, maintenance and restoration of the painted woodwork.

Painted font canopies are fairly rare: they range from soaring mediaeval spires to more solid canopies – some with shutters – which include a number of seventeenth-century examples. Their function has always remained the same, to provide an honorable setting for a great sacrament, and in earlier times also to secure the holy water which remained in the font all the year round.

The chancel screen has been most favoured at those periods in

---

3.1 Church of St Mary, Hennock, Devon. The restored ceilure and the screen after cleaning of late fifteenth century polychromy. (Photograph by Hugh Harrison, reproduced by kind permission of the vicar and churchwardens.)

history when the mystery of God and of Eucharistic worship has been emphasized. However, it may also fulfil a practical purpose. Like altar rails, it may serve to screen off the Holy Table when the rest of the church is in use for secular purposes, and for monastic communities whose frequent offices are the nearest earthly approach to the per-petual worship of the angels, screens and high stalls were very welcome in a draughty church on winter nights. As engineering developments in architecture enabled wide chancel arches to be built, parish churches emulated this enclosed sanctuary, and the rood screen developed. Side chapels proliferated with chantry benefactions and similar devotions, and could be fenced in with parclos screens. It was natural, whenever an image painter could be afforded, to represent in this prominent position the saints of the Church in Heaven whose prayers enhance those of the congregation.

From a musical point of view, the loft above the screen must have provided a wonderful position for the choir of a mediaeval parish. At the Reformation, however, musicians were moved, usually to the west gallery. Unfortunately, in the nineteenth century attempts were made to apply the intimate seating arrangements of monastic and collegiate choirs to the parish church, with the result that the congregation in the nave often cannot hear the choir in the chancel and the unfortunate screen receives the blame. To move it, however, in a church with a long chancel, is seldom a good solution, as the effect will merely be to lengthen the visual perspective. (In Eastern Orthodox churches, the choir usually stands in front of the high screen.)

For the mediaeval layman, hearing Mass in the nave, the visual focal point of worship would have been the Rood, the great crucifix standing or hanging above the screen, and surrounded by the burning votive lamps which served as memorials before headstones and the 'in memoriam' columns of newspapers took their place. At the Elevation of the Host he knelt and gazed devoutly eastwards, sometimes drilling a hole in the screen in order to do so. The symbolism of entering the sanctuary, signifying heavenly things, only by passing under the Cross, must have been powerful.

The Rood was often given a canopy of honour or 'ceilure': this is why the eastern bay of the nave is sometimes more richly decorated than the rest of the roofs. Nowadays, a mediaeval ceilure may find itself appropriately forming a canopy for a nave altar. Sometimes the whole roof was painted, and this was often done in a distemper technique which was cheaper, and less durable, than oil paint. A

3.2 Church of St John the Baptist, Metfield, Suffolk. Ceilure after conservation of fifteenth century polychromy. Note the pulley wheels behind the western truss. (Photograph by Anna Hulbert, reproduced with grateful thanks to the incumbent and churchwardens.)

ceiling wholly carved, or painted with figures, is rare indeed, and denotes a wealthy church.

Liturgical arrangements following the introduction of the 1552 Prayer Book are a subject of considerable speculation: certainly screens and ceilures did not figure large at this time, the Roods having been destroyed by order in Privy Council in 1547/1548. In Archbishop Laud's time attempts were made to restore the dignity of the Chancel. Laud was executed for his efforts in 1644, but from the Restoration of the Monarchy and the 1661 Prayer Book dates a new era of angel-painted ceilings and other rich furnishings. Often these have suffered over-painting, and it should not be assumed that altar rails and the like require to be stripped to the bare wood, as they were frequently once painted to resemble rich marbles.

The exuberance of this period later became unfashionable, and nineteenth century restorers intent on reinstating 'correct' mediaeval furnishings usually swept aside those of the seventeenth and eighteenth centuries. Victorian interiors are not uncommonly of high quality and carried out with great conviction. Screens and roofs are often parts of elaborate decorative schemes. All too frequently these have conflicted with the requirements of modern worship, but they should be adapted with sensitivity.

In the latter part of the Middle Ages many parish churches acquired fine pulpits to accommodate increasingly popular preachers. Post-mediaeval pulpits are seldom coloured, but quite possibly seventeenth century paint has sometimes been lost during later cleaning. Where evidence survives of a mediaeval pulpit's original situation, this was almost always at the side of the nave, maybe half-way along. Many pulpits have now been repositioned so that they block the view of a finely painted screen.

THE ENVIRONMENT OF THE BUILDING

Most of what is said in Chapter 5, on the care of wall paintings will apply to screens and roofs. Overflowing gutters will damage not only plaster, but also the timber wallplate along the top of the wall, and the ends of beams and rafters. A lead roof that is laid directly onto oak planks is liable to become corroded with the tannic acid in the wood. Treatment for death-watch beetle and other infestation has to be undertaken with especial care where the timbers are painted, and the choice of insecticide and fungicide must always be approved by a

3.3 Church of St Mary, Uffculme, Devon. Rood screen with mediaeval polychromy during removal of mid-nineteenth century brown oak graining. (Photograph by Anna Hulbert and reproduced by kind permission of the vicar and churchwardens.)

paintings conservator. Oil paint is relatively robust, but distemper is porous and very easily stained.

A damp floor will often cause the sill of the screen to rot, and the end posts adjacent to the walls are also vulnerable. When the oak is softened by fungus attack it becomes palatable to insects, which normally only eat sapwood edges, and the paint layer may become a mere shell with nothing to support it. A conservator can still consolidate such a surface, but the decay is best avoided. When the ends of the beam along the top of the screen are damaged, the whole structure may become unstable and unsafe, especially where the posts have dropped into a rotten sill. It is best, when plastering the walls, to feather the plaster off just short of the timber: wood that is buried in impervious render will be forced to absorb all the damp present in the wall. To preserve the sill, it may be supported on thin slices of slate, so as to create an air gap underneath the screen.

Stone screens and pulpits need much the same care as the monuments. Sometimes colour survives on stone vaulted ceilings – in one church, patches that had been mistaken for algae turned out to be the remains of mediaeval blue. Provided there is a dry space above the vault, condensation is probably the worst enemy here.

Heating appliances placed near the screen will cause wood to shrink each time they are lit. No matter how long the wood has been seasoned, it has become acclimatized to one state of atmospheric humidity (the relative humidity in village churches is often around 80 per cent) and if this changes, the wood will move. When it shrinks, it becomes slightly smaller than the paint that it carries, which is then forced off.

Central heating systems which rapidly lower the humidity throughout the church, often cooking the ceiling while the congregation still shiver below, will cause similar damage. In particular, blown hot air collects dust particles which become, as it were, magnetic as they travel, and stick to the roofs. Even newly conserved paintings will not last long in such an environment.

CARE AND INSPECTION

The greatest danger to a painted surface is the loosening of the paint itself. Once it has fallen off, it is gone for ever: only rarely can the conservator retrieve flakes from the floor. So only a surface that is in sound condition should be dusted.

3.4 Church of St John the Baptist, Wickhamford, Worcestershire. Details of lion's mane from James II Royal Arms, painted in distemper on a mediaeval ceilure, during fixing of loose paint. The area at the bottom of the photograph has been consolidated. (Photograph by Anna Hulbert, reproduced by kind permission of the incumbent and churchwardens.)

If the binding medium has decayed, which happens easily with old distemper, and occasionally also with oil paint which has been treated with an unsuitable cleaning agent, the surface may be powdery. Alternatively, the paint may be peeling off, as often happens with East Anglian screens. These were probably painted with oil, but artists favoured a glue and chalk priming which, like glue-bound distemper, deteriorates with damp. In any case, animal glue does have a limited life, often only five hundred years, so some fresh glue or other adhesive will eventually have to be introduced.

First, therefore, take an inspection lamp or a bright torch, and look closely at the whole screen, and also the roof whenever you have an opportunity to reach it. Inspect it even if you had not previously imagined it to be painted: numerous screens now dull with blackened varnish, or covered with the oak-graining effect popular in the early nineteenth century, do, in fact, retain rich polychromy underneath. Look for little chips where the colour may show through. Slant the beam of light at a sharp angle, so that any curling flakes and blisters are thrown into relief. Do not be tempted to touch them: call a conservator, who will inject an adhesive between the paint and the wood, and gently press the loose blisters, thus securing the colour for the future.

A stone screen presents more complex problems, as it is seldom possible to consolidate loose paint until the source of damp has been cut off, and any accumulation of salts poulticed out. This type of work is described in Chapter 7, Sculpture. The loosening of paint on stone is normally caused by the evaporation of moisture, and the consequent formation of crystals of various salts between the stone and the paint. The damage will be more rapid if there is a heating appliance near the screen.

Do not despair even if the whole surface is blistered, for you may be astonished at the transformation once all the flakes have been flattened. Picture restorers are so accustomed to this problem that many different methods of fixing loose paint have been devised, and these are often less time-consuming than might be imagined.

The causes of flaking paint can very often be avoided if the nature of the materials is understood. More information will be found in Chapter 4, Paintings on Canvas and Wood. Whatever the cause, very clean pale spots denote recent losses, and should be regarded as a danger signal.

MAINTENANCE: DOs AND DON'Ts

Supposing that the painted surface is in good, sound condition, it should be given its own pure bristle dusting brush which must be washed at intervals. A soft brush with white bristles and a plastic ferrule is best; a metal ferrule should be padded with sticking plaster. An ordinary paintbrush serves very well. Feather dusters and impregnated mops should be avoided, but on intricate carving a rubber puffer with a soft nozzle, known as a 'rat-tail syringe', will be found very useful. (This can be obtained from a medical shop.) A cloth duster is not good as it can rub particles of grit into the painted surface, which should not be dusted more than necessary.

Never apply polish to a painted surface without professional advice. Many polishes contain solvents which could affect the paint, or other ingredients which harden until the accumulation is difficult to remove. Never attempt to freshen the surface with linseed oil, as once it has become old and brown there is no solvent which will remove it that does not also endanger the original oil paint. The same applies to mop oil, which will quickly collect dirt. Azurite blue turns khaki when oiled; it was originally mixed in a glue medium and is ruined permanently by a single application of oil. The old furniture restorers' concoction of linseed oil, turpentine, and methylated spirits has potential for disaster. Modern varnishes frequently have a frightening capacity for shrinkage, and can pull the paint off. Those which contain resins that dry harder than the paint are an expensive nightmare to remove; moreover, some types of polyurethane tend to dry white and opaque when applied in a church that is very cold. In short, do not apply any coating whatever to a painted screen, and for unpainted wood keep to beeswax-and-turpentine. (Varnishes used by conservators are carefully chosen for texture and resolubility.)

Cleaning is equally hazardous. Even plain water is dangerous, because animal glue, the many uses of which are mentioned above, is soluble in water. This is why so little blue survives on mediaeval screens: glue-bound azurite was quickly washed off even when oil-bound pigments survived. Some of the richest gold is burnished water-gilding, which is extremely vulnerable.

Remember that household cleaners labelled 'suitable for paintwork' are designed for modern paints that will be renewed anyway within twenty years, and never be misled into using them to clean anything antique. Caustic soda converts oil into soap, and may go on acting for years after it was believed to have been rinsed off. Even cleaning fluids sold in art shops especially for pictures are not adviseable, as they are designed for removing artists' varnishes. Your screen may have been exceptionally lucky and have escaped any really stubborn coating, but almost all varnishes used in churches over the centuries are now so hard that a mild picture cleaning fluid would have to be used in huge quantities, enough to put the original colour itself at risk.

Be warned that some insecticides can leave tide-marks, and others leave brown stains and an oily residue which may preclude the subsequent penetration of an adhesive or consolidant. If you do want to nip an insect attack in the bud, make sure the fluid goes down the holes and nowhere else, or alternatively wrap the affected area in a polythene tent containing an insecticidal vapour strip. (Avoid applying masking tape to a painted surface: the paint can be looser than it looks.)

If you have bats in the church, try not to let piles of droppings accumulate. It is difficult to check the roof, but the top of the screen at least can be kept clean. This is particularly important if it retains fan vaulting, which may lack floorboards to protect it.

Bird droppings can be eased off sound paint with cotton wool, which may be very lightly damped if you are certain the paint is oil, but it is better not to persist if they are very hard to remove.

Distemper paint cannot be touched at all, especially if it is powdery, without professional advice.

Be very careful that electricians do not nail wires along carved or painted beams. They should be placed along the top, out of sight.

Be careful not tie prickly branches to the screen with wire or hard string, or cover it with damp flowers and leaking vases. This is known as lilying the gilding, and is unnecessary. Never use drawing pins, even on unpainted woodwork. Although soft wool may occasionally be used when decorating unpainted screens, every effort should be made to dissuade enthusiasts from attaching anything whatever to painted ones.

HISTORIC EVIDENCE WHICH MAY BE OBSERVED

During your inspection, you may note features which illustrate the richness and variety of mediaeval worship. A roof may retain pulley wheels, which, depending on their situation, may mark the site of a lost font cover, a Lenten Veil converting a festal reredos into a sombre Passion scene, a hanging Pyx, or a votive lamp before the Rood. Fittings for a sanctus bell may be encountered, or for the long lost scenery of a mediaeval play. On all of these, any surviving paint may provide the best proof of antiquity.

Screens are even richer as sources of such evidence. Any part of the wainscot or dado which has been left uncarved or unpainted may have

3.5 Church of St John the Baptist, Metfield, Suffolk. Mediaeval pulley wheels on the ceilure above the former rood; photographed before conservation – note the holes between the planks on the left. (Photograph by Anna Hulbert, reproduced with grateful thanks to the incumbent and churchwardens.)

been hidden by a bench or an additional small altar. Holes in the dado are not infrequently older than the mediaeval paint, and must have been drilled for the viewing of the Elevation of the Host as soon as the screen was installed.

The pattern of over-painting, or of old repairs, may reflect a period when the screen was incorporated into box pews. Very old restorations may be of great historical interest.

Legends abound of the exotic origins of beautiful rood screens in village churches, because we cannot now envisage the strength of the mediaeval devotion which was manifested in such lavish gifts. If mediaeval paint survives over the heads of the dowels, this is proof that the object has never been dismantled, but was painted in situ.

The individual saints depicted may have been chosen for many reasons, often now hard to evaluate when the accompanying statuary has been lost. Their survival may depend on the preferences of reformers, who often allowed prophets bearing biblical scrolls to escape the iconoclastic attacks levelled, for example, at saintly Popes and Cardinals. Floral designs and stencil patterns also deserve close study, for when they are recognized in another church they can provide clues by which the travels of a particular band of painters may be traced.

Get to know the saints on your screen, because when you want to clean them, individuals may like to sponsor a particular figure.

Although there is no end to the historical evidence which may be found in a church, screens are particularly vulnerable when any radical restoration or re-ordering is planned, and it is essential to begin by acquiring as full an understanding as possible of the information which they contain.

THE RESTORATION PROGRAMME

If the painted surface is not deteriorating there may be no urgency to clean it, but a screen which appears black and gloomy and very much in the way in the middle of a church, may be found to be bright with colour and gilding underneath the dirt and varnish. Cleaning can effect similar transformations on a roof, and bring a great deal of light into the church. A conservator will make a cleaning test and assess the feasibility of uncovering the whole object.

Every roof and screen is unique, and will not necessarily give the same results that were obtained in a neighbouring church. The original technique may be different, and it may have suffered different vicissitudes.

You will need to find a suitable conservator, whose work is approved by the Diocesan Advisory Committee and the Council for the Care of Churches. A report and estimate must be obtained first; possibly a conservation joiner will be required as well as a conservator of paintings, so make sure they will work happily together.

Exceptional skill is required when blending in woodwork repairs without damaging adjacent paint. Sometimes a roof requires a structural engineer as well. The church's architect must be kept informed, and involved as necessary.

It is seldom possible to say in advance of cleaning, how much retouching will be appropriate. When debating the merits of conservation versus restoration, the liturgical function of the object in our own time should never be forgotten. Often money is better spent elsewhere, once repairs and cleaning are complete, leaving the historic object neatly preserved and retaining evidence of a chequered ecclesiastical history.

The defaced features of saints present a particularly tricky problem, tragic though it is to have lost them. A modern artist will have been trained in a totally different way from his mediaeval predecessor, and cannot recreate a style that is no longer a living tradition. The mediaeval artist, too, was supported by the ideas of the whole Church, while most saints who were popular in the Middle Ages receive little public devotion today.

Colour will always create a point of emphasis, so the desired restoration should be kept in balance with the rest of the church. Fortunately mediaeval and Victorian colour is normally sufficiently mellowed and creates no problems when cleaned, but this is not the case with unwisely chosen new colour. For example, heraldry is frequently repainted, thus forcefully directing our attention to the armigerous status of the gentry and nobility of the past, perhaps not the most relevant function of a church building today.

A conservator's skills lie in knowing how to consolidate fragile surfaces in a way that is compatible with the original technique, how to remove obstinate dirt and hard old coatings without damage to the paint and gold leaf underneath, and how best to protect the object for the future. In order to assess these matters, he or she will require adequate access to reach the object, without trying to balance (possibly illegally) on an unsteady ladder. For most screens, a sturdy stepladder is enough for an initial inspection, but a roof will require a tower scaffold or an hydraulic lift. Very tall screens will also need a small scaffold. A good light is also extremely important; the conservator will probably bring his own, but will need a handy electric socket. When a long inspection has to be carried out in winter, you will be warmly thanked for a flask of coffee and a stove! Requirements for the job itself will be discussed when the report is made.

Techniques available for cleaning include the use of selected solvents and reagents for removing old varnish, oil, and over-paint. The rate of evaporation and the time for which each is applied is vitally important. When the layers to be removed are harder than the original paint, they can only be softened, not dissolved, before continuing work with a scalpel. There are several useful methods of dry-cleaning, notably with extremely soft rubbery erasers which can be wonderfully effective in separating soot from powdery distemper colour. Long practice may make a process look easy, but it is very seldom possible to accept offers of amateur help.

Once you have found a conservator you can trust, you will be guided by his report. The problems that may be encountered are too varied to go into further detail here. But be sure to seek professional advice at an early stage: too often, a conservator is not consulted until much money has been spent on preparing unsympathetic plans.

Every church needs a roof of some kind, but it is sad when a screen is regarded as an outdated hulk, to be abolished together with all memory of its misguided donors, rather than as a treasured legacy awaiting a new role. Whatever the preference of an individual church in matters of liturgy and re-ordering, a sensitively preserved painted screen or ceiling will always enhance worship and provide an encouraging witness to the devotion of succeeding generations of worshippers.

ANNA HULBERT

With a degree in History of Art from the Courtauld Institute of Art and after volunteer work following the Florence flood, Anna Hulbert trained in the Conservation of Easel Paintings and then began work in mediaeval churches and cleaning rood screens and other painted objects and later working on wall paintings. She specializes in conserving polychromed wood, stone and plaster in situ, and has a special interest in the historical use and development of church furnishings.

4

PAINTINGS ON CANVAS AND WOOD

✳

Pauline Plummer

In churches across the country one may find a very varied collection of paintings of all types, on both panel and canvas. They include single devotional figures and religious scenes, historical and genre scenes, and portraits, as well as a large amount of heraldry in the form of Royal Arms and hatchments. From the late seventeenth century onwards there are numerous examples of commandment boards, sometimes combined with figures of Aaron and Moses, the Lord's Prayer and the Creed, benefaction boards and commemorative panels in ringing chambers.

Of the innumerable, portable, religious paintings which must have existed before the Reformation and the wholesale destruction which followed, little remains. Of mediaeval paintings in situ there is a wealth of fine examples on wood among the polychromed rood screens of East Anglia and the south-western counties of England. These may bear single figures of saints on individual panels, or scenes covering more than one panel, or have non-figurative decoration. Saints and divines also appear on the panels of several mediaeval pulpits. A certain number of paintings survive on the underside of tomb canopies, and there are groups of paintings on the backs of some choir stalls, as in Carlisle Cathedral. Occasionally one comes across a few loose panels

---

4.1 Fifteenth century rood screen from Barton Turf, Norfolk. Photograph shows detail of a panel with ancient scratches. (Photograph by Pauline Plummer.)

salvaged from a dismembered screen or other piece of furniture. Sometimes they have been re-used in an altarpiece, or even built into the walls of a vestry cupboard. A few dooms survive, painted on wooden panelling which formed tympanic inserts in chancel arches. A rarity is the painting on the door of a banner stave locker at South Cove.

During the disturbed times of the Reformation and Commonwealth, little religious painting was created for display in churches. After the Restoration, especially with the rebuilding of City churches following the Great Fire, there was a revival of the decorative arts, and the custom of painting altarpieces was resumed.

In the late sixteenth and early seventeenth centuries, family memorials replaced devotional pictures, but in three surviving instances the early triptych form was retained to combine central portraits of the deceased with poetry, heraldry and *mementi mori* on the wings.

There also date from this period interesting scenes such as those of the Armada and the Gunpowder Plot.

In succeeding centuries the variety of surviving subjects increases. Some revered incumbent, or noteworthy village event might be commemorated, while views of the interior or exterior of the church before some drastic nineteenth century remodelling, are of great historical interest.

In addition to these native works, there is a rich collection of paintings originating from many other countries. Patrons returning from their continental travels in the eighteenth and nineteenth centuries brought back a wide range of art objects of various periods, many of which they subsequently presented to their local churches. One example of such a gift is the sixteenth century Flemish triptych presented by his brother in memory of Gilbert White of Selborne.

The artistic quality of paintings ranges from the sophisticated work by masters of all periods, through that of lesser, but still professional, artists, to the products of anonymous, local amateurs – from Constable to the parish clerk. Copies abound, Raphael's *Madonna della Sedia*, Corregio's *Mystic Marriage of St Catharine*, and Rubens' *Descent from the Cross* being especial favourites. There are, too, many reproductions on paper, which, if mounted on panel or canvas, and covered with heavily discoloured varnish, might be mistaken for genuine paintings.

Paintings can suffer all the problems found in any ancient collection, augmented by the traumas due to their position in damp and leaking buildings accessible to all manner of people, and over the centuries being in the care of those who would not necessarily have any respect for them, or any knowledge of how to look after them.

PAINTINGS ON PANEL

Panels are usually composed of several boards joined together. Mediaeval screen panels are normally rather narrow and two boards butt-jointed, grain running vertically, are sufficient. The thickness is approximately a quarter of an inch. On larger paintings the boards are more likely to be fixed horizontally. The joints might also be feathered, that is the boards are tapered at the edges and overlapped, forming a flat surface at the front, but one slightly stepped at the back. This system might be used when the back of the panel was not to be visible.

In the mediaeval period and into the seventeenth century English panels were almost all of oak, while later coniferous wood might be used. In the eighteenth and nineteenth centuries mahogany was common. Imported paintings might be of lime, poplar or willow, if from Italy, oak and later mahogany if they came from the Low Countries or France; lime, beech or spruce if from Germany. In the twentieth century first plywood, and then after *circa* 1950, hardboard was frequently used.

Wood, however old and well seasoned, continues to move if conditions change. It expands and contracts across the grain, about a quarter of an inch on a twelve inch board. So it is advisable to avoid extremes of humidity and dryness. If the timber is constricted in some way when it tries to move cracking may occur. In the nineteenth century many problem panels were cradled, that is, they were thinned and a framework attached to the back. In this system the bars parallel with the grain are glued, while those which run across the grain are loose in slots. These often jam, causing strains and splitting.

Early panels were given a ground and painted on both sides, which helped to counteract any tendency to warp, as well as for visual effect. It ensured that the stresses were equal on both sides, and that one side could not absorb more moisture or dry out more than the other. One often finds that the paint on the reverse of screen panels has been planed off in the course of some 'restoration'.

Imported panels may be quite thick, an inch or more, if they are lime or poplar, and they may have bowed considerably even though they are of quite small dimensions.

The ground on early panels was very often chalk, or gypsum in glue (gesso), sometimes applied over an intermediate layer of cloth or parchment, which covered joints and flaws in the panel, and helped to

(a)   (b)   (c,   (d)

4.2 Relief ornament on sixteenth century East Anglian rood screens, incised (a and b) and cast in mould (c and d). (Photographs by Pauline Plummer.)

reduce the risk of cracks opening up on the face of the painting. Sometimes the ground was oil-based.

Many pigments were minerals ground up to a fine powder. Common types were yellow and red earths, which could be heated to form darker versions. More rare were azurite, malachite and lapis lazuli. Black was made from soot, or formed by burning bone or vine twigs. White lead and other colours such as crimsons, vermilion and some brilliant yellows were manufactured chemically. Gold and silver leaf was used in large amounts on mediaeval paintings. The metal was hammered until it was cobweb thin and stuck to the painting with some type of mordant, vegetable gum or oil. Since silver oxydizes quickly, it was usually glazed to protect it. It might be used as a substitute for gold, when the glaze would be golden in colour and provided a very convincing imitation.

Pigments might be bound in egg tempera, various forms of protein and oil emulsion, gum or oil.

The panel was isolated with size, given several coats of ground, which, if of gesso, were rubbed down to form a smooth surface. The design was drawn on the ground with a pen or brush, and then the colours were blocked in. Gilding, if part of the scheme, was done at this stage. Sometimes the gilded areas were tooled, sometimes decoration was painted on the gold. Motives cast in a chalk/oil or wax paste were frequently stuck on. Then the rest of the painting was completed with layers of body colour, and finally coloured, oil/resin glazes were applied over both painting and gold and silver leaf.

In the sixteenth century there was a gradual transition to a general use of oil, and the use of metal leaf on pictures slowly went out of fashion. Eventually oil for both ground and paint layers became the most common technique though the build up of layers differed from one period to another.

Protective varnishes of natural resins, dissolved in hot oil, or in turpentine, according to date, might be applied after the painting was quite dry.

There was a revival of interest in early techniques in the nineteenth century, and many altarpieces were created on panels, with gesso grounds, gilding and so forth, some extremely well painted.

One may come across copper panels which were used from the seventeenth century, tin or zinc in the nineteenth century, when we also find large panels of slate, used both for figurative paintings and texts. Paintings on paper may have been stuck to panels or canvases. Of contemporary work one might find collages comprising a variety of materials such as fabric, paper, leather with paint, ink or chalk decoration. All these materials have their own problems and distinctive types of damage.

PAINTINGS ON CANVAS

Occasionally one finds fifteenth century works painted in size medium on finely woven cloth. By the late sixteenth century oil on heavier canvas became common, and similar techniques are still in use.

The best canvases used for oil painting are linen, but less valuable work might be on cotton, jute or hemp, all of which are very susceptible to and respond differently to changes in humidity. They are normally stretched over frames, either strainers or stretchers, and secured with tacks along the thickness of the chassis. In quality work the edges of the canvas may be protected with tape or leather strips before the tacks are inserted. Of the two types of chassis, the earlier, more basic strainer is permanently fixed at the corners, which sometimes have diagonal braces. The stretcher which appears in the eighteenth century is composed of separate members which interlock at the corners, and are slotted to take wedges/keys. At first the stretcher joints were butt-ended, but in the nineteenth century mitred joints were introduced. A slack canvas can be tightened by tapping in the keys slightly, while a strainer does not allow of any further adjustments.

The general structure of a canvas painting consists of a priming coat, or coats, of size to seal the canvas, followed by a ground of chalk in size, or white lead in oil, or in the seventeenth century a red clay (bole) in size. Sometimes a semi-absorbent ground was used which was composed of half chalk and half white lead in oil. The decorative painting is built up with layers of various pigments mixed with the chosen medium, in most cases oil. The oil is generally linseed, though sometimes artists use poppy or walnut. The final touches of the painting can be transparent glazes of pigment in oil and resin which modify the tone or colour of the opaque body colour.

One might find contemporary pictures on synthetic canvases, and executed in a variety of synthetic paints.

GENERAL PROBLEMS

As may be imagined, such complex structures age and become less flexible at different rates according to the materials, and after a while no longer accommodate themselves to the fluctuating movements of the panel or canvas support as they respond to changing climatic conditions. This results in cracking, cupping, tenting, flaking and eventually paint loss. The network of cracks which is indicative of age, and varies in pattern according to the original medium, is called the craquelure and does not necessarily mean that the paint is in a dangerous condition. Once the paint begins to lift away from the ground or from the support then the situation changes, and action should be taken.

There is also the damage caused by pests. Panels are attacked by wood boring insects. Screen panels which stand at ground level, and so are often quite damp, can be heavily infested by death-watch beetle, while furniture beetle is active with all types of panel, and also attacks the stretchers of canvas paintings. The furniture beetle is particularly fond of the glue in old plywood, which is often riddled with holes.

The dust excreted by the grubs is frass, and a fresh sprinkling of frass is an indication that the pest may still be active in the timber. If, when rubbed between the fingers, the frass feels gritty, that is an indication that it is fairly recent.

On canvas one finds evidence of attack by moths and other insects, and even mice.

DAMAGE DUE TO INCORRECT TREATMENT

Apart from the effects of natural aging, the painting can gather numerous accretions over the years, such as deposits of dust, mud, and droppings of birds, bats and flies. Mistaken attempts at preservation have resulted in the application of every conceivable product at one time or another. Coats of spirit varnish, oil varnish, neat linseed oil, glue, egg white, casein, or wax may have been applied in successive layers on top of the original protective coating. Retouching has been spread liberally over undamaged areas as well as over paint losses, and, being in oil, has not only darkened considerably, but become very tough and difficult to remove. Much repainting has gone on, some in an iconoclastic attempt to obliterate images, some in lieu of cleaning, in order to brighten up the appearance of the work, some to change the subject matter from religious to secular, or to modernize the costume in a portrait, or to change the sitter's identity. In spite of the availability of information and advice, linseed oil and proprietary products such as O'Cedar polish have been used within the last few years, and no doubt somewhere someone has used insoluble polyurethane varnish in an attempt to do a really thorough, lasting job – the worst thing they could do.

4.3   Relief ornament on sixteenth century rood screen from Bramfield, Suffolk, piped and cast. (Photograph by Pauline Plummer.)

I have seen people handling objects in churches as though they were completely indestructible. In fact they are extremely fragile and vulnerable. Most should be in the controlled conditions of museums. Both wood and canvas are sensitive to damp and excessive dryness, heat and light. A slight blow can dent the support and chip paint, on a canvas causing a web-shaped pattern of cracks. Nails and pins may cause splits in wood, and if left, the eventual rust can stain. Canvas may be torn. Liquids such as oils and varnishes can form tough skins which are a problem to remove from sensitive paint. Paint may be water soluble and so suffer from the casual swipe over with a damp cloth. It may be absorbent, purposely painted with very little oil, or in a size medium to create a very matt effect. This would be ruined if it were varnished, since varnish dulls the luminosity of matt painting and can never be totally removed from an absorbent surface.

On mediaeval panels one often finds a combination of oil-based gilding, and water-based gilding and painting, so that varnish or wax, glue or water could all damage the decoration.

I have seen such horrors of mishandling as a flaking panel carried casually by its edge, the clothing of the bearer brushing it as he walked; a flaking screen brushed with a stiff carpet brush by a helpful child, while its mother chatted to someone else; a flaking panel wrapped in a woolly cardigan for transport; a flower arrangement in front of a screen where the vase was overflowing, and the water had soaked the carpet, and was seeping under the screen; flower arrangements being sprayed to freshen them up over the several days of a festival, the spray going onto the painted panels, risking the softening of glue-based paint, and certainly likely to leave a deposit of calcium on the surface; Easter arrangements of primroses and moss perched on the flat transom of a screen, so that the moss overhanging its container syphoned the water down over the paintings; flower vases wired to the posts of screens and leaking down them.

Many aspects of maintenance in churches can be compared with domestic maintenance. Would you let flowers overflow on your carpet, or bang nails into your best furniture for hanging Christmas decorations, or let the gutters stay blocked until the wallpaper started peeling off your walls?

There are many things, however, which a layman would not expect to cause problems, and I propose to describe a list of points to watch, which I trust will be helpful.

GENERAL ADVICE

As mentioned above, there are some very important and valuable paintings and frames in churches, and, of course, no one would dream of doing any DIY on them. Always contact the Council for the Care of Churches (CCC) or your local city art gallery, if you suspect anything might be amiss, however minor.

There is much that can be done in the way of basic maintenance, and regular checking is extremely valuable since any deterioration may be spotted, and the causes remedied, before any serious damage is done.

Before anything is done, think carefully through the procedures, set out whatever tools and equipment you are likely to need, and then proceed slowly and systematically. Never start on a project without considering whether you have all the facilities you will need, whether you and any assistants will be able to spare the time, and not have to leave in the middle, and whether there will be time before the church is next in use for a service. Move any furniture or carpets out of the way so that nothing else is damaged while you are at work.

Protective coverings

If building work is taking place within the church, and anywhere near or above paintings, then they should be removed, or securely boxed in.

Decorating has to be carried out from time to time. Whenever possible take down any paintings, rather than risk damage from ladders or scaffold poles. Poles have been known to go not only through stained glass, but right through wooden panels. However, if it is really difficult to move a picture because of its size or weight, make sure it is securely wrapped. Try to avoid touching the surface of the painting in case it is flaking. Use lightweight plastic sheeting and tape it tautly across the frame. Tape the plastic to itself, not to the frame, otherwise the tape will pull off the paint or gilding when removed, whether it is sellotape or masking tape.

Similarly, wrap up rood screens with plastic sheeting. Ladders should not be leant against any painted sections, nor against any carving, and certainly not if the structure is unsound. Use two tall step-ladders or a tower scaffolding. Sometimes, if the screen has lost its gallery and vaulting, one can tie several balls of string along one edge of the plastic, toss them over the screen, and haul up the sheeting. That is, of course, assuming the screen is not flaking so badly that such wrapping would cause paint loss.

For lack of such simple precautions I have seen screens which I had recently treated, either covered with sticky plaster dust or spattered with paint.

If flower arrangers wish to spray a display in front of a painting or screen, they should get someone to hold up a plastic sheet between the flowers and the painting.

Taking down pictures

One must have adequate labour on hand, sound in wind and limb. If the painting is large and heavy, two men with two ladders, or a tower scaffold, might be needed, using ropes or pulleys. Others would be needed standing below to receive the picture as it comes down. Keep it upright, and avoid any vibration or shock. Take care that the wire or chain does not fall against the paint and damage it, or hit one of the workers. It would be wise for those waiting below to wear protective goggles, since there is likely to be a rain of dirt and plaster fragments. Never try to jerk the picture away from the wall, the hooks might come out with some plaster. Steady the picture at the top and support it at the bottom. Do not hold the frame by one side only, it might come apart. Never take chances, if the picture is damaged it could cost far more to repair than the hire of scaffolding or payment for a half-hour's labour, nor will it ever be the same again, however skilfully restored.

When handling a painting which has been restored recently, always wear clean cotton gloves. Sweat and grease in the skin can attack the varnish and build up a grimy layer on the paint. (Note the grime which collects round a domestic light switch.)

When carrying the picture it should be held by the short end, with the paint towards the person carrying, so that they can check what is happening. If it needs two people to carry it, then the front person steers, while the second watches the painting. Once at the storage area, the painting should be propped on padded blocks. Use pieces of cloth, or preferably old carpet or underlay, wrapped around short lengths of timber, of minimum dimensions $2 \times 4 \times 18$ inches, or larger according to the size of the picture. This keeps it off a damp and possibly dirty floor, prevents it from slipping, and ensures that the frame does not grind on the floor. It is very easy to damage the projecting mouldings of an elaborate frame. Lean it against a flat surface, face inwards, avoiding any projections. Do

4.4   Ranworth – detail of St Peter's robe. (Reproduced by kind permission of the Courtauld Institute of Art.)

not lean it against, or behind a door, in case someone forgets and walks in. Never lean anything else against it, unless it is protected by a board larger than the frame. One might cut a piece of hardboard as a temporary protection. The wires may be taken off at this stage, if so, keep a record of their length, to avoid problems when the picture is rehung. Never leave the picture in direct sunlight, or near a radiator or heating pipes. If using a lamp to do some repair, do not leave it close to the surface. Paint can be blistered by a 60 watt bulb, if it is left too close.

It may be that the picture has been too close to a damp wall, or that the plaster has bulged since the picture was hung up, and the back may be covered with mould. It should be left to dry out slowly before dusting. You may find rot has attacked the back of the frame.

While the picture is at ground level, do not leave it alone in an unlocked church. Theft of church treasures is a booming business.

Before doing anything more to the painting one must make absolutely sure the paint is sound. Put the picture on a table and look at it carefully with a strong, raking light. Hold a 150 watt lamp almost level with the paint surface to throw all the irregularities into relief. It should give you a good idea whether or not the paint is flaking. If it is beginning to lift, dust and cobwebs may well be caught on the edges of the flakes. Paint loss may show first as minute, triangular holes in the paint surface, holes little larger than a pin head to start with. If the surface has lumps and possible flakes, do not touch it, or press the bulges, the paint may be very brittle. It should be treated by a specialist, paintings conservator, otherwise it will continue to flake. If it is sound, then, using an artist's watercolour brush, or similar soft, clean, brush of oxhair, badger or sable, dust the paint very, very carefully. If there is a lot of dust, one might hold a vacuum cleaner nozzle well away from the painting, twelve inches or more, to suck up the dust in the air. A cloth wrapped over the end of the nozzle would reduce the suction. *Never* put it anywhere near the paint. Never turn to speak to someone while continuing to work. Stop what you are doing and then turn round.

Animal droppings might be removed with a small swab of cotton wool, just dampened, no more, with water.

It would be desirable if the same person checked the paintings regularly, every six to twelve months. Then they would recognize any changes in the condition. Make sure the person, who is checking, has good eyesight. Preferably use magnification with a strong light at the same angle each time. One should check at the same time for renewed insect activity.

Dusting the back of the picture

The back may be dusted very gently. A two inch wide decorating brush may be used together with a vacuum cleaner, the nozzle being held a few inches away to catch the dust disturbed by the brush. If it is a panel there would be less risk, but with a canvas one must make sure the paint is not flaking, since even a gentle brushing at the back might cause sufficient vibration to dislodge some flakes at the front. *Never* let the vacuum nozzle touch the canvas. Always watch what you are doing, and do not let yourself be distracted.

It is important to keep a permanent record of what one does to the picture. Any inscriptions, labels, collection numbers, seals should be carefully noted, and preserved. One often finds the name of the artist on the back of a Royal Arms. Be careful not to suck any labels up into the vacuum cleaner. Ideally it would be useful to take photographs of the picture when it is down, of the back, and of any interesting details.

Removing the picture from its frame

Do not do this unless there is some compelling reason, and having made sure that the paint is not flaking. Should it be necessary, then make four padded blocks, put them on a table and place the picture face downwards, with the corners of the frame supported on the blocks. This will protect any decoration on the frame from being crushed. Do not let anything touch the paint surface. One can then work on the back without any risk of damaging picture or frame.

It is very likely that the picture is fixed in the frame with large, rusty nails, either knocked into the frame and bent over the edge of the painting, or driven through the panel or stretcher. They have probably damaged the picture and the frame. Where the picture does not fit the frame exactly, the gap may have been filled with slices of old bottle corks. It can take some time to extract all the ironmongery. Take care not to split the panel, stretcher or frame any more than they have been already. As nails are removed they should be put immediately into a container, so that there is no risk of their slipping out of sight, and causing damage later. If your tools are damaging the wood, use a piece of card to shield it.

Once the picture is out of the frame, carry it with the flat of the palms against the edges as though it were sticky both sides.

The layman should never attempt to secure flaking paint, remove

4.5   Late Georgian Royal Arms painted on canvas. Note the blanching of the varnish caused by dampness and the unusual frame with its original bottom member missing. (Photograph by Pauline Plummer.)

varnish, put on any type of varnish or retouch damages. Never let anyone struggle with a ladder near paintings, or wash the floor while they are at ground level.

The frame can be cleaned further, once the picture is out and standing safely on its blocks again. The frame could be treated with insecticide or fungicide at this stage, if necessary. If any pieces have broken off and have been saved, they could be glued back. Animal glue should be used, as synthetic glues do not hold to surfaces which already have glue on them, and many fractures have been repaired before. The gluing should be done as neatly as possible, since any strings or drips of glue falling onto paint, or gilding, will eventually contract and pull away the surface.

Sometimes on a Royal Arms or hatchment the frame is flat at the back and just nailed on. One would not remove it unless more repairs were necessary to panel or canvas, but once off, a rebate can sometimes be formed by fixing four strips at the back. This is only possible if the frame overlaps the painting.

After treatment, the frame should be put on blocks, separately from the picture, until required.

Re-framing

When re-framing, put the frame back on blocks on the table and replace the picture, making sure it is the right way round for the hanging rings, hooks etc. Instead of the rusty nails use brass strips approximately three to four inches long, with two holes at one end, bend them so that they will press against the back of the painting and hold it in place, and secure them with brass screws. If the picture projects far above the back of the frame, it might be necessary to fit little blocks of wood to raise the brass strips. The painting should not be fixed to the frame, just held gently and securely. One would need three or more strips on each side, depending on the size of the picture. Screw into the thicker part of the frame. Gaps at the sides could be filled with cut up corks, but strips of balsa wood can be bought in different thicknesses from hobby shops, and are much more satisfactory. White glue, such as Evostik Resin W, can be used to stick the cork or balsa to the frame.

Never try to force a warped panel flat, the frame can be adapted to fit it.

Before rehanging it would be desirable to fit a protective backing. A suitable, rigid, lightweight material is Correx. This can be found in builders' suppliers, but there is a conservation grade available, Otherwise polypropylene or terylene sailcloth may be used. Brass screws and brass cup washers should be used for the Correx, and some stainless fastenings for the cloth. Stainless staples are available for tacking guns.

Rehanging

Before rehanging check that the wall fittings are secure, and use strong wire or chains, do not risk metal fatigue. Never rehang if the plaster has been renewed and is still damp. Allow it to dry out thoroughly. Hang the painting out of reach from the ground, to avoid the risk of theft or vandalism. The painting must be at least two inches from the wall to allow air to circulate easily behind it. If necessary fit distance pieces. Do not hang in strong sunlight, or over a radiator, where there is not only rising heat, but dust is also carried upwards in the warm air current.

Valuable pictures should be fitted with some security device to prevent unauthorized removal.

SPECIFIC NOTES ON PANELS

A panel, once removed from its frame, might warp, so it is better to avoid taking it out, or, should it be necessary, to replace it as soon as possible. Another risk is that the glue or pegs between the component boards might have failed, and, if taken out of the frame, it might fall to pieces. Should that happen, of course, never try to re-stick it yourself, this task must be left to the specialist conservator. Similarly, such a specialist could release the jammed bars of cradles, and add supports at the back of inadequately supported panels. They might be able to reduce a warp slightly, and could adapt the frame to accommodate a warped panel which could not be flattened.

Metal panels are easily dented and the corners bent over, and they could be fitted with a supporting frame by a conservator. They should certainly have a rigid backboard.

Active beetle in the back of a panel might be treated with insecticide injected by hypodermic syringe. Seek advice beforehand as to whether it would be safe for you to go ahead. Chose a type of syringe, such as a glass and metal one, which is not affected by the solvent in the insecticide, and always wear protection over your eyes. Keep the insecticide from running onto the paint surface, and check that it is not going through the panel onto the paint. Should it do so, mop it gently with a small piece of cotton wool, or pad of kitchen roll. Do not rub. I do not recommend that you treat the front of the painting. If the infestation has gone so far, then a conservator should be called in. Sometimes panels can be treated in a gas chamber. Even when that is done, there is the risk of reinfestation from outside, (there is usually some timber in the building with active beetle), and the painting should be checked every year for signs of frass or fresh beetle holes. Furniture beetles emerge in April/May, and death-watch beetles a little later in the year.

SPECIFIC NOTES ON CANVASES

Paint is more likely to crack if jarred or vibrated when the temperature is low, so try to avoid moving pictures in cold churches in the winter.

Often one can see that the tacking edges are crumpled and rotted, like unravelling fringes. They may have a second set of tack holes which show that the canvas has been adjusted, the shape altered, and put on a new stretcher. They may have been lined, or re-lined, when the original tacking edge would have been cut off, and a new canvas stuck on the back with glue or starch paste. Wax has also been much used for lining. Sometimes in the past pictures were put through heated rollers to make the lining canvases stick, with the result that all texture has been lost, the paint surface is flattened like linoleum.

Sometimes the canvas has failed round the edges of the stretcher, and is only held in place by the frame. It would be best not to take it out of its frame in that case.

If a lot of debris has collected between canvas and stretcher which you need to clean out, and your initial inspection shows that the paint is not flaking, once the picture is out of its frame, check it against the light. You will see if there are any small holes. The more light shows through, the more dangerous the condition. If the paint and canvas are both sound, then turn the picture upside down, facing away from you. Lean the upper edge towards you, tap gently and dust and debris will fall out. Since the canvas is likely to be rotten and very brittle it might be dangerous to do more. However tapping might not dislodge larger objects. The usual way to deal with them is to take a flat, *round ended* spatula such as a painting knife, and probe along the gap between canvas and stretcher to hook out anything wedged there. One could easily poke right through the canvas on the turning edge when doing this.

When the foreign matter which caused distortions in the canvas is removed, the canvas will not go flat, it will have been permanently distorted, but it will not get any worse. Vacuum clean again.

If you find any loose wedges put them back in their slots in the stretcher. Hold a piece of card behind them and tap each wedge gently, working systematically round the stretcher. This will key out the canvas slightly and make it more taut, if it is sagging. As canvases move with the changing humidity and stretch over the years, they begin to rest against the stretchers and then to drape and sag round them. If such a flapping, sagging canvas is moved about there could be a risk of losing paint. However, if you tap too much, the canvas might not be able to take the strain, it might shed paint, or split, and if you enlarge the stretcher too much, it might no longer fit the frame. If the canvas is puckered in waves at the corners, it could be due to a butt-ended stretcher pushing the canvas unevenly on one side. Tape the wedges into place with strips of gummed paper holding them to the stretcher.

If the stretcher has failed, without taking off the canvas, one might be able to ease the two members back into position and join them with brass strips or mirror plates, and brass screws. No matter how rickety the stretcher it is safer to leave the canvas on it than to take it off. It is likely that both paint and canvas would be too brittle to stand being rolled, and a large canvas once off its stretcher is very inconvenient to store flat. (When pictures are rolled, after being faced up with tissue and an adhesive, they should always be rolled with the paint outwards so that it is not crushed, and a supporting cylinder should be used.)

Any insect infestation might be treated with insecticide using a syringe as for panels. Once again one should seek advice. It would be very easy for the liquid to seep into the canvas.

Tears have often been repaired with patches, frequently of canvas much thicker than that of the picture, and stuck with glue which has contracted and caused puckering. The patch usually becomes visible on the front after a few years, since there is a double thickness of canvas which moves differently from the single layer of the rest of the picture. In more recent years sticking plaster or insulating tape have often been thought suitable for a repair. If tears are not repaired then one can get differential shrinkage between the torn flap and the rest of the canvas, pieces hang down and gradually curl up, shedding paint. There is little the layman can do in this case, most attempts in the past have caused more problems than they have solved.

One must leave to specialist, painting conservators all interventions such as the treatment of flaking paint, repair of tears and bulges, lining, removal of varnish and overpaint, retouching and revarnishing.

If you do have a damaged painting, or a hatchment, or Royal Arms badly torn and the canvas distorted, do not regard it as beyond repair, and push it haphazardly into a damp, neglected corner of the vestry or tower room. Nearly everything can be repaired, and it is astonishing how remarkable the results can be. If you cannot afford to have it conserved professionally now, set it aside carefully, on blocks and protected by a board as described above, or hang it back on the wall with a backboard, until repair work can be commissioned.

FRAMES

The treatment of frames is also full of pitfalls, and usually requires the services of a specialist. The best period frames are carved, and have a glue and chalk ground on which the gilding is applied with either an oil-

4.6 Ranworth — the rood screen. (Reproduced by kind permission of the Courtauld Institute of Art.)

or water-based mordant. Less valuable frames may have had the ornament cast in moulds and stuck on, before gilding. They are as vulnerable to heat and damp, jarring and dropping as are the pictures. The water soluble elements are easily softened, the cast ornament cracks into sections, while the oil gilding may become brittle and curl up. They can be gently dusted, and any loose pieces secured, and that is all. Never imagine you can improve the appearance by painting with gold paint, you will ruin the frame if you do. If the frame is very plain, never be tempted to discard it for a smarter, modern one. The original might not be very interesting, but the design would be correct for the period of the painting.

LIGHTING

Often, after an object has been conserved, the Parish wishes to illuminate it, having seen the brilliant effect of the conservators' lamps. However, it is really unnecessary to pick out one aspect of the building in this way, be it roof, mural or monument. It was intended to be seen in natural daylight or by candlelight, and if lighted from the wrong angle, it may look uncomfortable. If everything, which has just been restored, is given a special spotlight, the building will in time be dotted with them. However, if the church is very dark, and there is a need to light a special object to allow study, then one must make a very careful choice of lighting. Of course, one needs a Faculty. One should consider where the lamps and cables may go to be inconspicuous. Remember there may be hidden wall paintings. Lamps should not give off any degree of heat, which might change the atmosphere, and, after a while, cause shrinkage of timber. They should have ultra-violet filters, and, if possible, be colour matching. The light level recommended for oil paintings is 150 lux. There are many types of lamp and lighting system on the market, and one needs a detailed knowledge of them to make the best choice. It is best to consult the CCC, and to take advice from a specialist in lighting works of art on site.

PAULINE PLUMMER
After graduating in Fine Art, Pauline Plummer studied picture conservation at the Courtauld Institute of Art. Since then she has specialized in the conservation of large, painted schemes in historic buildings. The medium is usually oil, but supports may include plaster, panels and canvases. She is a Fellow of IIC, and the Association of British Picture Restorers, and a member of UKIC, and its Wallpaintings and Paintings sections.

~ 5 ~

MURAL PAINTINGS
AND THE FABRIC

✳

Donald Smith

Wall paintings, probably more than any other objects or decorations within a church, are an integral part of the building, painted as they are on the very structure. They should not therefore be considered in isolation by those responsible for them. This can present a seemingly daunting predicament, sometimes needing knowledge and advice from different specialists. However, a great deal of necessary decision making boils down to common sense and a keen interest. Small changes can bring about great benefits. This chapter sets out to give some simple guidelines to those concerned with the matter, whether it be a fragment of ancient painted plaster or an interior filled with patterns.

As wall paintings are so acutely affected by external conditions and even design, it is wise to stand back from the building to look over its structure and observe how it functions; the direction of the sloping roofs; the position of tower and roof; the number of hidden gulleys; camouflaged parapets. Then follow the system of rainwater disposals, from top to bottom: how it escapes from the tower, whether over roof tiles below, into a hidden gully or hopper head, or directly to the ground; the number and position of downpipes (constantly relating this

---

5.1   From the Church of Holy Innocents, Higham, Gloucestershire. Proper cleaning can transform a wall painting. (Photograph by Donald E. Smith.)

to the murals within), if they empty into hard or pebble trenches at the base of the wall, into soak away pipes, or end abruptly half-way down the wall, or spout into an overflowing oil drum. Are roof tiles all in position and is the flashing and end-pointing sound. The external stonework may be broken, porous and the rendering or pointing crumbling or completely missing. Rainwater has an alarming ability to percolate great distances. Vegetation should be kept clear of foundations. A thicket of spreading ivy may look picturesque but it usually means simply that the drains are blocked or broken. Soil banked against a wall results in a higher level of moisture. An oil tank positioned alongside a wall leads to constant splashing from deflected rain droplets and hinders normal evaporation.

With the potential risks and problems found on the exterior it is then safe to venture inside to carry out a similar observation, and we are now better able to grasp how the two relate.

The presence of dampness, whether rising or falling, is the greatest and commonest curse to befall a wall painting. Painted on stone or plaster, it forms very much a part of the shell of the building. Signs of dampness are normally plainly obvious and there is no need to seek moisture reading instruments. Smell alone can detect much. While many churches are fairly damp, this seems to be accentuated by the cold. Heavy, thick, mouldy dampness is quite different and there is no better way of sensing this than by kneeling at the base of affected walls. Breathing in the odour from crumbling, moist plaster can leave a potent example. Always touch walls gently with the palm of the hand. Really damp plaster is very wet indeed, and although walls are cold and clammy, damp ones chill the hand immediately. Wet, crumbling plaster sticks together and does not fall away from fingers easily. Small bumps suggest a build up of salts underneath. Surface salts either brush off easily, almost floating away, or in more extreme cases, require scraping with the fingernail until they fall in lumps.

Visual detection is perhaps the most important way of searching for damp patches. High up, the plaster will appear darker, frequently surrounded by a ring of white salt efflorescence. Salts can be seen best under raking light from a strong lamp, and this is such an effective method of detection that it can transform a seemingly sound area of wall into an alarming sight. Even from a distance, salts are easily noticeable, especially along stonework where the moisture has darkened the stone and 'bled' from the jointing. Green algae will cover the base of the worst affected walls.

Leaks from gutters, downpipes and roofs can sometimes cause

5.2 Church of St Helen, Brant Broughton, Lincolnshire. Photograph shows how a leaking roof can wash away soft distemper decoration. (Photograph by Donald E. Smith.)

irreparable damage within a matter of days. A three foot thick wall which has become saturated from water gushing through a cracked downpipe can take months or years to dry out. Once inside the wall there is very little anyone can do. The simple rule must be to sort out the damp problem as soon as it is noticed. If left, a small leak will always result in more serious damage and involve even greater financial expenditure. It is irresponsible not to seek out the cause of a damp patch, nor question why streams of water cascade down walls, or accept that such a situation is the norm and has been in living memory. Countless schemes of decoration have been ruined completely because of a complacent attitude: distemper, gluebound painting can be wonderfully washed away and even durable, oil-bound surfaces can burst off like confetti. For the conservator it is a painful experience to be asked to inspect and estimate for damaged work after years of utter neglect. The cost of repairing damage in its early stages is negligible when compared with the daunting task of raising the funds for the repair and conservation of plaster, stone or woodwork at a later date.

It is a good idea to stand quietly in a church during a heavy rainstorm. There is no better way to discover how watertight the building is. Rain seeping through windows, either from broken or missing glass or poor putty, will affect decoration on the splays and sills. Blocked soakaways and water bouncing off saddle bars can spread water under plaster and paint layers and create a microclimate of humidity that, in time, will weaken the binding medium of the paint causing colours to powder and fall away and plaster crumble.

When repairs are necessary to walls, either in small areas or in great sections along the base, it is essential that in practically all cases the use of cement, or cement-based plaster should be banned. During the nineteenth century various types of cement for rendering and pointing were experimented with but the use of slaked lime and hair plaster was still largely the norm and continued well into this century. Practically all the great nineteenth century schemes on plaster have been created using a lime plaster. The use of cement is unheard of for earlier murals. Cement rendering is incompatible alongside lime plaster because of its hardness, inflexibility and impurities. Lower down, along the base of walls, moisture that would have tended to evaporate or breathe with a lime plaster, builds up and begins to travel slowly up the wall behind the impervious layer of cement, affecting areas that would otherwise have remained dry, dissolving in the process natural dormant salts within the wall or leaching out those present in the cement, and carrying them ever upwards until they escape through the older, more porous plaster, evaporate and deposit the salts into crystals on the surface and pores of the wall. Over time, salts harden into a shell forcing the moisture to escape even higher or until it eventually breaks down the plaster structure of the wall. Long before this the mural would probably have flaked off the wall.

In many churches, it is common to find the wainscot above floor level renewed with a hard cement rendering. This usually results in a band of hollow loose lime plaster where it abuts perhaps a mediaeval work. Cement infills create the same phenomenon. It is very much the job of the conservator to remove these hard blemishes. Therefore, it would be ideal if all cement plaster repairs could be removed where they meet early, lime plaster, or where the building is prone to dampness, and all lower sections should have a lime and sand mixture. There is hardly ever an occasion in the conservation of mural painting when a lime plaster is not used. For large and extensive repairs when building firms are sought, it must be a requirement that no cement is used – a spoonful of cement beckons a bucketful. If none can be found that are willing to use slaked lime, it is worth seeking out the services of specialist firms.

The atmospheric conditions of a church interior can play an important factor in deciding the fate of a mural. Some buildings are more humid than others and will always be so by their construction and location. All will be directly affected by inadequate and faulty conditions of the fabric. Measures can be taken to try to lessen overly moist interiors and by the same measure there is a sound argument against undue heating and measures to dry out a building. Paintings which have survived for hundreds of years in unchanged, rather moist conditions, such as the crypt of a cathedral, have probably done so because of the peculiar environment. In these cases, it would be wrong to produce temperatures that are too high with corresponding low air humidity as this would have a tendency to over dry the plaster and jointing.

A balance has to be found between providing a safe environment for the paintings and an acceptable regime for worship. Long-term monitoring by thermohygrograph, giving month long readings of temperature and relative humidity, is a good method to understand conditions, yet they are of greater value if they can be compared to similar buildings to appraise how unusual one particular study might be. For the conservation of wall paintings, while they may be of value to the conservator, they should never be used as an excuse to delay necessary action.

The common complaint of dripping walls and condensation is a direct result of the intermittent, once weekly sudden heating of the cold interior, normally once a week for Sunday worship but also for other services and activities in the week. This situation is the worst, but for the needs of the parish, seemingly the most sensible. It is far better gradually to build up the temperature over days and decrease it equally in the same manner. It also makes sense, perhaps, to keep the temperature slightly lower.

A balance has also to be struck between introducing fresh air, usually cold and therefore draughty in winter, and the preservation of the congregation. In most churches there are windows designed to be opened, yet so often the pulleys stick out, cordless from the wall, window frames firmly shut enshrouded in rust. Devices to open dormer shutters lie disused and partly broken and then as a final humiliation are swept away as bothersome during reroofing. All of these were designed for a purpose and should be made operational.

The question of dehumidifiers is vexed. Their efficiency is undisputed, as bucketfuls of water can be taken from the interior of a church, but whether they are consistently effective is another question. After the initial cost they are cheap to run, can often be automatically pumped away, though more often require regular attention by parishioners. They can be noisy, and more than one is usually necessary. However, they can never be a substitute for repairs.

Radiators set against the wall will always produce wide bands of darkness on decoration above, decreasing in soiling all the way to the roof. This is due to the upward convection current of various atmospheric pollutants. Where radiators are essential and permanent they are a constant yet unavoidable nuisance. A shelf positioned immediately above a radiator will help to deflect the dirt for a few feet. Whenever possible, new radiators should not be sited at the base of murals. In connection with a dusty atmosphere, large ducts under the floor of the church should be regularly vacuumed, as well as the area around recessed hot water pipes. Butane gas heating is the most detrimental form because of the amount of moisture produced by combustion.

Frequently, with the conservation and cleaning of schemes of mural decoration the parish turns to consider new wiring and lighting. Metal conduits are often used to feed cables through. Often they are ill positioned, crossing stonework and hiding paintings. For the last forty years, electricians have employed the simple aluminium clasp with galvanized nail to attach flat cable to the edges of the wall. This effective design now seems to be out of favour and is increasingly replaced by the white, plastic snap on conduit, inflexible and without the advantage of bending into odd shapes and corners that its predecessor had. These new conduits should be avoided like the plague. Site new switches after a good deal of thought and if they cannot be positioned away from the mural, then place them where the older switches were. Opt for cabling alone, or thin copper tubing and think very seriously about re-using the older conduits no matter what the electrician might say. Any rewiring will involve a certain amount of repair afterwards by the conservator, such as newly exposed strips of plaster to be cleaned, old splashes of paint removed, holes filled and retouched.

In the day-to-day running of the church there are a great many routine things to be aware of, all of which will help to preserve the paintings. Unskilled intervention on more serious problems can result in irreparable damage or severely complicate the task of the conservator.

1. Wall paintings should never be cleaned by unskilled hands. This may sound obvious, yet it does happen. Colourful window splays are often thinned by enthusiastic rubbing.
2. Cleaners should be on the look out for white, sometimes translucent, salt efflorescence which has landed on the floor. Flakes of paint and plaster, both of which, if large enough, should be stored for the conservator in a box with padding. Decorated plaster fragments can frequently be refixed into position during repair.
3. Avoid dusting off the surface of the wall painting as this can dislodge fragile paint or catch on the edge of loose plaster.
4. Abandon the old cobweb cleaning poles attached with stout hard bristles. Both mediaeval and nineteenth century schemes, especially if painted with distemper, have been gradually scratched away to the underlying plaster. If, on entering the chancel, the paintings high up in the corner are strangely thin with broken patterns, it is almost always because of this. Similarly, never store these poles against decorated walls. Use instead an extended vacuum pipe with soft brush attachment to dab the cobwebs free.
5. If floor polishes are sparingly used avoid the edges of the floor in contact with wainscot decoration.
6. If brass tablets secured to painted plaster and stone are to be polished use a straight edge template, even plain card, to protect the surrounding murals from smeared polish and rubbing.

7. When mopping and brushing avoid knocking the walls.

8. Do not stand furniture against plaster nor lean banners and implements in corners.

9. In churches prone to rising dampness, never allow rubber-backed carpets. Mostly confined to the sanctuary area in small interiors, these will force the damp to collect underneath, create mould, help rot woodwork and cause problems to adjoining walls and stone and above all to the tiles below. Far better to expose the rich polychrome tiles and roll down a strip of carpeting for the communion service.

10. Oil and paraffin lamps are rarely used now but candles are still necessary and important for worship. All of these have contributed to the layers of grime now being removed by conservators. Over the high altar the walls and east window splays are usually some of the most soiled in the building. If candles are to be used (as they ought) the incumbent should consider reducing their number and positioning them as far as possible from wall surfaces. A flickering flame from a constant draught will produce more smoke. Candles should be extinguished with the proper instrument rather than by blowing which only deposits wax droplets that are difficult and time consuming to remove.

11. Generally, keep a look out for leaking windows and roofs, and condensation down walls or puddles at the base of walls.

12. Place several grouped buckets under a regular leak.

13. Bat droppings, usually around the high altar or chancel arch ought to be considered more a matter of rejoicing than horror. In the most extreme cases, bats could be encouraged to roost in less sensitive areas. The damage to wall paintings caused by bat droppings and urine is negligible when compared with that achieved by the human hand.

14. Beware of impulsive redecoration. We have inherited walls covered by limewash, sometimes hiding fourteenth century fragments or seventeenth century cartouches. While it has protected many paintings, the sheer number of layers has meant that not all layers are possible to preserve. For old buildings it is wise to insist on limewashing for any redecoration, distemper to a lesser extent as this is affected more by damp environments. Countless schemes of important murals have been obliterated by ruthless and ill-judged redecoration. Nineteenth century murals have suffered most. Distemper

5.3 Church of St Nicholas, Little Braxted, Essex. The photograph demonstrates numerous problems: subsidence, rising damp, leaking windows, cement repairs, cracks, salts, flaking paint, surface grime and an over-painted ceiling. (Photograph by Donald E. Smith.)

and limewash can be removed without damaging underlying oil-bound paint but emulsions and oil paint is quite another story. The term 'whitewashing' is increasingly and wrongly used to mean the use of modern white emulsion. Never, for example, paint over a Victorian wainscot in a chancel or sanctuary. If it is drab and grubby, it needs cleaning. Consult the conservator. If it is damaged and rubbed have it professionally restored. (It might then look better as a backdrop for the flower arrangements.) Victorian paintings require a rich, deep wainscot to settle on, not the sterile yards of empty, white space.

At some stage, the parish will want to seek further advice from a conservator of wall paintings. He or she is contacted through various channels: appointed church architect, Diocesan Advisory Committee (DAC), the Council for the Care of Churches (CCC), English Heritage, the Society for the Protection of Ancient Buildings (SPAB) or the conservation departments of the County Council. They are invariably freelance, private concerns, working individually or in small teams. Although they come recommended, they are independent and do not represent any official body. Two reports or estimates may be needed and a fee may be asked, either fixed, hourly or negotiable, to cover work and travelling costs. It is most helpful to meet on site with churchwarden or incumbent and have at hand ladders, or, on special occasions, a tower scaffold, for the inspection. At least several hours will be needed so light switches should be explained. The conservator will always want to gain access to the worst affected areas and carry out small cleaning tests to assist with the calculation of the final cost. If plaster is flaking near the roof, a tall enough ladder should be available.

How helpful it is when parishioners and clergy realize what an important role they play in assisting the conservator to understand the history of the building and its decoration. A brief explanation of recent small maintenance tasks and major building work can be immensely valuable: when gutters were last inspected and cleaned; which down pipes are broken; which hopper heads tend to overflow in heavy rain; whether the drains soak away efficiently; which windows leak and is it a result of broken glass or crumbling grouting; if the walls have a tendency to drip with condensation, when and in which part of the building; how often the church is heated and the method; when the new boiler and radiators were fitted; how long since the plaster fell from the wall; when the walls were last painted over or limewashed and an approximate date for the over-painting of the mural decoration.

The answers to many of these questions could be solved during a close inspection by the conservator, with time, yet the functioning of the building is best explained by the custodian. It can be very productive if, by chance, the visit is carried out during a torrential downpour.

It is quite amazing what a wealth of vital information many churches possess on their decoration, all essential for the conservator to assess accurately what needs to be done before undertaking the project. Most take the form of original cartoons and drawings or watercolour views of the interior and photographs, invariably looking eastward down the nave and into the chancel. Many hang high up on vestry walls, some are displayed in the nave or tower, yet countless lie huddled in heaps behind cupboards or stacked on shelves, forgotten, mouldy, half-eaten by insects. There are occasions when such astonishing records have not seen the light of day for decades. Before they are lost forever, every parish should at once take stock of what it might have, then dust and rehang, or clean and remount.

For nineteenth century buildings, old photographs provide perhaps the most important clue to the appearance of the original scheme, more so than architectural elevations submitted for the decoration, as they show how it really looked once completed. The great nineteenth century schemes of decoration all too often suffered from the hand of changing fashion; partly over-painted, scraped away, redecorated and at its most savage, obliterated. Such practices continue today.

The eyes of the conservator can at once identify: the presence of two or three layers from different centuries; the dating of old plaster; identification of pigments; style and original method of painting; alterations; old retouchings, repairs and reconstructions; old varnishes and plaster needing fixing or pigment consolidation. The conservator should be able to show what can be achieved by cleaning, and how the paintings could look with proper attention. Over-painted schemes can be uncovered with stunning results, but it is only those able to carry out such work who can assess the situation accurately and confidently.

For paintings hidden under limewash, grant support is less likely to be forthcoming (even if restoration is desired) especially now when resources are stretched even for those visible fragments most in need. When called upon, the conservator should establish the probable extent of the hidden decoration, the size of the likely areas, their condition and whether they are worth uncovering.

When seeking advice on the cleaning of a complete series of wall paintings, from ceiling to floor, beware of those who recommend total redecoration. This is over-painting and little more than vandalism.

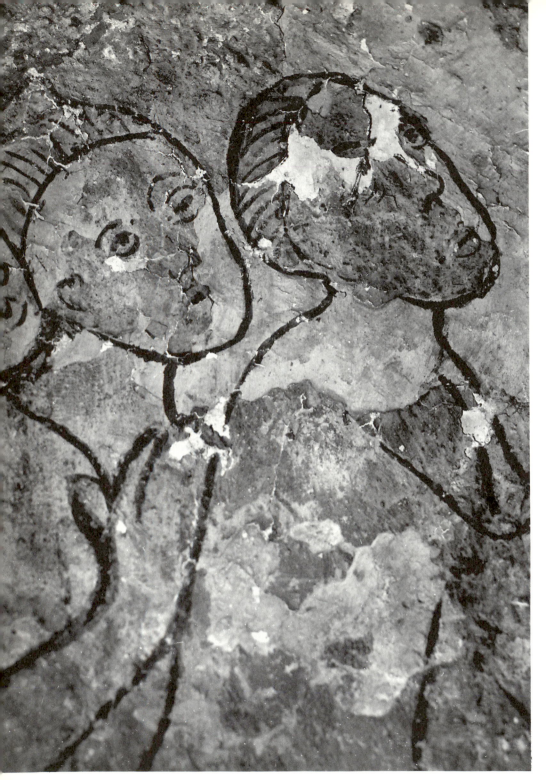

5.4 Church of St Nicholas, Stanningfield, Suffolk. An over-painted, thickly waxed and seriously peeling mediaeval painting. (Photograph by Donald E. Smith.)

An understandable question to a conservator nearing the end of a project is: 'Are you going to seal it with a protective coating?' This may come after many weeks spent removing a dark layer of varnish, at quite considerable expense. The answer must be that, on practically all occasions, a layer of varnish of whatever kind should never be applied to paintings on plaster and stone. The word 'seal' is most apt, for this describes and anticipates the potential risks associated with it.

The fact that old buildings, by their construction from porous materials continuously 'breathe', accepting and releasing moisture from the atmosphere, is increasingly recognized by parishioners and clergy. The application of a varnish will therefore only succeed in accelerating the decay.

Warnings against the use of preservatives were voiced as early as the 1920s by the Society for the Protection of Ancient Buildings (SPAB) but it was not until the 1950s that an organized response, in the form of guidelines, was issued. It is telling that a formal letter to *The Times* on 21 February 1953 by the Central Council for the Care of Churches and the SPAB, warning against the use of any varnish coating, was directed primarily at the conservators of their day. Until then, it was common for mediaeval fragments of painting, often freshly uncovered, to be sealed with copal, shellac or wax varnish, sometimes applied hot, so that a thick, visible layer rested on the surface. The colours may have looked fresh and bright for a short time but soon the varnish darkened and became brittle, pulling off the fragile layers of paint, or held in moisture previously allowed to pass through overlying limewash causing a build-up of salts, blistering efflorescence and bursting of plaster.

Those dark ill-defined squares of plaster, with their faint ochres and murky reds and blacks, which typify so many surviving examples of mediaeval wall paintings in our parish churches, are the legacies of past and usually well-intentioned endeavours to preserve these vital clues to our ancestry of religious decoration.

A great deal of a conservator's time is now spent trying to reverse this predicament. Perhaps we now have a better idea of what action to take if we have a mediaeval painting in our care which is peculiarly dark and shiny, pitted with dusty white salts, flaking in scaly shapes or is flanked by irregular cement repairs.

DONALD SMITH

With a degree in the History of Art from the University of Warwick, Donald Smith trained under Robert and Eve Baker. He worked extensively in southern Germany and studied with the Bavarian State Office for the Conservation of Historic Buildings. He has completed major conservation and restoration projects throughout the British Isles.

~ 6 ~

DECORATIVE
PLASTERWORK

❋

Jane Schofield

Ornamental plasterwork, whether modelled by hand or cast in
moulds is not particularly common in churches and so it is of the
utmost importance that any still surviving is looked after and treated
carefully. While mural paintings on flat plaster have survived later
'improvements' quite surprisingly often (they are usually painted over),
relief plaster is not so easily disguised and changing fashions have led to
its destruction in vast quantities by well-meaning architects, builders
and incumbents over the years.

Flat painted plaster survives from almost every century and with its
obvious classification as art it has been treated with a certain amount of
respect in most (but not all) churches for many decades. Ornamental
plaster has not been regarded in the same light – falling somewhere
between building work, craft and applied art. When problems with it
occur they are likely to be more serious structural ones, apparently
threatening life and limb through the imminent collapse of ceilings or
the bombardment of the congregation with large and extremely heavy

---

6.1   Church of St Mary & St Gregory, Frithelstock, Bideford, Devon (1677). The
Abbot family of Frithelstock were famous and skilled West country plasterers for
four generations. This superb coat of arms in their local church is a fine example
of their work. Despite the many coats of paint which are beginning to blur the
inscription, it remains in excellent condition. This robust early plasterwork
should never be coloured.

sections of mouldings or monuments. Its repair is (or can seem) complicated and awkward. By its very nature plaster obscures and makes inaccessible its means of support, so that nails can rust and timbers rot away hidden from scrutiny. The first evidence of a problem may be a dramatic hole, crack or pile of rubble on the floor. This should not be taken as an excuse for neglect, however, as many hints can be observed before damage becomes too serious, and nowadays it is possible to save plasterwork in virtually any condition.

Although Vitruvius, writing in around 30 BC, gives instructions for preparing plaster which are pertinent today, there was no ornamental plasterwork in Britain until the sixteenth century when the fashion was started by Henry VIII who brought the Italian Nicholas Bellin over from Fontainebleau to work on the new palace of Nonsuch (started 1538). Although Italian stuccoists worked at other great houses, the only surviving fragments are those at the ruinous Hardwick Old Hall. The vast majority of plasterwork dating from the sixteenth and seventeenth centuries is by the hand of native British craftsmen whose naive and delightful details were drawn from patternbooks, textiles, heraldry and life around them and include all manner of plants, animals, religious scenes and symbols.

There are various reasons why plasterwork became popular in churches. The ornamental work was fashionable and it was a means of achieving a richly patterned finish without a large investment in expensive or elusive materials such as marble or fine timber. The ingredients required were cheap and available locally and they were the most basic building materials of the time: lime, sand or earth, hair or straw, and small section lathing timber or even reed in some areas. The skill of the plasterer was the special requirement and, relatively speaking, labour was the cheap element of any work. He was able to run out mouldings in situ, model freehand decoration in the slow-setting lime plaster and also make pre-formed cast elements which were incorporated into the overall design. The result was a lively handmade applied sculpture which the later mechanically-produced work could not hope to improve on in spirit, although it was usually far more accurately repetitive.

Fashion had its influence on churches just as it did in the great houses. Mediaeval timber roofs, however splendid, were perhaps thought out of date and they were certainly dark and draughty for the congregation below. 'Ceiling' this roof (the verb 'to ceil' is derived from the French for 'sky') meant the church was warmer, lighter and given a face-lift all in one go. Exposed stone and structural timber were hidden under limewash and plaster until well into the nineteenth century.

In some more remote and rural areas the rumbustious style of this early work was still in vogue into the eighteenth century but the more sophisticated architects and designers of the time had rejected such old fashioned methods and motifs in favour of classicism, Palladianism and restrained Adam designs. This was better achieved through the hands of professionals from the continent, and Italian plasterers again came to dominate the trade in Britain. With them came increased mechanism and the use of hard, gypsum plasters to turn out numerous identical casts. Although this faster setting plaster initially released the experts to create some remarkable almost freestanding modelled work, it inevitably led to a decline in the individual artistry of the plasterer and an increase in the use of pre-formed sections which could be prepared in a workshop off site, and installed with relative speed where required. The eighteenth century Gothick revivalists used plaster to imitate the stone vaulting of the past. This rather stage-set-like construction was presumably not intended to last indefinitely as the sealed areas within the vaults provided the perfect (and inaccessible) environment for decay.

Apart from an attempt at a revival of the old methods by the Arts and Crafts movement in the nineteenth century, by Victorian times most plasterwork was of a pre-formed fibrous construction – lightweight gypsum sections reinforced with scrim or hessian and small sections of timber. These techniques form the basis of the methods of virtually all plaster restoration companies today and, until recently, were the only known means of repairing (by replacement) even the earliest lime plasters. While these methods may well be suitable for the repair of the similarly constructed Victorian or Edwardian plaster, they are not appropriate for the early lime-based work. More sophisticated (but not necessarily more expensive) methods of conservation are possible which result in far more (and usually all) of the original work being saved and repaired with durable and sympathetic materials.

Ironically, the Victorians, with their love of things historical, probably destroyed many early plasterwork ceilings in their desire for restoration: in some cases not only pulling down the ceiling to expose the older mediaeval roof timbers, but then restoring those with new copies – effectively depriving later generations of all the original work. At the same time, any plasterwork which escaped was often painted up in different colours in another attempt at a new mediaevalism. This is most common on wall panels, monuments and coats of arms (possibly

6.2 Overmantle from Higher Rookabeare, Barnstaple, Devon (1630). Early plasterwork is frequently described as crude, but the removal of hundreds of years of paint can be most revealing. Although this is a time consuming job, it can sometimes be carried out by a dedicated amateur under the guidance of a conservator, with rewarding results.

because they were more accessible). Admittedly, years of limewash and distemper would have obscured the design and it is arguable that such painting-up defined the information and detail and increased an interest in its survival. However, very little, if any, early plasterwork was intended to be painted and the removal of later colours and accreted layers underneath can often reveal a dramatic amount of detail and subtlety of modelling. In some cases tiny pecks and careful hatching accurately represent heraldic colours – a fine pattern which would be lost under even a couple of layers of paint.

The most important contribution to be made to the survival of old plasterwork is through careful and sensible observation by those who look after the buildings in which it is housed and through prompt action being taken when appropriate. Plasterwork that is in reasonable condition stands a better chance of staying up if it is left alone. One way or another, most problems are caused by human interference.

Recognizing serious faults is not always easy – which cracks matter? The following is intended to be a general guide and starts with a description of the basic construction.

The most important constituent of plaster until the nineteenth century was lime. Limestone rock was burnt in limekilns to produce quicklime. This was then slaked (mixed with water which made it boil) and the resulting slurry (lime putty) was kept carefully protected from air until use. Lime makes its set by exposure to carbon dioxide in the atmosphere. To make the plaster, lime was mixed with sand or earth and hair (often tough soft fibre from oxen) or, less successfully, with straw to give it a tensile strength and help to bind together the other ingredients. In very high quality work the plaster might be very rich in lime throughout, but more usually the first and second coats had a much greater proportion of earth and hair. This sticky mixture was applied to laths, usually of riven (split) oak but also chestnut (and later softwood). The laths were first nailed to the underside of the joists or across a framework on the wall. In some areas bundles of reed were used in place of wooden laths; these were secured by strips of wood fixed along the bottoms of the joists. The plaster key (the vital anchor) was formed from the part of the mixture that squeezed through the laths and made a series of hooks as it flopped over.

The layout of the design would be marked out on the first or second rough coat and the geometry of the pattern adjusted to fit the available space. The next and final coats comprised a mix of clean sand, lime and often selected white hair. Repeated elements of the design might be cast and stuck into position with a plaster slurry, and mouldings such as ribs and cornices would be run at this stage. The casts and ribs would also be held in place by the final flat coat of plaster on which any freehand modelling would be carried out. The items which were made in moulds must have been turned out before they were hard as on some there is evidence of tidying up and undercutting. Deep holes were also made in the surface to emphasize the design. (Both the selection of the white hair, and the use of holes – which paint would block immediately – are factors indicating that the surface of the plaster was considered the finish, and intended to show.)

Wall panels and monuments were sometimes plastered straight onto stone walls, but more often onto a timber framework fixed in place first.

The problems associated with lime-based plasters are often to do with materials other than the plaster itself which is surprisingly robust. One of the greatest dangers is damp in some form or other. Rising damp and surface moisture caused by condensation are often a result of human intervention through the use of the wrong (waterproof) paints or the introduction of impermeable surfaces with cement or hard gypsum plasters. Ground levels are allowed to build up outside the church or the building is heated and filled with singing, breathing people one day only to be shut up and cold the next.

Damp also causes problems where the air is consistently humid and the plaster contains ironwork. Lath nails are an obvious candidate for rust, but there can also be built-in (and plastered over) straps, hangers and wall cramps. Rusting metal expands and splits the plaster around it as well as causing brown stains.

Water also gets into various parts of the church through leaking roofs, overflowing gutters or failing leadwork. This damage is often localized – a gaping rotting hole may appear in one place while a short distance away the timber and plaster are still sound. This situation does not remain static, however, and softened wet timbers are much more palatable to both death-watch and furniture beetle.

Infestation by these pests is sometimes a result of infected softwood used for repairs or even left in roofspaces as crawler boards, and can reduce the structural support of a ceiling to dust. It should also be remembered that treatment by professional pest eradication companies that involves de-frassing timbers and sweeping out between joists can do more harm to a ceiling in a day than a hundred years of beetle attack. Oil- or spirit-based sprays can also cause staining of the plasterwork itself.

Bats are natural predators of the grubs of wood-boring beetles (it is the grubs who cause the damage), and should be encouraged to increase their populations. As they are a protected species what better way to deal with a problem than to put the belfry tenants to work? Where chemicals really are necessary, they should be used as selectively as possible and at a time of year that will cause the least disturbance to the bats. There are a small number of products that are supposed to be harmless to bats. Information on this is available from the County Council, County Wildlife Trust or local Bat Group.

Damp can also encourage the onset of wet and dry rot which is possibly the most difficult problem to deal with to the satisfaction of everyone involved. As always, prevention is much better, and invariably cheaper, than cure.

The last, but not inconsiderable, cause of damage is man in his physical form. A misplaced foot, a hammer slipping from a chilled hand or a dropped slate are so common as to seem almost inevitable. When work to any other part of the church is taking place plasterwork becomes vulnerable. Protection and a thorough briefing of everyone working on site (especially those erecting scaffolding) are essential to its survival. A verbal word of caution is probably more effective than a note somewhere in the depths of the specification which is unlikely to be read by those on the ground.

The various problems outlined above can often be identified by observation of the patterns of cracks on the surface. Somewhat simplified, they fall into three main types.

1. A regular pattern of straight cracks, often at right angles to each other, and especially along the lines of main beams or at the wall top is usually indicative of a failure in the supporting structure. Birds-mouth joints may have shrunk so much that joists have lost their connection. The building might have moved sufficiently (especially through roof thrust) to pull the joists out of their seats, or they may be rotting at wall-top level. Connecting nails or straps may have rusted away. The joists and plaster are moving together.

2. A seemingly random pattern of cracks around large plates of plaster, often drooping at one edge, frequently shows the loss of connection between laths and timber support. This can be through beetly laths, beetly joists (especially when sapwood is left along the lower edges) or rusting lathnails. It can also be caused by the loss of the plaster key – either through damage or occasionally because the laths were put up too close in the first place for sufficient plaster to squeeze through.

3. Thin surface layers of plaster laminating away from the coarse backing coat can be caused by deflecting joists sagging in the middle and springing the harder top coat away from its backing. Sometimes brittle gypsum repairs have been applied in the past and are now peeling away. In the case of vertical plaster which has had a sustained soaking, the backing coat can be physically washed away, leaving the surface crust without support. Bad workmanship in the eighteenth and nineteenth centuries meant that occasionally new ornamental ceilings were slapped over roughly keyed old ones, often with the paint still in place. Obviously these are vulnerable to splitting and collapse.

6.3 From 'Adcocks', Taunton, Somerset (*c* 1620). Plasterwork which has fallen and broken is still not beyond repair. This spray was reassembled from over 70 fragments, with no restoration of missing details, and is now reinstated in its original position. All fallen fragments, should be saved and labelled.

Other symptoms of damage have a range of causes such as previous repairs failing, surveyors' feet missing their step on scaffolding and ladders, to impact on the face of the plaster and so on.

Where the problem has gone beyond suggestive and worrying cracks and the collapse of plasterwork has occurred, it is still not too late for conservative repair to be carried out. If possible it is best if conservators can pick the pieces up themselves – observing how and where they fell – but if this is impractical *all* the fragments should be transferred (without turning if they are face down) into shallow boxes or trays and labelled clearly. Even small, unmodelled fragments can be vital clues in the ensuing jigsaw so are worth retaining. Bread delivery trays are useful: they can be lined with newspaper and then stacked without damage to the fragments inside.

If collapse looks imminent, but has not actually happened, the short-term measure of spreading old carpets, cushions or straw on the floor beneath can save a surprising amount of damage and thus reduce the final repair bill. Photographs taken at this stage provide information which will be vital during reinstatement if the ceiling does fall. Placing the camera flat on its back on the floor at regular intervals will result in relatively undistorted images. Alternatively, lying flat on the floor oneself can be effective, but obviously great care should be taken if the ceiling is really unsafe. A strong directional light will help to increase the contrast in the relief.

Propping is not as simple as it sounds. A good system of props is the first part of any conservation project and any put up initially must work with the whole scheme. The ideal prop is well padded with sheets of foam or several layers of carpet underlay, and raised until it is barely in contact with the surface of the plaster. It should be self-supporting, and there should be no attempt to lift drooping areas however tempting this may seem. Where a section of plaster has started to come away, debris will have fallen into the opening cracks and any lifting may lever off an even larger section. It is often possible to push an area back up during the repair work when access from the back will have enabled such debris to be removed. The complications of propping (especially something like a distorted vaulted ceiling) should not be underestimated. This can absorb a substantial amount of the repair budget.

Once an area of plaster is safely propped, further investigations can be made to establish the cause of the failure and the scheme of repair.

It is not within the scope of this chapter to describe the solution to every possible problem that might be encountered but a number of basic principles apply to most of them.

Repair is nearly always carried out from the back, as this is the only way of dealing with the supporting structure without damaging the face of the plaster. Although there are sometimes reasonable grounds for drilling through plaster from the front, it should be the last resort. It must always be remembered clearly that it is the retention of the original plaster that is the object of our work, and that any filling, modelling-up or casting is the result of our inability to save it all, and should be avoided if possible. Missing details need not be replaced doggedly – most designs work just as effectively with substantial gaps, provided the condition is sound. Old work can and should look old and dignified, not modern and smart.

Getting access to the back of a ceiling can be a trial. Where ceilings are fixed to the undersides of roof timbers or where the roof void is inaccessible or very cramped, the only reasonable solution is that an area of roof must be stripped. The advantage in this is that most of the repair work will be carried out effectively outside the building, and mess and disruption inside will be reduced. The disadvantage is obviously that of cost especially if scaffolding and a temporary roof are necessary.

If the plaster and laths prove to be sound and the movement and cracking is due to the shrinking, rotting or other failure of the timber supporting structure then a straightforward system of ties and splints can be devised. If possible, timbers, even where they have no structural function, should be left in place, and, if appropriate, they should be treated to prevent further decay. Materials should be of the best possible quality, and fixings of stainless steel. If and when the plasterwork is repaired, stainless steel will be used and it is important that other metals, particularly brass, are not combined with it in the presence of gypsum, or electrolytic action and salting may occur. Repairs to the timber must be carried out with due care – no hammering or levering against joists should be allowed. Any holes or cuts should be made with high-speed power tools; there should be no nails on site. Any debris should be vacuumed from the back of the plasterwork, avoiding brushing the vulnerable key.

Most other problems require the provision of a new connection between the original plaster and the existing (or repaired or strength-ened) timbers. In the past this was attempted in a number of ways using plaster-soaked scrim (often draped over ceiling and joists alike, sometimes leading to the decay of the timber through lack of ventilation) or, even worse, chicken-wire and plaster. Where these old repairs occur it will probably be necessary to remove them to effect a proper rehanging although if the ceiling is in a really dreadful state this may cause even more damage. Where chicken-wire is rusting it really is essential to remove it, probably by patient unpicking and the con-trolled use of a small grinder to cut through replacement plaster and wire together.

Once the back of the original plaster is visible a survey of the laths can be made. Ironically, if they are not in good condition it is better that they are really awful as this makes them easier to remove without damage to the plaster and key. It is not unknown for laths to be so beetle-infested that they can be removed completely with a vacuum and paintbrush, leaving the key intact. This is ideal. Where laths are moderately decayed they should be cut through at either end (close to the joist) with a tiny circular saw and carefully winkled out. A simple hoof-pick (from a saddlers) with the end ground flatter and sharper is a cheap and useful tool for this. The odd resistant lath can be left in place and beetle treated without harm. If more than one in three resist removal then they should probably not be being taken out anyway, and the problem must lie elsewhere. When the back of the plaster is revealed it should be scrupulously cleaned, especially the undercuts of the key. The paintbrush and vacuum nozzle are ideal tools. A very dilute mix (say 1:5) of polyvinyl acetate (PVA) or 'Unibond' in water should be brushed thoroughly over the clean surface – attention again being paid to the area under the hooks of the key. This has the effect of consolidating any dusty areas and also helps prevent the water from the repairing plaster being too quickly absorbed.

A trough the width of the joist bay is formed from stainless steel expanded metal lath with an upstand of two to three inches each side (it should not come up higher than the joist tops). The high-rib type of lath should be cut so the ribs run from joist to joist. The troughs are positioned as close to the back of the old plaster as possible and screwed in place with stainless steel screws and large washers into the sides of the joists. If any dust or sawdust has fallen into the bay, it should be vacuumed out before the troughs are fitted.

Gypsum casting plaster (Plaster of Paris) is then properly mixed (that is the plaster added to the water and agitated to remove air bubbles) in amounts of about a gallon at a time and poured through the stainless steel lath to run under the old plaster key and finish just covering the new lath. One bowl will cover between one and two feet in an average fifteen-inch bay, obviously depending on the depth. The plaster should make its initial set within about five minutes of pouring.

This procedure can be carried out exactly where it is needed, in sections as small as six inches. There is little to be gained by rehanging areas which do not need it. When the new plaster has dried out (after perhaps a week) the props can be struck and any necessary work to, or cleaning of, the face may be carried out.

Where plaster is fixed directly to a wall then obviously access to the back is more difficult. If it is in serious need of attention then it may be necessary to remove the plasterwork, attend to the repairs, and refix it. This drastic action should be a last resort as, however carefully the job is done, a small loss of the original work is inevitable as it will usually require drilling to refix, and, in the case of a large piece, may even need to be cut into manageable sections. The technique used is glueing-up.

The paint surface (if any) of the plaster must be adhering well or else removed before glueing-up starts. Layers, first of muslin, and then scrim, are built up over the plaster using a water soluble glue which dries hard but can be relatively easily removed later. The layers incorporate pieces of timber in gradually increasing sizes so that the plaster becomes monolithic and rigid. Plaster is extremely heavy and a specially designed structure will be needed to support the section, undamaged, when it is removed from the wall. If the plaster is in a sufficiently parlous state to warrant this treatment, then removal from the wall may be fairly straightforward as its fixings will be in a poor condition. Once removed the problems (probably rotting built-in timbers, beetle or rusting metalwork and nails – or all these) can be assessed and a method of consolidating and refixing be designed. When the plaster has been reinforced and refixed in position the strengthening timbers and scrim can be removed gently after softening with warm water; any necessary attention may then be paid to the face.

In some cases, such drastic structural work (which really must be carried out by an experienced conservator) is not necessary and the problem lies with unsuitable paints or surface treatment. Generally speaking any paint which forms an impermeable layer should not be used in churches as moisture in the walls, or from condensation, builds up behind it. The plaster cannot breathe or dry out and, in serious cases, can break down under the surface skin. When the moisture eventually does burst through, a section of plaster will have crumbled away and been lost.

A dramatic reduction in condensation levels in a church may be made by the removal and wholesale substitution of emulsion, gloss paint, 'Sandtex', 'Snowcem' etc. with limewash or distemper which will absorb and evaporate moisture gently.

Removing paint from ornamental plaster is a laborious, and in many cases specialized, job – the crucial skill being in recognizing the various types of paint applied, and knowing which technique to use to remove each type without damage to the plaster. In some cases, water, kitchen paper and patience are all that is required and it may be possible for the conservator to establish a technique which can be followed by a dextrous and dedicated volunteer. In other examples, the chemical complexity of the paints may require a chemical cocktail to remove, all of which must be safely neutralized before another is applied. It is also vital to know the constituents of the plaster. Some strippers which are ideal for use on lime plaster will actually dissolve gypsum – with disastrous consequences, even on seemingly 'safe' early plaster if it has been restored at an earlier date.

It is so much easier and cheaper to apply paint than remove it, and this should be remembered during any decorations. Plasterwork is

6.4a Church of St Mary, **East Brent**, Somerset (1636). This plasterwork ceiling by George Drayton still looks much as it would have in the seventeenth century. Natural light is reflected from the ceiling down into the church, while enhancing the main design of principal ribs, pendants, bosses and sprays. A more subtle secondary pattern of small cusps on the main ribs creates a detailed background of squares, triangles and quatrefoils. The soft white distemper allows moisture to evaporate from the plaster without damage, and prevents the formation of condensation droplets so the ceiling remains in good order. Comparison with Figure 6.4b is most revealing.

actually better visually for being a bit dusty and grubby. The dust gathers in the hollows and enhances the details. I suspect that this dust was considered and allowed for in the original design.

However, there are occasions when paint is necessary. After structural works have been carried out any cracks or holes in the face will have been repaired with a lime plaster mix. This, even when carefully chosen, may be obviously brighter or cleaner than the original plaster, or there may be stains or marks left by the removal of earlier paint. In these circumstances a new coating should be applied which allows the plaster to breathe, and will be easy to remove in the future when details

6.4b Church of St John Baptist, Axbridge, Somerset (1637). Dark blue and white emulsion paint with touches of gold on pendants and bosses have destroyed the character of this once beautiful ceiling. Only one year later than East Brent (Figure 6.4a) and also created by George Drayton, it is hard to believe the two ceilings are almost identical. The crude outlining has lost the subtle hierarchy of the design and the quatrefoil negative spaces now dominate. Emulsion paint has caused the inevitable damp to be trapped in the plaster which is starting to break down in small blisters. It is sad that in a church where such love and care have been lavished on the fabric, this kind of misplaced enthusiasm is not only making the building darker, but actually contributing to its decay.

have again become obscured. The ideal paint is a soft water-bound distemper. Not only is this visually good – very matt and not too brilliantly white – but it is easy to remove with water. As plasterwork is invariably out of reach of hands or shoulders, the softness of the paint should present no problem. Distemper may be home-made, but a good ready-made version is available (Potmolen Distemper Super). It should not be applied too thickly, and it is often a good idea to go over the plaster after painting to clear out any blocked holes or undercuts. Distemper can safely be applied over other paints as a visual interim measure, but, of course, its breathing quality will depend on what is underneath.

Different colours should never be used on early hand-modelled work. All the evidence I have seen through cleaning plasterwork suggests that initially the plaster itself was the finish, and only after it became intolerably dirty was it given a facelift of white, cream or pale buff limewash or distemper. Apart from the eighteenth century plasterwork which was designed to be coloured, most colour dates from the Victorian period as mentioned earlier.

Over-painting bright colours may prove disappointing if they were applied in the first place because so much detail had been lost under centuries of paint. In this case it will be necessary to remove the old layers to regain the subtleties of the design.

Once repaired and repainted, plasterwork is best left alone. Apart from removing cobwebs with a feather duster, the only attention it needs is a routine check that there are no damp patches caused through leaking roofs or gutters or an alteration in ground level. These should be identified during the quinquennial inspection, but by then severe damage may have occurred. A simple, regular check can mean that potential dangers are recognized and dealt with before problems with the plasterwork have a chance to develop. Prompt action can save both ancient fabric and modern funds.

JANE SCHOFIELD
After a degree in sculpture, Jane Schofield developed her practical skills to repair ornamental plasterwork, specializing in the conservation of early lime-based plaster. She also makes and sells mature lime products from her Devon smallholding.

~ 7 ~

SCULPTURE

✽

Michael Eastham

Monuments and sculpture found in churches differ considerably in design, structure, material and location but it is their position within or outside the building which is the prime consideration for the conservator assessing their condition and treatment. Monuments inside the building stand as independent structures yet take support and weather protection from it. By the same token they are affected by factors controlling the climate of the building, a leaking roof, rising damp, high humidity and fluctuations of temperature. Sculpture performs a commemorative, decorative, instructional and often functional role in the building, whether inside or out, and is equally subject to appropriate mechanisms of decay. Churchyard monuments and crosses, which sadly suffer widespread neglect and vandalism, fall prey to mowing machines, subsidence, organic growth and sometimes wholesale removal.

INTERNAL MONUMENTS

There are many variations of form but a limited number of basic structures and they form a useful means of classification.

7.1 Neale Monument (1621), Church of Our Lady, Warnford, Hampshire. Alabaster monument shown after conservation.

1. Wall monuments.
2. Ledger stones.
3. Tomb chest or table monuments.
4. Canopied tomb chest monuments.

Wall monuments

Wall monuments can be very simple in design comprising a slab of stone with a carved or painted inscription. Relatively light in weight, they can be fastened to the wall with metal tie bars known as cramps. Simple inscriptions of great antiquity are found, but there are many eighteenth and nineteenth century examples surviving. Wall monuments can be very ornate, ranging from contrasting white and black compositions to extravagant use of coloured marbles combined with flamboyant carving of brackets, portrait busts or medallions, lanterns, swags and cherubs.

As the monuments grow in size and complexity it follows that they increase in weight and can no longer be supported by wall cramps. A cantilever system of support is employed, where blocks of stone known as corbels or brackets are set well into the wall with their protruding ends taking the weight of the monument. Cramps are still used on the large wall monuments, but when associated with corbels, they simply tie back the top of the monument to the wall and prevent any forward movement.

Ledger stones

These are stones with inscriptions or bearing incised, low relief carving let into the floor and forming part of it. Generally they mark the actual place of burial or an entry point to a vault. They can also be bedded directly into the earth and pointed with a lime mortar to separate the stone from adjoining slabs.

Tomb chest monuments

Free-standing versions rely for stability on the tomb chest and the substantial core to be found inside which is constructed of brick or rubble. The core gives support to the table top set above it and provides for the attachment of the tomb chest panels which adorn the sides of the monument. The table tops are sometimes plain, perhaps carrying a chamfered inscription, or provide the indent for an inlaid monumental brass. Life-sized effigies, reclining, kneeling, or sitting, are a regular feature and the tomb chest panels below may be carved to reflect the architectural style of the period or to display heraldry, weepers, or effigies of children.

Canopied tomb chest monuments

A further variation on the tomb chest type is found where a canopy is raised above the effigies by means of columns, as many as eight in number, supporting a ceiling with entablature to provide an elevated platform for the display of heraldic achievements, allegorical figures, pyramids, putti, and inscriptions. More elaborate versions occur where, in addition to the columns and canopy, an adjoining wall is used, hollowed out and lined with panelling to form a niche complete with coffered ceiling. The niche provides space for an inscription and for two or three effigies to be displayed in stepped arrangement from the table into the alcove. Tomb chest monuments can be quite complex structures combining many sections of panelling, moulding and carved decoration in the manner of a small building. The constituent parts are fastened together and to the core by metal cramps and dowels set in a variety of mortars and sometimes secured with molten lead. If original, these fastenings are found to be almost always of iron, but dowels were occasionally made of wood or animal bones. Replacement fastenings fitted during periods of renovation and repair are found in steel, copper, bronze and brass.

CARVED DETAIL

Internal sculpture can be closely associated with the building in material and structure, or free-standing and independent in material. Capitals, voussoirs, door and window mouldings, fonts and pulpits have always provided scope for sculptural expression. Sculptural detail on the outside of the building can function in the form of drip mouldings, gargoyles and balustrades but also provide expression as figure sculpture on tower or facade.

Churchyard monuments

The earliest surviving headstones, monuments and crosses in the yard may be carved from the type of stone native to the parish, in common with the church building. Later monuments, reflecting changes in taste and a wider availability of stone through improved transport, will show much greater variety of material. Incised headstones, tomb chest type and canopied monuments can be found, all built directly on the ground with bases below ground level to gain stability.

POLYCHROME SCULPTURE

Interior monuments were frequently painted, disguising, enhancing and transforming the stone used in their construction. Many monuments still exhibit painted surface decoration but the paintwork has often been so altered by over-painting during one or more schemes of renovation as to bear little or no relationship to the original scheme. Flat colour finishes applied with modern gloss or emulsion paints are no substitute for the rich and subtle artistry generated by the craftsmen first employed to transform the carved stone into flesh, textile and metal. Overlays of colour, translucent glazes, gilding and wax applique techniques were used to dazzling effect and the evidence for such technical and artistic accomplishment can be found beneath the layers of over-paint.

MATERIALS COMMONLY IN USE

Limestone

This is one of the sedimentary rocks widely available and suitable for building, carving and monument construction. Composed principally of calcium carbonate, it varies in colour, composition and durability. In the past the selection of the stone would have depended very much on local availability or the convenience of water transport. Certain limestones, notably Purbeck and Sussex stones, are composed of marine snail shells in a matrix of calcium carbonate and are sufficiently hard to take a polish. Purbeck was prized for colour and decorative surface and was transported by sea from the quarries in Dorset to locations throughout Britain. Derbyshire fossil limestones, from the Carboniferous series, have similar characteristics with a myriad of fossil forms revealed by polishing the stone. Hard limestones displaying these qualities became known as marbles although in geological terms they are fossil limestones. Black carboniferous limestone, a tough, durable stone with a slightly waxy polish found favour as suitable material for table and inscription panelling in monument construction.

Sandstone

This is a primary source of building stone from the sedimentary series, principally composed of quartz grains bound in matrices of varying composition. A matrix of silica produces an extremely durable stone, whereas one of clay makes the stone liable to rapid disintegration. Colours vary through buff and brown to red, yellow, and green/grey.

Marble

A metamorphic rock which is formed by subjecting limestone to heat and pressure, changing the crystal structure, hardness and colour. Not native to Britain, but many black, white and coloured marbles were imported for monument and sculpture production. Surfaces were polished and the qualities of colour, veining and mottling used to great effect. The hard, compact nature of marble allows for very precise carving, where sharp arrises and crisp detail are characteristic.

Alabaster

A fine-grained granular form of gypsum or calcium sulphate, it is soluble in water. Alabaster was popular for the building of interior monuments because, although massive and essentially nonporous, it is extremely soft and easily carved. The surface is so soft that it can be cut with a finger nail, a fact illustrated by the number of alabaster effigies having surfaces disfigured by incised graffiti. The impervious quality of the surface made it especially suitable for polychrome decoration. Early alabaster, carved from plentiful deposits, was almost pure white in colour although always with a measure of translucency compared with marble. When the white alabaster had been worked out, other grades were used, tinted by iron and copper oxides and having a creamy, dappled appearance modified by characteristic veining of red and green. It is often confused with marble, but a touch test reveals it to be comparatively warmer.

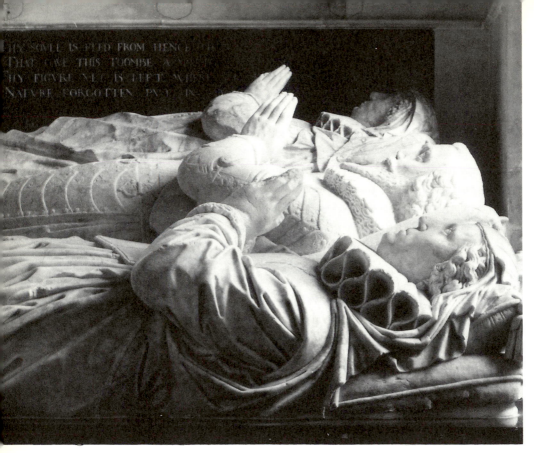

7.2 Neale Monument (1621), Church of Our Lady, Warnford, Hampshire. Detail of Sir Thomas Neale and his wives, Elizabeth and Mary, in alabaster.

Plaster

This is a prepared form of gypsum used in monument work for casting and modelling small detail, for repair and for setting stones together. Plaster sets quickly and firmly but grows brittle with age and is prone to fracture. It breaks down under prolonged moisture attack.

Terracotta

Terracotta is a fired earth rather similar to earthenware. A clay fired at relatively low temperature and varying in colour from pale buff to strong red. Terracotta sculpture was frequently painted but is not a common material in use for church monuments. Exceptions are to be found at Layer Marney, Essex where the monuments to the two Lords Marney have panelling and a canopy in terracotta.

Coade Stone

This is another fired clay body, but to high temperature, producing a material of high strength and durability. Pale cream in colour and crisply modelled with a fire hardened surface. The Coade Stone company produced large quantities of sculpture, monuments and architectural detail between 1769 and 1836. Coade Stone monuments are not unusual in churchyards, and many examples will be found impressed with the company name and date of manufacture.

DETERIORATION AND CONSERVATION

External stone is subject to weathering by atmospheric pollutants, notably sulphur dioxide. Erosion, and the growth of impervious sulphation skins, leads to considerable loss and damage to surfaces. The movement of soluble salts through the stone and their subsequent crystallization at the surface results in significant damage. Soluble salts in the form of carbonates, chlorides, sulphates and nitrates can be present in groundwater and in water percolating through masonry walls from where they transfer to sculpture and monument. The salts are thought to travel by capillary action through the pores of the stone, eventually being drawn to the surface by evaporation. A wetting and drying cycle, brought into play by periodic rainfall externally and periodic heating internally, serves to increase the rate of evaporation and encourages the salts to crystallize out of solution. The pressure generated by crystal formation is sufficient to loosen particles from the matrix and a friable surface is initiated.

The solubility of limestones in acids has led to their steady, slow dissolution through acid rain attack decade by decade. It is instructive to inspect a weathered limestone surface where resistant fossil shell protrudes above the level of the stone indicating the amount of material lost from the carving line. The performance of sandstones undergoing weathering is affected by the strength of the binding matrix. Calcareous and argillaceous sandstones, having predominantly lime or clay matrices, erode severely if placed in close proximity to limestones where the decay products of calcium sulphate wash into the sandstone to disrupt the matrix and loosen the quartz grains. A typical weathering pattern on sandstone is the formation of 'contour scaling' where the face of the stone is lost in areas parallel to the face of the carving. The erosion is a result of soluble salt movements accelerated by wetting and drying cycles. Surfaces affected may exhibit efflorescence as well.

Dense pointing material in the form of hard, impermeable mortars prevents water escaping through joints and directs it through the stone margins at the edges of the joint, accelerating decay in the stone. External sculpture has generally undergone repair, usually by the application of rich cement mortars, and these impermeable fillings trap moisture, increase decay and fail prematurely. Sculpture may be fixed in position originally with iron dowels and repair work can deposit astonishing amounts of metal in the sculpture. Steel, brass and copper cramps, dowels, wires, tie bars and braces are all likely additions. The ferrous metals will rust and expand when wet, staining the stone and exerting great pressure upon it, sufficient to cause severe damage. Copper salts leach from copper, brass and bronze fixings and stain green.

Terracotta and Coade Stone sculpture withstand weathering exceptionally well if a glazed or fire hardened surface skin remains intact. Damage, fire cracks and disruption from metal fastenings can affect the integrity of the surface and allow moisture to penetrate the body of the material. In the churchyard, headstones may exhibit erosion and loss of surface in a band just above ground level, indicative of a drying zone where salts carried up from the ground crystallize and accelerate decay. Power mowing the confined spaces between headstones and monuments has led to abrasion damage. Exposure in the yard has left monuments prone to attack by vandals. Even minor subsidence can lead to instability and collapse. The vigorous growth of ivy and other invasive plants can be very disruptive if left unchecked.

INTERNAL SCULPTURE AND MONUMENTS

The principal agent of deterioration is moisture which reaches monuments in the form of rising and penetrating damp from the floor and walls of the building. The moisture saturates structures and activates soluble salts, damaging the stone and attacking ferrous fastenings in the monuments to cause corrosion, expansion and a threat to stability. The porous nature of many limestones, sandstones and marbles makes them susceptible to damage by moisture attack and alabaster is at even greater risk because it is soluble in water. Condensation and drips of water can quickly degrade a surface while prolonged contact can lead to sugaring of the alabaster where crystals are disturbed and displaced.

7.3 Monument to Thomas White, Church of St John the Baptist, Bristol.
Extreme decay of polychromed abalabster.

The movement of soluble salts through alabaster is restricted by the
dense nature of the material and efflorescence is usually confined to
natural fissures in the stone and to associated joints. Plaster, when
affected by moisture loses strength, softens, and breaks down to damp
powder.

Condensation causes problems with polished and painted surfaces.
Temperature and humidity levels fluctuate inside church buildings
and, when the dewpoint is reached, moisture is deposited from saturated
air upon the cold surfaces of monuments. When combined with dust,
dirt and salts the water serves to etch surfaces, dissolve alabaster and
disrupt paint films. Corroding and expanding iron fastenings present
serious problems with monuments leading to immense disruption,
particularly of the complex canopied structures. With a simple wall
monument the corrosion and weakening of cramps can cause the panel
to fall from the wall with potentially disastrous results. Tomb chest
monuments depend upon iron cramps inserted into the structure at all
levels to secure them together and are liable to great disturbance when
the monument comes under attack from rising and penetrating damp.
Base stones are generally linked together with cramps, tomb chest
panels tied back to the core in the same way, and dowels used between

table, column, capital and entablature. Cramps, rods and braces are found at canopy level securing the ceiling, attaching decorative elements together and sometimes fastening the canopy back to an adjoining wall.

Early repairs can contribute to the problems of decay. The use of hard repair mortars causes as many difficulties with internal sculpture as with external ones because of the interaction with moisture. The disparity between the strength of hard cement mortar and that of alabaster, for example, makes the removal of the cement extremely difficult without inflicting further damage upon the alabaster. The problem is compounded by moisture leaching from the mortar to sugar and weaken the alabaster in contact with it. Early repair work may have attempted only cosmetic treatment and not addressed underlying reasons for the disturbance and it is not unusual to find open joints repointed with plaster and no attention given to a rusting iron cramp within. Where radical repairs have been completed in the past, correcting the problems can be a daunting task. For example, at Warnford in Hampshire, the Neale monument (see the illustration on p.102), a large canopied tomb chest in alabaster, had the canopy strengthened in 1930. Two rolled steel joists were laid on concrete beds over the canopy and tie rods inserted vertically through the ceiling to connect with the joists. The remainder of the monument, in almost pristine white alabaster, was then pointed throughout in hard Portland cement mortar.

It is surprising to find that monuments move position and are not always to be found where they were first constructed. Re-ordering, modifications and rebuilding can cause them to be removed from one setting to another. There are cases where a monument has moved from one building to another. At Preston-on-Stour Warwickshire, the Kempe monument was transferred from a London church and then fastened to the wall on corbels attached by cramps to blocks of oak set into the wall. The oak decayed to dust and only one corbel remained effective in keeping the structure attached to the wall before major repair work was undertaken.

On occasion, a free standing tomb chest monument has been moved against a wall to increase floor space and the rear panels have been lifted and placed on the wall above and behind the tomb chest. Such an alteration makes a nonsense of the design, but more seriously leaves the monument open to attack from penetrating damp. Painted surfaces can suffer considerable disruption from moisture attack, especially where the stone beneath the paint layer is porous. Infiltrating water can disturb the bonding between paint and stone as well as between layers of paint. Oil bound paint films which are commonly found on monuments are impermeable and restrict the passage of moisture through the stone. Sections of paint lift, craze, bubble and flake away as the surface beneath the paint is disrupted. Floor standing monuments and ledger stones can be adversely affected by the type and condition of the flooring in the building. Where hard Victorian tile is laid to the margins of a monument the floor can act as a waterproof barrier preventing rising damp travelling through it. In consequence, the damp is directed into pathways through which it can escape, the monuments, ledger stones, walls and piers, and the effect upon them is magnified.

CONSERVATION TREATMENTS

The sculpture conservator can initiate a number of treatments and procedures when the condition of a monument or sculpture gives cause for concern. A conservator will inspect the monument thoroughly in order to report upon its condition and give an estimate for the cost of the work. The resulting conservation report will locate the monument in the building, give the dimensions, material and description of the piece, record the condition, attempt to analyse the reasons for deterioration and provide recommendations for treatment.

Where an internal monument has been subjected to moisture attack to the point where the stone, surface decoration and fastenings have all been affected, the most radical form of treatment and one frequently necessary is the dismantling of the monument to allow corroding fastenings to be removed, repairs to be completed and a damp-proof membrane to be installed. Before embarking upon such a procedure the conservator will make a photographic record of the monument and, in all but the simplest case, make a measured drawing of the structure to ensure accurate rebuilding to the original dimensions and location. Dismantling proceeds through opening joints, cutting through or releasing fastenings and lifting sections of stone away. As each piece is removed it is numbered and the position recorded on a working diagram. In situations where surfaces are friable, paint flaking or detail in a fragile condition dismantling can only take place after preconsolidation treatment.

Preconsolidation is a method used to secure vulnerable surfaces prior to handling, cleaning, or repairing them. The surface requiring treatment is strengthened by the application of an acrylic resin from brush or dropper. When dry, the surface can be further strengthened by applications of facing tissue. When cleaning begins the resin and tissue layers are readily removed. After cleaning, delicate surfaces may require further consolidation and acrylic resins are most effective for the purpose.

After dismantling an internal monument it is normally cleaned by removing remaining fastenings, cutting away mortar and old fillings and dusting off surfaces. The type, surface finish and condition of the stone will determine the method of cleaning to follow. Where preconsolidation has been necessary, the consolidant may serve as an aid to cleaning by strengthening a friable surface sufficiently to allow a solvent to be introduced and dirt to be removed. On the other hand, the consolidant may have to be removed to allow cleaning to take place. The following categories of material and appropriate cleaning programmes indicate some of the possibilities.

Limestone

Water-based methods are both appropriate and effective, but there are always exceptions and magnesian limestones can produce spectacular efflorescence when water cleaned.

Water is usually applied by brush, swab or spray, in poultice form, and by steam generator. A conservator will clean a surface by applying small quantities of solvent in a controlled manner, avoiding flooding and the risk of driving dirt deeper into porous limestones. The solvent may be worked with a brush or swab and collected with a second swab to lift loosened dirt from the surface. Poultices are used to draw deep-seated dirt from limestones and marbles and can also be effective in reducing soluble salt levels. A poultice is mixed by adding water to an Attapulgite or Sepiolite clay and then applied to the wetted surface of the stone. As moisture evaporates from the surface of the poultice it draws further moisture from the stone, capturing the dirt and salts in the clay. When cracked and leather hard, the poultice is removed, the surface washed and the process repeated until cleaning is completed. Where the intention is to reduce soluble salt levels, deionized water is used in the poultice and batches of used poultice can be sampled with a conductivity bridge to indicate the quantity of salts in solution. The device measures the conductivity of a solution and relates directly to the concentration of soluble salts forming the electrolyte.

If grease, oils, or wax deposits are encountered at depth they can be poulticed out using an appropriate hydrocarbon solvent but the evaporation of the solvent will need to be controlled by covering the poultice with cling film. Paper poultices, made from high-grade blotting paper can sometimes be substituted for clay and are thought to be particularly effective in removing soluble salts. They are clean to use and very easily and quickly removed from a surface.

Steam is a useful cleaning method on limestones. There is little risk of over-wetting a surface and as the dirt is dispersed into the condensing water both can be gathered by swab and removed. Residual heat dries the stone quickly, reducing the risk of disturbance. Steam can sometimes be used to remove surface grease and wax without recourse to hydrocarbon solvents.

On external limestone sculpture cleaning can be achieved by the use of lime in poultice form. Poultice and sculpture are kept damp and air excluded over a period of two to three weeks before the lime is removed. Friable areas can be treated with lime water to provide some binding of the surface before applying repair mortars. Lime mortars are used to fill gaps, to hold loose fragments in place, to grout cavities and to eliminate water traps. Finally the sculpture is treated with a fine slurry of lime and aggregate producing a shelter coat, colour matched to the stone and intended to act sacrificially under further weathering attack.

Marble

The methods of cleaning applicable to limestone are suitable for marble cleaning but often extended by a wider range of solvents, cleaning paste and micro-airbrasive methods. Acetone and white spirit can be helpful as well as an emulsion formed from water, white spirit and soap. Solvol Autosol, a proprietary paste cleaner, can be useful but needs careful removal with white spirit and acetone to avoid a white residue remaining in crevices and detail. The porosity of marble can lead to dirt being deeply ingrained beneath the surface and poultice cleaning is often necessary. Micro-airbrasive cleaning can be helpful especially in the removal of hard sulphation skins. The micro-airbrasive tool directs a finely controlled stream of cutting particles at the surface by means of compressed air. Aluminium oxide is commonly used as the abrasive powder and the flow of powder and pressure can be regulated with great precision.

7.4   Font (*c* 1160), Church of St Mary Magdalene, Eardisley, Herefordshire. The sandstone font is shown after conservation.

Sandstone

Steam is especially useful for cleaning sandstones but if heavy soiling is a problem it may need to be followed by solvent or micro-airbrasive cleaning methods. The granular nature of the surface leads to dirt becoming trapped within crevices and interstices and makes it difficult to remove.

Alabaster

The solubility of alabaster in water precludes the use of water as a cleaning solution except as an emulsion with white spirit and soap which can be both safe and effective. Mixtures of white spirit and acetone can be helpful and so can Solvol paste, but the paste must be cleared very thoroughly from the surface to avoid a white bloom forming as the solvent dries. The extreme softness of alabaster leaves the surface vulnerable to scratching and abrasion so that any cleaning has to be very controlled to avoid accidental damage. Removing dirt from incised graffiti improves the appearance of a marked surface considerably and deep incisions can be filled to reduce their impact further.

Plaster

On a sound plaster surface it may be possible to clean with steam but if any additional moisture is likely to cause disruption then dry cleaning methods apply. A pencil eraser, Draft Clean, or bread worked gently across the surface can remove a considerable measure of grime.

Terracotta

Steam and water methods can be effective but the porous nature of terracotta leaves it prone to staining and a patchy finish after solvent cleaning. As with plaster, dry cleaning methods can offer a safer alternative but some terracotta surfaces can be very soft, liable to scratch and extremely difficult to clean.

Coade Stone

Steam and water methods together with chemical solvents provide the means of cleaning sound surfaces. Where the fire skin has eroded or broken away to expose the body of the material, porosity can be a problem and dirt is likely to be driven in, presenting great difficulty in cleaning.

Polychrome surfaces

Where paint is disrupted, flaking or cupping on the surface, cleaning is usually completed by a combination of methods combining consolidation, setting cupped and loose flakes back to the stone by heated spatula, followed by solvent cleaning. Acrylic resins are used to re-attach paint to the surface and to strengthen painted surfaces after cleaning. Solvents are chosen for their capacity to remove dirt films without attacking the paint. In some situations cleaning by micro-airbrasive tool is preferable, and on other occasions over-paint is effectively removed by scalpel. The large scale of polychrome monuments limits the amount of work that can be undertaken to paint surfaces where funding is limited, so that complete removal of over-paint is generally avoided. Disrupted paint films are given priority, light cleaning is undertaken and sometimes a 'window' is made to explore the paint layers in depth to discover and report on the earlier schemes in use.

REPAIR

Broken sections of stone are usually joined together with a polyester stone adhesive and reinforced by stainless steel dowels or cramps. Wherever possible, existing fastening holes are used to house the dowels or cramps but where fresh breaks have occurred the joint faces must be drilled to receive new dowels. Stainless steel to BS316 is generally specified as having the highest resistance to corrosion. A number of commercial brands of adhesive are available, developed specifically for use with stone. Thixotropic grades of adhesive fit many applications but low viscosity resins are available for fine jointing or long dowel settings. A repair is made by cleaning the break surface, drilling to accommodate the dowels, then cutting and dry fitting the dowels to ensure an accurate joint. The adhesive is mixed and positioned with the dowels and the joint held together until set. Adhesive will creep across a surface under pressure so the amount applied to a joint face is calculated to complete the joint without reaching the face of the stone. Polyester resins are affected by ultra-violet light and darken considerably after exposure. Where they are used to repair white marble and alabaster it can be helpful to modify them with titanium white pigment before application. Multiple fractures of stone requiring repair can lead to complex solutions with larger fragments being joined first and small sections fitted to them. A dry run will help to avoid the problem of locking out where the sequence of joining can prevent all the pieces fitting together accurately.

After breaks have been joined and set there will be gaps to fill to complete the repair. For external sculpture, a lime mortar combining sand and an appropriate stone dust can make a durable and colour matched filling. On internal sculpture there is a wide choice of filling materials available, with acrylic-based mixtures performing well. Marble and alabaster fillings have often been made from alabaster powder in clear embedding resin which can produce a body with excellent colour, translucency and sparkle. Some fillings of this type applied to church monuments have been found to discolour and acrylic resin is now more commonly used. The acrylics do not produce the translucent colour so effective on alabaster and need retouching when dry to adjust their colour to the surroundings.

REBUILDING CHURCH MONUMENTS

The essential part of rebuilding a church monument is the damp-proof membrane. The membrane, commonly of lead sheet, is used to isolate the monument from the floor and walls of the building. It is sometimes necessary to replace the foundations of a tomb chest monument, by excavating the floor, packing with hard-core and forming a raft of concrete to support the weight. The concrete is allowed to dry thoroughly before the damp-proof membrane is fitted above it. Lead sheet is laid down, protected from the fresh concrete by bitumen paint or liquid asphaltic composition. Vertical damp-proof membranes are necessary behind wall monuments but sheet sizes and fastenings must comply with Lead Development Association recommendations to be effective. The monument will be rebuilt above the damp proof membrane using stainless steel fastenings set into polyester stone adhesive and bedded and pointed with lime mortar, PVA/sand or acrylic/sand mortars. The core material in tomb chest monuments will be replaced with building block or brick joined together with resin mortars to restrict the amount of water used in the construction. Marble and alabaster monuments are normally treated with microcrystalline wax to protect surfaces from handling, atmospheric moisture and dirt. Occasional careful dusting is all that is required to maintain clean surfaces.

External sculpture and decorative detail is sometimes found to have been disrupted to the point where any further weathering will lead to complete loss. In such a situation, conservators may decide to consolidate the stone in depth to prevent further damage and decay caused by moisture and the movement of soluble salts. Silane resins, with the capacity to penetrate deeply into the stone, are used for this purpose. The resins have a number of useful properties, including the ability to travel deeply into porous limestones and sandstones, to strengthen and line the pores of the stone and to allow moisture vapour to escape through the treated matrix.

Limitations on use are governed by the porosity of stone to be treated, some darkening of treated surfaces and the high cost of application. The treatment is never likely to be reversible and is normally considered as a last resort where the alternative would be to lose the sculpture altogether.

GLOSSARY

Allegorical figure Small figure sculpture found on canopies or cornice with emblems attributing them to the virtues of Faith, Hope, Charity, Patience, Justice, etc.

Arris The sharp edge where two surfaces meet.

Balustrade Coping or handrail supported by a series of small pillars or balusters.

Capital The top part of a column.

Corbel A projecting piece of stone designed to support weight.

Drip moulding A projecting moulding designed to direct water off the face of a wall.

Efflorescence Salt crystallization at the surface of the stone.

Entablature The horizontal structure comprising cornice, frieze and architrave in Classical architecture positioned above the columns and capitals.

Friable A loose deteriorated surface marked by powdering stone often associated with blistering and flaking decay

Fire-skin Hardened surface produced by exposure to extreme temperature in a kiln.

Gargoyle A waterspout carved into decorative or fantastic forms.

Micro-airbrasive Precision tool using compressed air to supply abrasive powder through a fine jet nozzle.

Thixotropic Viscous.

Voussoir A wedge-shaped segment of stone used to form a semicircular arch.

Weepers Small figures set along the sides of tomb chest monuments.

MICHAEL EASTHAM

Michael Eastham works as a freelance conservator of sculpture. He has extensive experience in the conservation of church monuments and architectural detail. He also works for museums and private sculpture collections throughout the British Isles.

~ 8 ~

METALWORK

*

Hazel Newey

Metalwork found in and around church buildings can fulfil a variety of functions: structural, architectural, functional, commemorative and decorative. Often one or more of these are combined in one object, for example, a brass altar rail, but there are simple guidelines which can be followed to ensure that the metal is preserved to the best effect. This chapter will not deal with structural metalwork, which is covered in Chapter 1 on the fabric of the building. Architectural metalwork, for example wrought iron railings, is a specialized subject in itself and consequently will be mentioned only briefly with information on who to contact for further advice.

Metals are utilized both for their qualities of physical strength and attractive appearance, the latter often in conjunction with their monetary value. It is sometimes assumed that metals are virtually indestructible. Under certain circumstances objects made of metal can be as fragile as china and as easily damaged, so it is important to handle metalwork carefully. By their chemical nature metals react with the

---

8.1 Mediaeval chalice with silver bowl and enamelled plaques on copper stem and foot. The dark patches on the bowl are silver sulphide or tarnish. This is easy to remove using a suitable cleaning method. Great care must be taken to ensure that any chemical chosen does not touch the delicate surface of the enamels. Likewise no solution should be allowed to run inside the hollow stem or behind the plaques where the corrosion process could continue undetected. (Photograph reproduced by kind permission of the Trustees of the British Museum.)

environment around them to form layers of oxides, sulphides and other minerals on the surface. Sometimes these produce a stable, decorative patina of age, valued as part of the object itself. In different circumstances the layers are unstable and the metal continues to corrode until eventually the object will become unrecognizable or totally disappear.

The purpose of this chapter is to identify the main causes of deterioration of metal objects, how to recognize that it is taking place and then how to deal with it. Simple cleaning and housekeeping methods will be described but it is important to stress that conservation or restoration of complex or historically important metalwork should only be undertaken by trained and experienced conservators, who are always willing to advise on suitable treatments.

CHEMICAL DETERIORATION

Very few metals exist in nature in the metallic state. Instead they are found as mineral ores from which the metal is extracted, for example, by smelting or heating. This produces a higher energy, unstable state which tries to revert to the ore by reacting with the chemicals in the environment around it. The metals can also be arranged in order of their chemical stability which will predict how two metals in contact with each other will behave, the baser one corroding in preference to the nobler. Two or more metals can be combined to form an alloy and the original properties of each are subsequently modified to make it more useful for the production of artefacts.

Once the metal is produced, the method of manufacture can lead to problems. Poor quality workmanship, for example, the remains of soldering flux not removed, can result in corrosion taking place, either visibly on the object surface or inside the structure. The latter is obviously more difficult to detect and to treat but could lead eventually to the physical breakdown of the object.

In any building a metal will react with moisture and chemicals in the atmosphere to begin the corrosion process. It is important, therefore, to reduce these where possible by removing metalwork from direct contact with the source of moisture and materials which may give off harmful chemicals.

Finally, the chemicals present in polishes and cleaners can act as corrosion agents if not thoroughly rinsed off and residues removed after use. Worse still the wrong cleaner can actually harm the object by attacking the metal itself. Chemicals present on human skin in sweat can also affect metals, especially those with a polished surface. It is sometimes possible to see a fingerprint etched into the surface of an object. Good housekeeping procedures such as the wearing of suitable gloves when handling the pieces, correct cleaning methods and good storage conditions can ensure that many of these problems do not arise.

PHYSICAL DETERIORATION

Despite their impression of physical strength, all metals to a greater or lesser degree are subject to physical damage. They can be scratched, bent and broken. The surface will be abraded away by overvigorous cleaning or rubbing with the resulting loss of incised or applied decoration. Careful handling can prolong the life of metal objects and ensure that damage is kept to a minimum. Objects should always be handled with two hands where possible and excessive manipulation of moving parts such as hinged lids avoided so that undue strain is not put on them. Likewise handles, stems or necks of vessels may prove to be areas of weakness in older metalwork and should not be used to pick up the object without supporting it underneath.

CLEANING

Dust that settles on a metal surface can attract moisture and thus act as an initiator for corrosion. It is important therefore regularly to dust all metal objects on open display. This should be done with a soft, lint-free cloth which may also help to remove fingerprints if the object has been handled. For more delicate or intricate objects a soft bristle brush could be used in conjunction with a vacuum cleaner to take away the dust. It is not advisable to use a feather duster as the sharp section of the quills may scratch the metal surface.

Washing with water and a non-ionic detergent like Synperonic NDB, followed by thorough rinsing and drying can also remove dust and some surface deposits. This should only be used for robust modern silver because the water may initiate corrosion in the other metals.

Conservators often recommend that hollow objects are not immersed in any liquid because of the difficulty in ensuring that all chemicals are totally removed and the interior of the structure dried. Needless to say that if the metal is associated with another material, for example wood, the object must not be immersed at all.

Candle grease may be removed either by gently warming the candle stick with a domestic hairdryer and absorbing the wax onto paper tissues or by careful application of white spirit on a cotton wool bud. If the wax is hard it may be possible to pick it off the metal but there is a danger of scratching the surface if this is done too roughly.

The majority of metal objects have a shiny, reflective surface and this is achieved, and maintained, usually by polishing or rubbing the surface with an abrasive material. The disadvantage of polishing is that by removing tarnish it also removes a small part of the surface metal. Gradually the metal is worn away so it is extremely important not to overclean objects. Ideally cleaning should only take place when the object needs it and not as a matter of routine.

CORROSION INDICATORS ON METALS

This section describes the common corrosion layers found on those metals likely to be found in a church. Some may be easily and safely removed by non-conservators using the techniques described below but others indicate that something more serious is occurring and professional advice should be sought.

Gold

Gold is one of the most stable and valuable metals. It is yellow in colour and extremely soft in the pure state, so it is usually alloyed with another metal such as copper to increase its hardness and durability. Baser metals like silver or copper are sometimes gilded and a thin layer of gold applied chemically or electrolytically to the surface. Gold itself does not corrode or deteriorate under normal circumstances but it becomes covered with the corrosion products of the associated metal. This can make identification of the nature of the object difficult and so it is extremely important to examine any piece carefully before deciding upon a cleaning method. Excessive polishing or rubbing of a gilded object will soon remove the surface layer, leaving the base metal visible.

Silver

Silver is a white lustrous metal that can be polished to a shiny reflective surface. Like gold it is a soft metal, easily worked and is usually alloyed with copper for hardness, the composition of the alloy being identified by the hallmarks stamped onto the surface. It is also found in conjunction with the baser metals in the form of Sheffield plate and electroplate, again, both identified by maker's marks.

Silver is extremely susceptible to the presence of sulphur in the atmosphere. Minimal quantities will react with the metal to form silver sulphide or tarnish which begins as an iridescent yellow-brown layer and gradually gets darker and darker. Eventually if left untouched it will form a thick black layer which obscures any decoration or detail. It is not chemically damaging to the metal, only cosmetically displeasing. Tarnish can be removed by a suitable proprietary metal cleaner, though consequently part of the surface of the object is also being removed at the same time. Therefore, the more the metal tarnishes and requires cleaning the more surface is removed and the thinner the object becomes. It is important to ensure that minimal cleaning is carried out and that the silver is stored in such a way that tarnishing is reduced.

It should be mentioned at this stage that there are two decorative techniques used in the fabrication of silver objects which are removed by certain cleaning methods. The first is niello, a black waxlike inlay inserted into incised patterns or designs on the metal's surface. It contains a mixture of silver, copper and lead sulphides. The second is a deliberate blackening of the surface to produce an artificial patina which can enhance detail or design. If either of these are likely to be present then expert advice must definitely be sought before attempting any type of cleaning.

Under certain conditions and when more copper is present in the alloy the metal surface may become covered with green corrosion. The treatment of this will be discussed next. A mediaeval silver chalice is illustrated at the beginning of this chapter.

Copper

Copper in the pure state is a soft, pinkish coloured metal that can be rolled or hammered into sheets which are then fabricated into objects. In the atmosphere dark oxide and sulphide layers are formed, which are brown and often considered to be a desirable patina of age. In the presence of excess moisture and chemical pollutants like chlorides corrosion will start to take place which can lead to serious disfigurement or eventually to total loss of the object if left untreated. If pale green powdery crystals are seen on any copper or copper alloy objects then professional advice must be obtained immediately. This indicates the presence of 'bronze disease', a problem usually associated with buried metalwork though it can be found where the environment is particularly damp and the object is in contact with ground salts. The treatment of this condition can only be carried out by a professional conservator in laboratory conditions because of the chemicals involved. Hard green deposits or spots on the metal surface resulting from water or other solutions dropping on to it can sometimes be removed by using a sharp blade or abrasive, but there is a danger of damaging the metal underneath. Similarly the use of chemicals can affect the alloy, so it is always important to consult a professional before embarking on any cleaning method.

Copper is also susceptible to organic acids and their vapours and will react with them to form basic copper acetate or verdigris. This is a dark green, waxy layer on the surface. Like tarnish, verdigris is cosmetically undesirable and will not affect the long-term chemical stability of the metal. It is easily removed by the local application of an organic solvent such as industrial methylated spirits using cotton wool pads or buds. When using any cleaning method it is essential to follow all the manufacturers' Health and Safety recommendations printed on the packaging. It is important to stress at this point that, like all copper compounds, verdigris is poisonous and great care should be taken when handling or cleaning objects. Ideally, plastic disposable or cotton gloves should be worn to protect both the metal and the handler. The two common alloys of copper are brass and bronze. Brass contains zinc and sometimes lead as well as copper and bronze contains tin and lead. Both can be cast as well as worked to fabricate objects. In addition the surface of each was treated to produce different decorative effects. Brass was sometimes given a coating of gold coloured lacquer, both to simulate the appearance of gilding and to protect it from tarnishing. The application of different chemical solutions to the surface of bronze produces artificial patinas of brown, black or green. These decorative effects can be easily lost by the wrong cleaning method or by indiscriminate handling, as can the natural patina of age mentioned above.

Bronzes and brasses were sometimes enamelled as well as gilded or silvered. The incised pattern or design was filled with a vitreous material which was then fired to fuse it in place. An alternative, cheaper method to enhance the decoration was to use coloured waxes or resins for this purpose. If the corrosion products conceal the surface of the object it will be difficult to see what is present and again the choice of the wrong cleaning material could seriously damage the object. Many of the commercial cleaners for copper alloys contain ammonia, recognizable by its distinctive pungent smell. If a brass object is immersed in an ammoniacal or alkaline solution the zinc in the alloy can dissolve out leaving behind a pink coppery surface. As a matter of principle objects should not be immersed in chemical or cleaning solutions because of the danger of reacting with the metal and any associated materials, plus the possibility of incomplete rinsing leading to further corrosion taking place.

Lead, tin and pewter

Lead is the softest of all metals, grey in colour, easily bent and shaped and leaves a grey mark on paper. It was used in the past to make pipework and butts for water and can be seen on the exterior walls of churches either left to weather and develop a natural patina or painted. Problems arise because of its softness and tendency to sag. In the past lead was alloyed with tin to produce a more durable alloy called pewter, but modern pewter is almost 100 per cent tin in composition.

Lead reacts readily with organic acid vapours in the atmosphere to form white, powdery lead carbonate. Like all lead compounds this is extremely poisonous and great care must be taken when handling objects made of the metal and its alloys. If active corrosion is seen on an object then professional help must be sought immediately. The object should be isolated by wrapping it carefully in polythene, wearing plastic or rubber gloves and a dust mask to prevent inhaling the powder. Any loose corrosion laying around must be carefully swept up, wrapped in paper and put in a polythene bag for correct disposal. Corrosion can sometimes take place under the top surface, especially if it is painted, and erupt out. It is possible to stabilize and preserve the object provided it is recognised early enough. This should only be done by an experienced conservator. Figures 8.2 and 8.3 show a corroding lead seal before and after treatment.

Pewter was, and still is, used to make plates and vessels such as jugs and cups. It is a harder, more stable metal than lead and can be polished to a high shine like silver. When it deteriorates it forms warts or pustules which push the surface away from the main body. If these

8.2 Lead seal before conservation. This picture illustrates lead corrosion in an advanced state. Some of the letters and the edge have become blurred as the metal turns to white powdery corrosion. Treatment of this object is further complicated by the fact that the seal is still attached to its document by the original silk threads. (Photograph reproduced by kind permission of the Trustees of the British Museum, with acknowledgements to the Dean and Chapter of Westminster (Collections of Westminster Abbey Muniments).)

8.3   Lead seal after conservation. The corrosion has been reduced back to lead and the surface consolidated with a synthetic resin without affecting either the vellum or the silk threads. It is still possible to read the letters but these would have been lost if the object had not been treated quickly. (Photograph reproduced by kind permission of the Trustees of the British Museum, with acknowledgements to the Dean and Chapter of Westminster (Collections of Westminster Abbey Muniments).)

warts are removed either chemically or mechanically a pit will be left which is aesthetically undesirable. If the wart is very large a hole will result.

Tin is a soft white metal which was used to coat other base metals, either to give the impression of silver or to protect them from corrosion. The inside surfaces of cooking vessels were also coated with tin to stop the copper contaminating the food. Coffin plates were sometimes made of tinplate, iron covered with tin, and because the tin is more stable than iron, as the iron rusted, the tin was pushed off the surface.

Iron and steel

Iron is alloyed with varying amounts of carbon to form cast iron, wrought iron and steel. Their differing properties of strength and workability mean that they are used for a variety of purposes. In the presence of excess moisture iron and steel corrode readily to form rust, a complex mixture of oxides, chlorides and other chemicals seen as a reddish-brown layer on the surface of the metal. As the corrosion proceeds unchecked the iron laminates and expands leading to the disintegration of the object. If the object is coated or painted this can give a degree of protection to the metal, although in the presence of excess moisture the iron can continue to corrode under the paint, the corrosion often concealed beneath it and finally erupting through.

If iron has been used to make an armature or cramps for a stone monument any expansion due to rusting will cause the structure to crack, as well as discolouring the surface of the stone by the absorption of iron salts. The problems of corroding iron in relation to the structure of the building and monuments is discussed elsewhere in this book. A thin layer of rust can be removed by simple abrasion using fine-grade steel wool and a thin household oil. The surface can be protected from further rusting by the application of a thin layer of oil or microcrystalline wax. Commercial rust removing solutions dissolve the rust and leave a passivated surface layer to reduce further damage. The final appearance of this may prove to be aethestically unacceptable and professional advice should be sought first.

COMPOSITE OBJECTS

These are objects made of more than one material, for example enamelled silver processional crosses with wooden shafts or iron bound wooden chests. Obviously the requirements of all materials present must be taken into consideration and cleaning methods selected that will not affect the other components. It is sometimes possible to separate each component and clean them individually. Where this is not possible the other material should be masked off with Clingfilm or Melinex and any cleaning solution applied locally on cotton wool buds, carefully rinsed off and dried. When in any doubt always ask the advice of a conservator before attempting any cleaning method.

RESTORATION

The repair of historically important metalwork must only be undertaken by a trained and experienced conservator or restorer, someone who will preserve the physical and historic integrity of the object, rather than approach a local jeweller or craftsman. It is not always essential to remove every dent and scratch from the surface as these are often part of the history and character of the piece. Small portable objects should be made physically safe and suitable for handling and use if that is necessary. Larger items must be made secure so that the church users are not at risk.

The aim is not to make an old object look like new but to conserve it for the future generations. In a museum repairs to metal objects are often made using synthetic resins and adhesives to avoid altering any evidence about how the piece was made. For objects that are in use, it is better to employ soldering or brazing as techniques for repair. If the object is very badly damaged then perhaps replacement should be considered and the original displayed or stored safely.

RESETTING MONUMENTAL BRASSES

Monumental brasses were usually set into precut stone slabs on monuments or on the floor of the church, using brass rivets and a layer of pitch or similar material to act as a damp-proof layer between stone and metal. Over the years, as people walked across the floors, the pitch was squeezed out and the softer slabs wore away leaving the edges of the brass exposed and the centre hollow. This meant that the brasses were vulnerable to accidental or deliberate damage and many were totally or partially removed from their true location and lost. Alternatively attempts were made to repair the slabs with cement, which reacted with the metal causing it to corrode. Many brasses whose slabs are unusable are sited on the walls of churches, screwed directly onto the brick or stone without a waterproof separating layer. Again, this led to corrosion of the back of the brasses as the moisture content of the environment increased and if the wrong type of fixing was used then further problems occurred. A method of avoiding these is to secure the brass to a chemically and physically stable board which is then fastened to the church wall.

Brasses set into the floor of a church should be protected by a layer of hessian-backed carpet over a good quality wool underfelt. Coconut matting or similar floor coverings are too abrasive and allow dirt to penetrate. Under no circumstances should cleaning fluids used on the floor be allowed to flow onto the surface of the metal. Likewise the brasses must not be polished or scrubbed at the same time as the rest of the floor. If possible visitors should not walk on them and rubbing reduced to a minimum. Figure 8.4 shows a monumental brass.

Advice on the conservation and restoration of church brasses may be obtained from The Conservation Officer at the Council for the Care of Churches or from the Secretary of the Monumental Brass Society.

STORAGE AND DISPLAY OF METALWORK

The ideal environment for storing or displaying objects made entirely of metal is stable, cool and dry. It should be free from atmospheric pollutants that will cause the metal to corrode. Where metal is found in association with organic materials, like wood, the relative humidity needs to be higher, between 50 and 60 per cent. In practice, these conditions are rarely found, especially in a building such as a church where both construction and use mean that the relative humidity and temperature fluctuate and pollutants cannot be excluded. Despite this, over the years many of the objects will have reached an equilibrium with their surroundings and sit happily in what appear to be unsuitable conditions. Problems will occur where microclimates are set up, for example on the back of a brass plaque screwed directly onto the church wall or where a damp object is stored in a sealed polythene bag. It is important to check regularly to ensure that no deterioration is taking place and to take immediate action if some indicator is found.

8.4 Detail of mediaeval brass of Sir John de Brewys. Taken before conservation, this photograph illustrates problems that can arise with monumental brasses. As the stone deteriorates and the surface spalls away the brass is left standing proud of the slab. Gaps around the edge of the metal make it vulnerable to loss and theft. The small tassel on the top right hand side is lying loose on the surface and must be removed to a safe place. The shield in the top left corner has already been lost and only its rivet and plug remain. The surface of the metal is covered in corrosion spots which, although not active, are unsightly. (Photograph reproduced by kind permission of B. Huntley-Egan, with acknowledgements to Wiston Estate Office and the Reverend Michael Walker, Rector of Ashington, Washington and Buneton.)

Objects which are neither used regularly nor displayed should be cleaned carefully, wrapped in acid-free tissue paper and stored in a suitable cupboard; lockable if the piece is valuable. Plastic bubble wrap can be used to prevent physical damage but it should not be tightly sealed. Corroding lead is the only metal that must be stored in sealed polythene bags. Silver can be placed in bags made of a special fabric containing a tarnish inhibitor, manufactured and supplied by Tarnprufe. An alternative method of reducing the rate of tarnishing or oxidation is to put a coating of clear lacquer on the metal surface. This is only suitable for objects that are not handled regularly because the film can be damaged, leading to accelerated tarnishing. Lacquering is an extremely skilled process and should only be undertaken by an experienced conservator.

Ideally objects should be displayed in closed cases to reduce the level of dust, pollutants and moisture around them. Any materials used in the exhibition must be tested to ensure that they will not affect the artefacts on exhibition. Similarly the methods of attaching or supporting the objects must be carefully selected so that they do not cause physical damage to them in any way. Screws or pins used to secure metalwork to a board must not be allowed to cause the original to corrode. Particularly sensitive objects may require special environmental conditions within the building or case. Advice on all these matters should be sought from professional conservators or the bodies listed at the end of this book.

CARE OF METALWORK

In conclusion, there are some basic guidelines that should be followed to ensure that metalwork is preserved for the future in the best way possible. Regular and thorough monitoring of all objects will bring present and potential problems to light so that they may be dealt with quickly and effectively before a situation gets too serious.

Minimal handling and careful packing of metalwork can reduce the occurrence of physical damage. Ideally polished metals should be handled with cotton gloves whenever possible so that transfer of chemicals from human skin is minimized. For plate that is in regular liturgical use, careful washing or cleaning, followed by thorough rinsing and drying is the recommended preservation method.

It is important not to overclean objects so use the mildest cleaning agent (for example, water and a non-ionic detergent such as Synperonic

NDB). Polishing and cleaning gradually wears away the surface of the metal, dulling the design and making the object thinner. Cleaning should be carried out when necessary, not as mere routine. When the metal is in association with other materials then a decision on the choice of cleaning agents must take all components into consideration.

Finally, it is recommended that professional advice is always sought for the treatment of pieces that are heavily tarnished or corroded and before any restoration of metalwork is undertaken so that the physical and historical integrity of the object is preserved.

HAZEL NEWEY

After 21 years at the British Museum, Hazel Newey recently joined the Science Museum as Head of Conservation. Since 1984 she has been advising the Council for the Care of Churches on metalwork conservation and is the current Chairman of the UKIC Metals Section, a professional group of conservators and restorers. She was Head of Metals Conservation at the British Museum for 11 years.

BELLS AND BELFRIES

✱

Christopher Dalton

With an Appendix

TURRET CLOCKS

John C. Eisel

O f all aspects of an old church, the belfry has received the least attention and study. This is a pity. For those who have the patience and persistence to seek permission and keys, and the energy and agility to cope with awkward stairs (often having to sidestep brooms, pans, boxes of Christmas decorations and – these days – sometimes altar brassware too), or climb long ladders (with the odd missing rung), and who are prepared to get dusty and dirty and often to share an ill lit belfry not so much with bats but with pigeons, starlings and jackdaws, the upper parts of the towers of most old churches have a great deal to offer.

First, of course, there are the bells themselves. These, at least, have been the subject of some specialized study and most counties of Great Britain have had a volume devoted to their bells, starting in the mid-

---

9.1 Seventeenth century bell in early twentieth century frame and fittings with canons removed, at Exeter Cathedral.

nineteenth century and continuing to the present day. However, the great majority of these county bell books concentrate mainly on the inscriptions borne by the bells and what these tell us about the founders who cast them. Notwithstanding the appearance in 1912 of an excellent general book, *Church Bells of England*, by that great bell historian H.B. Walters, other aspects of bells such as their moulding techniques and casting quality, their shape and general appearance, and more particularly their tone and tuning, had hardly been touched upon until George Elphick's pioneering book *The Craft of the Bellfounder* was published in 1988.

Similarly, most of the county books say nothing about the frames in which the bells are hung, which can range from marvellous examples of mediaeval carpentry in oak to fine specimens of Victorian technology in iron and efficient modern frames of cast iron and steel. Again it was George Elphick who pioneered the serious study of bellframes, first in *Sussex Archaeological Collections* (Vol. 84) in 1945 and later in his book *Sussex Bells and Belfries* in 1970. Nor does 'bell archaeology' stop with bells and frames: there are also bell fittings and these have at last had a book devoted to them by Trevor Jennings in 1991.

Lack of wide knowledge and appreciation of bells and their accoutrements, even among those who take most interest in old churches, has been reflected in such policies and provisions as exist for the preservation of the best and most interesting or rare examples. For each diocese there is a *Schedule of Bells for Preservation*, prepared under the auspices of what is now the Bells and Clocks Committee of the Council for the Care of Churches and which is principally a labour of love on the part of Ranald Clouston, one of the most knowledgeable and experienced bell historians of the present day. Those schedules which have been revised in more recent years reflect a gradual widening of interest in bells, and are a good deal more comprehensive than when they first began to be issued in the 1930s. The CCC has also produced a Code of Practice entitled *The Conservation and Repair of Bells and Bellframes* (published in 1993). This is a new, very much longer, and in some ways controversial edition of the 1981 version of this publication. The combined effects of the diocesan Schedules and the Code, although both are only advisory and not mandatory, mean that most important old bells are reasonably well protected. Parishes generally abide by the faculty jurisdiction and most (but unfortunately not all) Diocesan Advisory Committees, bell advisers, archdeacons and chancellors abide by the provisions of the Schedules and the Code.

Where bellframes are concerned the picture is not so rosy. Only recently have important frames, where indeed any information about them is available, begun to be included in the Schedules; and the 1981 Code had much less to say about frames than its successor which, as we have seen, has recently been published. As a result, ancient oak bellframes are being lost, as was shown by a recent survey by Christopher Pickford and myself covering the period from 1970 to date, at a rate of more than one a month – a rate which has been fairly consistent over the last two decades and continues unabated today.

Not all of these frames could – or should – have been kept in use, least of all where bells hung for full-circle ringing are concerned: this is usually not so much because of their condition as on account of their design. Weak frames which do not adequately resist the considerable stresses set up during ringing can make bells difficult or impossible to ring properly and, worse, they can damage a tower. But the worry is that without proper investigation and recording of old bellframes nation-wide, we have no clear idea of what we can afford to lose and what we ought to be trying to preserve. A valid criticism of English Heritage when that body started to be involved in bell schemes, not because it was grant-aiding them but because it had grant-aided the church, was that lack of specialized knowledge meant that it was insisting on the retention of frames of second- and third-rate interest and quality while first-rate frames elsewhere were slipping away. However, the balance here has begun to be redressed in 1992 with English Heritage grant-aiding and in other ways assisting with the repair of an important early bellframe at Pakenham in Suffolk for continued use for full-circle ringing.

In view of its obvious interest and involvement in the subject there had been hopes that English Heritage would take some sort of a lead in organizing, and arranging the funding for, a national survey of bell-frames. Much of the information already exists in the filing systems of specialists who have spent their spare time and money investigating the contents of belfries up and down the country; but there is a clear need for the data to be centralized – in the same way as it is for bells – and for the gaps to be filled, and then for the information to be made available to all those who need it, in particular to help with decision making. A working party was set up and for a while hopes ran high; but it then became clear that a combination of scarcity of funds and that peculiar brand of corporate inertia which afflicts statutory organizations was going to cause the project to founder. All is not lost, however, because much has been going on behind the scenes and thanks to the energies of officers of the Ancient Monuments

Society and the Society for the Protection of Ancient Buildings (three
cheers for 'the voluntary sector') a pilot survey of the bellframes in one
English county (Essex) is now in train.

Above I referred to full-circle ringing: this is the way in which bells
have traditionally been rung in this country for at least four and a half
centuries and probably longer. In earlier times bells at first were swung
through a small arc by the use of levers fixed to the stocks on which
they were hung, the stock being fitted – as now – with axles (known as
gudgeons) rotating in bearings. Later, the lever gave way to the wheel,
or rather a segment of a wheel: a few 'half-wheels' still survive either in
use or on display. We know from the early churchwardens' accounts of
several parishes that the full wheel did not come into use, generally,
until the late seventeenth century. But we also know from clearance
grooves cut into the walls of certain towers where bells were obviously
packed in tightly that they were being swung through anything up to
360° (that is, full-circle) from at least as early as the fifteenth century.
This is corroborated by the design of bellframes.

The earliest bells were hung, where indeed there was a tower rather
than an open cote or turret, across a pair of beams. However, certainly
by the early fourteenth century bellframes of various designs were
being made, to accommodate bells which were both larger and swung
more vigorously. Typically, bells were now hung on top of trusses, each
truss consisting still of a beam, or sill, but now with a central king-post
with two braces – often curved – going down to the sill. The trusses
were linked by transoms and the sills were supported by bearers, which
in turn were supported by the tower walls. This made a frame which
could cope well with the stresses set up by the ringing of three and
sometimes more bells through about 180°. Somewhat surprisingly, in
view of what I said earlier about the rate of destruction, examples of
such frames do survive in the more rural areas of counties like
Shropshire and Sussex where there has never been the money or the
desire to increase the number of bells, nor an unsympathetic architect
or bellhanger to persuade the parishioners to rip out their old frame and
install a new one.

The next stage in the development of the bellframe was to fit a short
horizontal top member (or *head*) to the truss to avoid having bearings
set into the end-grain of the timber, with the consequent risk of
splitting. Short-headed frames like this survive in plenty in some areas,
though hardly at all in others, either in their original form or converted
later to the long-headed type. Ranald Clouston, who has largely
surveyed the county, is confident that Suffolk retains some 60–70

9.2 Mediaeval short-headed bellframe, Church of St Michael and All Angels, Plumpton, Sussex.

mediaeval or partly mediaeval frames. John Eisel and I can confirm from our investigations in the counties on the Welsh border that about thirty survive in Herefordshire. In Dorset, however, I know that only one frame now remains which pre-dates 1500; and in Devon, Leicester-shire and Northamptonshire, for instance, I can vouch for the fact that the numbers of mediaeval frames which can still be seen can in each case be counted on the fingers of one hand.

An early variant of the normal, posted, frame is found in several eastern counties where the king-post is sensibly replaced by scissor-braces, producing a stronger truss. It is evident from the investigations of Paul Cattermole, Ranald Clouston and myself that the eastern counties were again in the lead with the next – and indeed final – main development, the long-headed frame or 'cage'. This was much better adapted to the swinging of bells through full circles than short-headed frames could ever be, and meant that each bell hung in a proper *pit* with heads on all four sides, linking the pits together to form a strong frame. Norfolk and Suffolk can still show several fifteenth century frames of this kind, both of the king-posted and the scissor-braced types. By the latter part of the sixteenth century most of the rest of England had followed suit.

King-posts, and indeed eastern-counties scissor-braces, gradually disappeared from the design of frames, though jack-braces were sometimes added to give extra strength and rigidity; and in this form bellframes continued to be made, and almost always in oak, until iron began to take over in the nineteenth century. Inevitably in a review like this I have had to omit mention of the many variants of the main types of frame: indeed it is one of the thrills of bellframe hunting to come across the amazing high-sided mediaeval frames of Dalham or Hitcham in Suffolk, the queen-posted frames of Nottinghamshire and Derby-shire, and the splendid late sixteenth century double-cross-braced frames to be found in south-east Somerset.

There is – in the opinion of many – nothing wrong with a well-designed, well-made and well-maintained oak bellframe and many important rings of bells still hang in one at the present day, including those at St Paul's and Southwark Cathedrals, to name but two. But in view of the rigidity and stability – both very desirable characteristics in a frame if the bells are to be safe and easy to ring – of cast iron, it is perhaps surprising that its use in bellframe construction did not really catch on earlier in the nineteenth century than it did. No doubt cost had something to do with it, along with the innate conservatism of most bellfounders and hangers. Also many architects and others felt –

wrongly, as it turned out – that iron frames would damage towers and adversely affect the tone of the bells. In 1828 George Gillibrand of Liverpool made a splendid iron frame for St Luke's church there. The church survived the bombing in 1941 and can still be seen, though it is now empty. In the 1850s Taylors of Loughborough were responsible for a few iron frames which they installed in towers like Waresley in Huntingdonshire and Kingweston in Somerset where space was tight. But it was not until the 1880s that cast iron frames began to come into general use. At first, oak was still used for sills and supporting beams but this soon gave way to steel. A disadvantage here, of course, is that steel (unlike cast iron) can rust very badly unless it is protected in some way, and regrettably it usually is not. This is as much a problem, particularly where steel beams enter damp stone walls, as is death-watch beetle in oak. The short answer is that if steel is to be used anywhere in a belfry, proper protection ought to be insisted upon.

In most cases where an old frame is destroyed, it is a cast iron and steel frame that replaces it, and the reason is usually that the oak frame is decayed or defective and the parish wishes to continue to have its bells rung, or perhaps to hear them again after a long silence. Often a new frame is the only realistic answer but if the old frame is significant on account of age, interest, rarity or quality, it is surely appropriate that all possible means of preserving or conserving it should be explored. Often the old frame can be left in situ with the new one installed beneath it (Cardington, Shropshire, or Nettleton, Wiltshire) or it can be hoisted to a higher level in the tower (Saham Toney, Norfolk, or Uffington, Berkshire). If it proves impossible to keep the frame in the tower, it is usually feasible to preserve it elsewhere, albeit with the loss of its context (Rempstone, Nottinghamshire, or North Wootton, Dorset). If all else fails, at least the old frame should be properly measured and recorded before destruction; and it is heartening to note that the Society of Antiquaries has for the first time, in 1992, made funds available for emergency recording of this kind.

In many cases the old frame can be, and I believe ought to be, carefully and conservatively repaired for continued use. A large number of frames dating from the early seventeenth century are still giving excellent service; indeed there are still some frames in use for full-circle ringing which date from as early as the fifteenth century (Middleton in Warwickshire and Twyning in Gloucestershire). To repair an old frame *properly* – and it cannot be over-emphasized that for a successful outcome it really does need to be done properly – can sometimes cost more than providing a new one and here the precedent

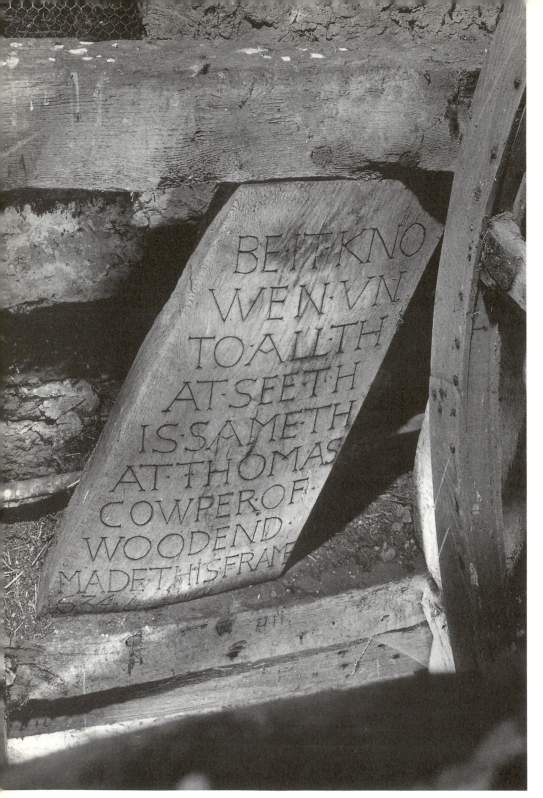

BE·IT·KNO
WEN·VN·
TO·ALL·TH
AT·SEE·TH
IS·SA·METH
AT·THOMAS·
COWPER·OF·
WOODEND·
MADE·THIS·FRAME

9.3   Inscribed bellframe of 1634, Church of St Botolph, Slapton, Northamptonshire.

of English Heritage grant-aiding such repair work at Pakenham is gratifying. It is encouraging, too, that there are now more church architects and others who are prepared to take a serious interest in old frames and their retention and repair, rather than necessarily going along with bellhangers who, I am afraid, have often misleadingly given the impression that a frame is only fit for the chainsaw and the bonfire. Part of the problem is that bellhangers in these days are no longer geared to repairing woodwork by traditional methods; but there are plenty of carpenters who are competent to do so, and with the necessary co-operation between the two, under the supervision of a good architect, there is no reason why the carpenter should not repair the frame and the bellhanger hang the bells. For too long, because of their low profile, which I alluded to at the beginning of this chapter, ancient bellframes in spite of their undoubted beauty, interest and quality, have not been subject to the same rules as have governed all other aspects of old churches and indeed old buildings generally.

In any bell restoration scheme it is clearly desirable to rehang the bells for continued full-circle ringing if at all possible: this is the way in which bells have traditionally been rung, be it in rounds (descending order of note), call-changes (changes which are called out by the conductor) or the mathematical change-ringing (the order in which the bells ring changing at every pull) for which England is famous. Change-ringing is indeed a national tradition which deserves to be fostered and it is therefore a pity even for lesser numbers of bells (in which ringers themselves are now showing more interest) not to be hung properly. However, it would be wrong to suggest that there are no other options: bells can be hung for swing-chiming by means of levers (reverting to early mediaeval practice) or they can be hung stationary and chimed with hammers or special clappers. It should be added that this last option has little to commend it on any grounds other than cost and the convenience of one person being able to sound any number of bells, and the practice of fixing bells in this way is only too appropriately termed hanging them 'dead'. I am referring here to the rehanging of bells which up until now have been hung for ringing. There is, of course, a place for *chimes* of bells where the tower or other receptacle is too weak for swinging bells, and there is a place also for *carillons*, the name given to chimes consisting of larger numbers of bells. These are common in the Low Countries but have never really gained popularity in Great Britain, other than in Scotland.

That I have written at such length about bellframes and am about to say rather less about bells should not be taken to imply that the latter are less interesting; but much more has been written about bells than about frames in the past and the balance needs to be redressed. It is to bell *fittings* that, in the space available, I must perforce do less than full justice. Briefly, a bell hung for ringing is fitted with a stock (or 'headstock'), gudgeons, bearings, a clapper and clapper staple, wheel, stay and slider, and pulley. Stocks were originally made of oak but by the eighteenth century elm was commonly used because it is less liable to split. In the present century cast iron has been very widely used for stocks The earliest iron stock I have seen is the mighty object, dated 1838, which now lies outside the tower at Crediton in Devon. But as with frames, iron did not catch on for stocks until much later in the nineteenth century, when Taylors of Loughborough went over to them in 1892. Occasionally steel is used for stocks: Naylor Vickers & Co. of Sheffield used it in the nineteenth century and Bond of Burford and Bowell of Ipswich in the early twentieth century; but nowadays its use is confined to cases where the *canons* on a bell (described below) are to be retained. Bells were at first fixed to their stocks with nailed straps, later with wedged bolts and later still with threaded bolts and nuts, and now normally by means of bolts passing through the crown.

The earliest gudgeons were driven into the end grain of the stock but later the *strap* gudgeon came into use, the inner end being bolted up through the stock and the outer end retained by a small iron hoop round a projecting part of the stock. In the late nineteenth century such gudgeons largely gave way to the more easily adjustable *plate* type, the gudgeon itself being retained in an iron plate bolted up four times through the stock. Bearings were normally made of gun metal (although, confusingly, they were usually called 'brasses') but generally gave way to ball bearings from 1914 onwards.

Clappers were traditionally made of wrought iron but when that excellent material went out of production some years ago, new clappers were for a short time made out of steel. The material now favoured is called spheroidal graphite cast iron; but there are many who prefer the sound of bells rung with wrought iron clappers and the majority of rings of bells are still fitted with them. Clapper staples were traditionally cast into the bells but, being of iron, they tend to rust and certain types of staple can cause bells to crack as a result. By the late nineteenth century most founders had adopted the *independent* staple, which passes through a hole drilled in the crown of the bell.

Bell wheels had generally developed from the mediaeval half-wheel to the full wheel by the latter part of the seventeenth century. Traditionally wheels are made of oak, but with ash used for the *sole* (rim) and elm for the *shrouding* (flanges). There is no excuse for not treating the sole and shrouding against furniture beetle or for not fixing them with stainless or non-ferrous nails and screws. The failure of wheels where these good practices have not been adopted is probably the most frequent cause of bells becoming unringable.

A stay and slider are necessary so that bells can be set in the inverted position ready for ringing: both are traditionally made of ash which has the right breaking-point if a bell is mishandled by its ringer, and will prevent more serious damage. The temptation to use other timbers must therefore be resisted. Finally a pulley (or on ancient installations, a roller) is provided to conduct the rope vertically through the belfry floor after it comes off the wheel at 'handstroke'; at 'backstroke' it normally travels vertically in any case. All these fittings are described more fully, and illustrated, in the latest edition of *Towers and Bells: A Handbook*, published by the Central Council of Church Bell Ringers in 1990.

The earliest bells surviving in this country are tall, with straight tapering sides and flared at the bottom, they are relatively small and they are seldom inscribed. Plenty of bells of all ages hang, of course, not in towers but in open or enclosed cotes, and it is in such cotes that most really early bells have survived. George Elphick's work on these bells has made it possible to place them in chronological order. For instance the bell of archaic shape at the remote chapel of Hanford in Dorset can now confidently be dated to the eleventh century. Few of these early bells weigh more than about a hundredweight but exceptions are one of about 1200, formerly at Monkton Deverill in Wiltshire, and another at the delightfully-named Ashby Puerorum in Lincolnshire. The earliest bell so far discovered which is inscribed with a date (1254) is at Lissett in the old East Riding of Yorkshire. (Generally bells did not bear dates, or the names of their founders, until the sixteenth century.)

By the early fourteenth century bells had assumed more or less their present shape, the curves and proportions being carefully worked out to produce three octaves in unison, and also a minor third and a fifth. In all succeeding centuries there have been some founders who have maintained, with a greater or lesser degree of success, this *true-harmonic* form of tuning, such as John Wallis of Salisbury in the period about 1600, the Bagleys of Chacombe near Banbury in the mid-seventeenth century, Thomas Osborn of Downham Market in the eighteenth century and his grandson William Dobson in the early nineteenth century. But generally speaking bell-tuning degenerated in the eighteenth century and it was not until 1896 that the combined efforts of a Sussex parson, Canon Simpson of Fittleworth, and the Taylor foundry

9.4   Ancient bell, *c* eleventh century, Chapel of St Michael, Hanford, Dorset.

at Loughborough perfected the art of true-harmonic tuning which is in use today.

Before the invention of the cope-case by the London firm of John Warner & Sons in the mid-nineteenth century, it was necessary to make a model of a bell before preparing the *cope* (outer mould) to cast it. Accordingly the lettering (and any ornaments) for the inscription were applied to the model rather than being pressed into the cope in reverse as is now the case. Bells began to be inscribed in the thirteenth century and for this various kinds of Gothic lettering, some of them of great beauty and elaboration, were used until the simpler black letter took over from about 1400 onwards. The thrill of seeing the marvellous ornamented letters on bells such as at South Somercotes in Lincoln-shire, Cranoe in Leicestershire and Stour Provost in Dorset is another reward for the visitor to these often dark and dirty belfries. After the Reformation in the sixteenth century, Roman – or more or less Roman – lettering gradually took over from the Gothic, black letter and various transitional styles. In the meantime in some parts of the country founders, especially those who were itinerant, used large sprawling letters for their inscriptions which were cut out of any suitable material (commonly parchment) and stuck onto the model bell. A fine example of the practice (in this case apparently using leather) is Richard Purdue's splendid tenor bell at Queen Camel in Somerset.

Almost all old bells were cast with an *argent* and *canons*, namely one large loop on top joined by six smaller ones. These were provided to facilitate hanging bells before the days of bolting them to their stocks through holes drilled in their crowns. Canons are an integral part of an old bell, as well as often being very attractive in their own right, and also a valuable aid in trying to attribute dates and founders to bells with no inscriptions or distinguishing marks. Although modern hanging practice has no use for canons, it is clearly against good conservation practice to remove them and the Code of Practice, referred to above, forbids this in the case of bells cast before 1700 or included in the diocesan Schedules.

A more contentious issue is re-tuning. The note of a bell can be flattened by removing metal from the inside surface or sharpened, to a degree, by removing metal from the lip. This was formerly done by chipping and filing but is now done, with a good deal more precision, on a tuning machine which is, in effect, a giant lathe. Indeed it was the use of such a machine that made possible the consistent achievement of true-harmonic tuning introduced in 1896. Where old bells are con-cerned, it then became possible to improve, or at any rate alter, their harmonic structure, as well as to bring the notes of a whole ring of bells better into tune with each other. However, there are those who consider that no old bell ought to be altered in this way, and that to do so destroys its integrity just as surely as cutting off its canons. Clearly a balance needs to be struck: while there are some bells which ought not to be re-tuned there are others which demonstrably need to be if they are to continue in use as part of a set, which is, after all, a musical instrument that parishioners and others have to listen to week by week.

Bell metal, being a relatively brittle alloy of copper (about 77 per cent) and tin (about 23 per cent) is prone to cracking. Most bells are cracked as a result of abuse: the use of too heavy a clapper, or one which strikes too near the lip, or worse still the iniquitous practice of banging a bell with a rope tied round its clapper which can therefore be held against it and check its vibration. Also there comes a time when indentation from the clapper reaches such a depth that it is necessary to turn the bell to present a fresh surface to the clapper, if cracking is not to ensue. The other main cause of cracks is the rusting and expansion of the iron clapper staples cast into old bells – a particular problem with some seventeenth and eighteenth century founders who cast sharp-cornered staples into bells with thin crowns. It has therefore long been considered good practice to drill out such staples when bells are being restored and to fit independent clapper staples such as have been provided in new bells since the late nineteenth century.

If, despite every precaution, a bell still becomes cracked, all is not lost. Recasting is no longer the only answer (and let us make no mistake: a 'recast' bell is a new bell, normally cast from different metal, no matter how much trouble might have been taken to reproduce on it the inscription from its predecessor). For the past twenty years or so, there has been one firm in this country, Soundweld, near Cambridge, that has been capable of successfully welding most cracked or broken bells, which can then usually be returned to use. Of late this firm has been kept hearteningly busy. There is the incidental advantage that welding a bell costs less than recasting it.

That is not to say that no old bell ought ever to be recast, far from it. For every bell that is historic, fine, rare or beautiful, and ought to be kept, there are dozens which have none of these qualities and therefore ought to be replaced with something better if the opportunity arises. As I hinted above, the CCC's new Code of Practice entitled *The Conservation and Repair of Bells and Bellframes* is controversial. This is chiefly because a sensible balance surely needs to be kept between enlightened conservation on the one hand and good new work on the other; and there are widely differing perceptions of what that balance ought to be. But with care, common sense, and the willingness (not always noticeable among bellringers, it has to be said) to see other points of view, conservationists' and ringers' objectives are actually seldom incompatible or mutually exclusive. But conservation must not be allowed to get out of hand and heritage does not stop at the present day: both of the two remaining bell foundries in this country today are capable of producing excellent and well-tuned bells; and there are large numbers of highly skilled ringers who can produce performances of a quality and sophistication never before achieved. Our churches deserve the best that we can give; and our bell founders and ringers alike deserve every encouragement to be able to contribute their own late twentieth century excellence.

NOTES ON MAINTENANCE AND CARE

- Keep all access ladders, stairs, etc. clear and in good order, so that they are available for inspection and maintenance.
- Keep belfry and other floors in the tower clean and clear of debris; but seek professional advice before discarding any old artefacts.
- Watch for leaks in the tower roof (or even walls): unattended, these can lead to decay of bellframes and fittings.
- Keep all birds out of the belfry: nests and droppings are generally bad for bell installations. Netting and its fixings ought to be stainless steel; plastic-coated galvanized steel is acceptable as second best but anything else is too short-lived to be worth using.
- Keep fully tight such bolts and nuts as are fitted to the frame and fittings. Guidance on this and other maintenance is given in *Towers and Bells: A Handbook*.
- Lubricate all bearings (bell bearings, pulleys and clapper joints). The ideal lubricant for plain bearings is castor oil; ball bearings are pre-lubricated and sealed and manufacturers' instructions should be followed.
- Keep all *steel* elements well painted.
- Check for active woodworm in fittings and frame. Minor outbreaks in fittings can be treated by amateurs (using bat-friendly chemicals where bats are present); but major outbreaks

are best left to the professional. *Overall* beetle treatment is seldom necessary or desirable.

‣ Never work in a belfry unaccompanied; never work in a belfry with the bells rung up.

‣ All major work on bell installations should be carried out either by professionals, or by competent amateurs under the professional supervision of an architect, bellhanger or bell adviser as appropriate. The faculty jurisdiction applies as much in the belfry as in the rest of the church.

‣ If in doubt or in need of advice, consult the church architect, the Diocesan Advisory Committee, the Council for the Care of Churches, or the bell founders and bellhangers – as appropriate.

Appendix

TURRET CLOCKS

John C. Eisel

A church is normally a quiet place, but often the person who is adventurous enough to obtain permission to ascend the tower is met with the comforting tick of an old clock. And, whereas the contents of the belfries of most counties have been surveyed and the results published, the same is not true of church clocks, so there are delights still to be discovered.

The frames of the earliest turret clocks are posted, and the majority of these are of birdcage form: a late seventeenth century example at Croft, Herefordshire, is shown in Figure 9.5. In a minority of clocks the frame is shaped like a doorframe or a field-gate, depending on the layout of the trains, and, typically, is made of wood. This type of clock is found in a wide belt across the midlands, from the Welsh border across to Northamptonshire and beyond.

Many different types of clock frame were used in the eighteenth and early nineteenth centuries; but from the middle of the nineteenth century turret clocks of flatbed form became increasingly popular. In these the trains are built up from a solid cast iron base, providing a rigid unit.

There is interest not only in the clocks themselves, but in the ancilliaries. Clock weights can be made of cast iron, lead, or even large lumps of stone. If the clock is connected to a dial on the outside of the

9.5 Seventeenth century turret clock frame, Church of St Michael, Croft, Herefordshire.

tower, this can have only one hand, a clue to interest inside the tower. There can be a chime barrel, rather like a musical box but on a much more substantial scale, which is released by the clock at regular intervals and plays a tune: larger ones can play a different tune for each day of the week. A derelict barrel from a barrel organ can be mistaken for the remains of such a chime: however, the pins on a barrel from a barrel organ are normally made of wire, not nearly substantial enough to operate a hammer on a bell.

The care of a mechanical clock is largely common sense. As with all pieces of mechanism, it is necessary to oil the pivots occasionally with a suitable clean oil. When a clock is cleaned, the wheels and pinions are polished and these should *never* be oiled. A tower is a dusty place and while most clocks are in a wooden case, this can never be airtight and dust can enter. The dust sticks to the oil and acts as a cutting paste, causing the pinions to wear rapidly.

The weights of a turret clock are generally very heavy, and the condition of the rope or wire suspending them should be checked occasionally. Obvious places to check are where the rope/wire is attached at either end, also the pullies and supporting timbers. For an older clock, it is well worth checking the condition of the 'click' on the winding barrel, for if this fails the weight will fall, and if it is near the top of its drop, then it will impact with tremendous force. If the church is throwing out any old hassocks, it is a good idea to pile a few of these at the bottom of the weight chute where they would absorb some of the force of a falling weight. Failing this, a bag or two of sand is an alternative.

In order for the clock to strike freely, the linkage between the clock and any hammers on the bells should be checked, and the pivots of the bell cranks oiled. When a clock hammer is raised and then released, it depresses a spring and strikes the bell, and is then held off the bell by the spring. In the course of time, this spring can become deformed causing the hammer to rest on the bell, with the consequence that the bell will be prevented from resonating and may eventually crack. A regular check is vital, and any hammer that is resting on a bell should be tied off until the spring can be reset.

Perhaps the worst aspect of a mechanical clock is the need for regular winding. A flatbed clock may only need winding once a week, and this is not too much of a chore, particularly as they are good timekeepers and generally need little attention. An older clock may need winding more often, and, in general, the older the clock the more attention it will require; this may be an advantage as minor adjustments may be made as necessary.

When there is no one willing or able to give a clock the loving care that it deserves, most clocks can be converted to be wound automatically by electricity. However, the clock may suffer from the lack of attention, and this should only be considered as a last resort. If it is converted, it is important that it is the winding arrangements alone that are altered and that the clock mechanism remains intact.

CHRISTOPHER DALTON

Christopher Dalton's interest in bells, frames and fittings developed from learning to ring in the early 1960s. He combines work for the Churches Conservation Trust (formerly the Redundant Churches Fund) with photographing historic buildings and writing, mostly about bells.

~ 10 ~

WOODWORK

✻

Hugh Harrison

Treasures on earth represent man's efforts at creating the hereafter.
Most treasures in churches are easily recognized, but wooden
'treasures' are often mundane things, like floorboards and rafters.
These are purely structural elements, and generally they have no
artistic input. Floorboards provide a level area to move about on, and
rafters were reckoned and made by a village carpenter, when he was
given the span of the building, and were no different from those of any
barn or house he was building at the same time.

But stand at the top of the stairs at the north end of Westminster Hall
and look at the roof construction, conceived for the same basic purpose
of putting a cover over the building. Do not be confused by the riot of
mouldings, clever spanning techniques or carvings, just look at the
basic element, the arch timbers. The sweep created by the width of the
span (artificially reduced by using hammer beams) and the height,
produced arches of sublime proportions.

Now go to All Saints, Langham Place, and look at the floor in the
sanctuary designed by Robert Potter in the 1970s. Perfectly ordinary
flat floorboards radiate in a segment around the sanctuary floor. The
segment of the circle used was not chosen at random, but with skill

---

10.1   Church of St Mary, Molland, Devon. Although the Georgian furnishings
are famous for their entirety in this small remote parish church, the plainness of
the woodwork requires a particularly sensitive touch if repairs are ever needed.

and judgement to provide a focus of attention for the whole church. It is unlikely that the casual visitor will be aware of this arrangement, but imagine the floor running straight across and see the concentration of energy lost.

To revert to the ordinary church roof, rather than the grand roof as at Westminster Hall, any ancient roof will reveal a wealth of detail and history. A few examples of information that may be gleaned by observation and inference are listed here.

1. Construction practice: carpenters' numbers, some easily understood, some obtuse.
2. Meanness: use of timber with a high sapwood content, or undersized.
3. Craftsmanship: beautiful joints, well considered for the job in hand.
4. Botching: nailing of doublers onto the sides of old timbers rather than renewing.
5. Pride: carpenters' marks.
6. Artistry: sweeps, either unnecessary or never seen.
7. Saw marks: depending on what they look like they can indicate the type of saw originally used and can therefore help date the timber.
8. Cleft marks: showing the timber was split out of the log using wedges.
9. In the round (i.e. bark and all): no effort taken by those who inserted this timber, merely the cheapest most ill-chosen material available.
10. Re-used timbers: expediency, or sensible cost cutting.
11. Previous restorations: always informative, some were good, some bad.

I frequently have to spend, as do many historic building architects, whole days crawling around extremely dirty, often hot, always – or nearly always – stuffy, pitch dark, cramped roofs, and am always amazed at the information, history and conundrums offered by each roof. Each the result of village carpenters working over the centuries, rarely the leading royal carpenter of his day, as at Westminster Hall.

The point I am trying to make is that history is enshrined in all about us including the most humble elements.

This book advocates the ideals of conservation and maintenance, it must also impart judgement. That is the key; what do you save and what renew? We must never get into the 'conserve everything' state of mind, but we must equally be firm and keep as much as is feasible. This latter approach is actually the most likely to receive grant aid, if that is being sought, so it can make financial sense as well. My particular topic covers the mundane and the glorious: some floorboards are glorious, some ancient furnishings mundane; whereas the objects easily identifiable as glorious are normally accepted as worthy of maintenance, the mundane is rarely appreciated and therefore most in need of our help.

By starting at the most down to earth level of woodwork I have tried to highlight the breadth of use of wood in our churches; the fact that it is often doing a structural job, often a mundane job, often it cannot be seen or only from a considerable distance, and yet it is almost always the unseen parts where trouble starts.

Let us therefore make a list of places where we are likely to find woodwork:

Structural and exterior items
Floors
Walls
Doors
Windows
Roofs
Bellframes
Tower floors
Spires
Flag poles

Interior furnishings
Organ cases
Screens
Pews
Choir stalls
Altar crosses, candlesticks, aumbreys, tabernacles, missal stands
Lecterns
Pulpits
Reredoses/retables
Memorials
Chairs, stalls, kneelers, chests
Text boards/charity boards/hatchments/royal arms
Panellings
Flower stands, banner stands

Pascal candlesticks
Font covers
Sculptures
Vestment chests, vestry cupboards, book cupboards, para-
phernalia

There is no need to take each item and prescribe and proscribe individual courses of treatment. Many items can be put into groups which will have similar problems. Also, items of the same timber are likely to display the same problems. I have made my recommendations at the end of the chapter; I do hope, however, that you will not skip the technical information that follows, as even in this abbreviated form, it should help you make the right decision when problems arise.

At this stage I am excluding problems caused by human intervention (past restorations, bad repairs or just changes in fashion) so the problems we are most likely to be confronted with are rot (wet or dry) and woodworm (death-watch or common furniture beetle) or both.

DECAY

Wet rot

Wet rot is the most common fungal attack. It will occur in all timbers which have a constant high moisture content. Once the wood gets sufficiently wet for a significantly long time, it is almost guaranteed to be invaded by this particular fungus (*Coniophera Puteana*). It converts sound hard timber into soft crumbly material which is usually darker than the original and has cracking across the grain. Cracks 2–3 inches (50–75mm) apart, usually indicate deep decay; small cross checking, say, a half inch apart and much more numerous, indicates surface decay to a depth of a quarter inch or less. The drier the timber is, the less attractive it is to this particular fungus, and at a specific moisture content within the wood the fungus will not survive.

The cure is simple, isolate the object from the source of moisture and the fungus dies and the rot stops. Treatment of the decayed material is another matter.

Dry rot

Dry rot is a much more complex and dangerous fungus (*Serpula lachrymans*). In churches it is rarely found in connection with long-term areas of damp and more usually breaks out where leaks cause local areas of dampness within an otherwise warm, dry building. The moisture content within the wood is much lower than in wet rot (hence the name) and it needs conditions of warmth and darkness. Thus if a central heating pipe springs a leak behind panelling, or a roof develops a leak behind an enclosed cornice, these would become danger zones. What makes dry rot so much more dangerous than wet rot is its ability to invade perfectly dry wood at a considerable distance from the source of moisture and even on the other side of masonry walls.

The cure is extremely difficult if immediate results are required though the first action is always to cure the source of dampness. The normal approach is for the whole affected area, including the walls, to be sterilized with fungicide, all affected timber has to be discarded and new material should be impregnated with fungicide.

However, I strongly recommend a recent development is considered whereby more sympathetic techniques for dealing with dry rot are used. Where traditional treatment involves destruction of ancient or original material, the new approach first cures the source of the dampness, then closely monitors the area, both by continuous probes and visual inspection for long periods (years rather than months) after the damp has been cured and the fungus has died. This treatment takes the logical view that if you cure all the conditions that allowed the fungus to survive, it must die of its own accord. If we take, for instance, the case of the glorious rococo Chapel at Wardour Castle where the dry rot emanated from a leaking internal drain pipe, and totally destroyed the battens and lathes supporting the superb moulded and cast plaster over a substantial area of the wall. The traditional cure of cutting back and destroying infected plaster and other material would be disastrous. In this case the thickness of plaster made it virtually self-supporting, and with gentle assistance it hardly need be disturbed.

The recording of environmental conditions throughout the building or that area of the building, is required as any development of conditions conducive of fungal growth will quickly lead to new outbreaks of dry rot. On the basis that the detection of leaks and so on at an early stage must be the best policy of maintenance, it is still better to save money on the traditional destructive dry rot curing techniques and to spend it on monitoring equipment. I must, of course, qualify my advice on this specialist and potentially dangerous agent of building destruction by saying that a top class unbiased technical consultation must be sought whenever this problem is found.

There may be no external signs of dry rot, though if a mushroom-like smell is detected this should set warning bells ringing. The first sign one is likely to see of dry rot is a staining of the surface followed by the growth of a white/grey/purple furry fungus, which in its fully developed state is truly disgusting. The surface is often covered with orange dust which are the tiny spores waiting to drift off in air currents to invade another part of the building. The fruiting body (as it is called) will be glistening with droplets of moisture, hence its Latin name, *Serpula Lachrymans.*

Woodworm

From the tearful fungus, to the ever hungry woodworm. The name of the most destructive type is itself sinister: the death-watch beetle. This and the common furniture beetle are the two most common varieties found in our churches. Table 10.1 lists their characteristics for easy comparison.

It is necessary to know the following details of the life cycle of these bugs if we are to try to make judgmental decisions, rather than purely reactive decisions.

1. The female lays her eggs in crevices in the timber or old exit holes normally in the spring or early summer.

Table 10.1

	Death-watch beetle	Common furniture beetle
Size of exit hole	2–3mm (old fashioned drinking straw)	1–2mm (tapestry needle)
Time within timber	Up to 7–8 years	Up to 2–3 years
Size of beetle	Cylindrical diameter: 2–3mm; length: 4–6mm; wings rarely visible (hidden beneath wing)	Cylindrical diameter: 1–2mm; length: 3–4mm; wings rarely visible (hidden beneath wing casing)
Colour	Dark grey/brown	Dark grey/brown
Variety of timber in order of preference	1. Oak 2. Other hardwoods 3. Softwood	1. Softwood 2. Hardwoods other than oak 3. Oak

10.2   This is an oak log used as a banner stand. The photograph shows the infestation of common furniture beetle (small holes) and death-watch beetle (large holes) confined entirely to the sap wood. When the sap has been consumed there is a tendency if the conditions are suitable (damp and fungal decay) for the infestation to migrate into the heartwood. If it does so, the piece will be totally consumed. I would expect only the death-watch beetle to tunnel into the heart-wood. This is a good example of infestation in the sap wood only – at this stage.

2. After a few weeks the eggs hatch out into maggot-like creatures.
3. These bore into the wood making tunnels. They eat the wood in front of them and extrude it at the other end in pellets called frass, which is the dust one sees on the surface of actively infested timber.
4. They go on doing this for years (see Table 10.1) until one autumn they have had enough and they pupate, turning into a chrysalis. By some supersonic means before pupating, they tunnel towards a surface, but never through it.
5. Approximately six months later they emerge from the chrysalis, bore through the remaining barrier of wood to the surface, fly or walk short distances (metres rather than miles – death-watch beetles hardly move at all, common furniture beetles fly short distances) and within one or two days find a mate and then die. It is at this stage that the well-known tapping is

10.3   The sill of the rood screen at the Church of St Paul-de-Leon, Staverton, Devon. This is the restored sill installed in the 1890s. No effort was made to isolate the sill from the damp floor so infestation by death-watch beetle has already become heavy as can be seen by the number of exit holes. Note also the white deposit which is evidence of fungal decay. It will not be dry rot but some form of wet rot. Note how the death-watch beetle is infiltrating into the lower part of the posts. If this attack is not addressed all woodwork at this level will become infested and destroyed to a greater or lesser extent. This is a good example of damp led infestation.

sometimes heard in churches, as this is the noise made by both sexes of death-watch beetle to tell each other where they are. The males and females tap at different speeds to avoid unwelcome advances.

So whenever you see a beetle hole, you will know that beneath the surface there is a 3–10 year tunnelling operation beyond it.

Here are a few more important features of woodworm infestation.

1. Death-watch beetles usually only initiate infestation of oak in the sapwood. (Normally the outer 25–50mm of the tree immediately beneath the bark.) If the wood is perfectly dry, infestation may never or only slowly invade the heartwood in the same piece.

2. If oak becomes damp and infected with fungus, existing infestation by death-watch beetle will move rapidly into the heartwood.

3. Death-watch beetle does not like paint, particularly old paint. This is not to say that you will not find death-watch beetle holes in painted wood, it does mean that where you have death-watch beetle infestation in painted wood, you are likely also to have substantial tunnelling just beneath the painted surface. The surface becomes an incredibly thin veneer supported only by the few surviving walls between adjacent tunnels. What looks like a fine painted surface may actually be very weak and vulnerable to damage. If the paint is in good condition, very delicate tapping with a finger nail, or the lightest brushing of the surface by the tips of ones fingers will often reveal hollow areas beneath the surface. (It sounds as though one is brushing one's fingers over paper.)

4. Chestnut is often difficult to distinguish from oak, it was also quite often used as a cheap alternative to oak in nineteenth century restorations. A guide to whether the piece is chestnut or oak is given by the woodworm, in that if it is infested with common furniture beetle it is more likely to be chestnut, and if with death-watch beetle, oak.

5. When commissioning new work, if new oak is being used, insist with the greatest determination that all sapwood is cut off before use. This will cost more money, but it is worth every penny. It is particularly important to observe this rule with new green oak being put into roofs. As sapwood becomes more apparent with age, your building contract can actually state that if sap is found at any time in the future, the contractor or his heir remains responsible for its removal, and substitution with new clean oak.

As an object lesson, the beautiful new nave roof built in the early twentieth century in Lydford, Devon, has a tiny percentage, say 1 per cent or less, of sapwood throughout all the new oak used. Without exception, this sapwood, distributed evenly across the roof, is heavily infested with death-watch beetle. At the moment it appears that the infestation is limited to the sapwood, if it transfers, or when it transfers, the entire roof will become riddled with death-watch beetle which will be difficult to eradicate. In this case, either the dishonesty of the builder, or a paring of costs to win a tender, created a saving then (hardly measurable in cost) compared to the cost now of treatment, and the likely early failure of a roof which should last hundreds of years.

6. Old storage cupboards in vestries and towers were usually made with ply, glued together with animal glues. These are particularly favoured by the gourmet grub who will devour the ply with gusto. The infestation is normally so bad the only remedy is to remove the cupboard entirely. If in doubt and as an interim measure, treat immediately to reduce the capacity of the infested area for spreading infestation elsewhere.

Treatment consists of applying an insecticide in liquid form, or depositing it on the surface in powder form. Here is the great problem. We know from the life style of the woodworm that it never comes to the surface and the practical difficulties of flooding every tunnel, metres long and at some depth from the surface, is practicably impossible. So how does one eradicate woodworm? The insecticides used up to, say, five years ago, killed the infestation in three ways.

1. By impregnating the surface of timber with insecticide. This kills those beetles that eat the treated timber as they emerge before mating, it also sterilizes them.
2. Beetles are deterred from laying their eggs on treated timber, and it is further protected in this way.
3. The short-term fumes kill any beetles active in the vicinity of the application.

New pyrethroid insecticides which are currently used are much more specific to insects, and do not harm humans or bats. They work on a contact basis, so that as the beetle emerges, or as soon as it lands on a treated timber it dies.

How does one deal with the beetles in the backs of wall plates or in mortices or joints in woodwork? One cannot, other than by drilling into the infested wood and pressure injecting. This does work if done comprehensively, and conscientiously, though with unseen voids and barriers in large structures it is impossible to guarantee total impregnation of every part. Every pocket of infestation untreated, is a source of continued destruction.

Tests by the Forest Products Research Laboratory, realizing the impossibility of 100 per cent success by application and injection of fluid, actually showed that the infinitely cheaper smoke bombs, used annually for at least ten years, were much more successful. Success was measured by the simple process of counting dead beetles found on the floor each year. At King's College Chapel for instance after seven years, the number of dead beetles found had reduced by 65 per cent.

Summary of the visible characteristics of
woodworm infestation

> Big holes: death-watch beetle.
>
> Little holes: common furniture beetle.
>
> Frass: light colour wood dust. If this is coming out of holes which are also light coloured, then infestation is almost certainly active.
>
> Sapwood (particularly of oak): signified by huge numbers of holes in a clearly defined area only on the edge of a beam or a board means 'look out'. If exit holes are also in adjoining wood, it means that the infestation has passed from the sapwood into the heartwood, and the problem has become significant.
>
> Damp staining: all timbers in contact with masonry are at risk. A few holes in floor sills, or wall plates should not be automatically indicative of low or negligible infestation. They could be the only outside signs of serious infestation in the hidden parts.
>
> Dead beetles: always in April, May and June, inspect all sweepings from floors. As soon as even one dead beetle is found, next time look for others and then check all woodwork in the vicinity of the dead beetles. Don't forget they could easily have dropped from the roof above. But still note the places of high discovery rates.

Let us now return to our list of woodwork but this time we know what to look for and where, and we should understand what we see. As the same problems are likely to beset all the items in the same category, we can group these under main headings and discuss their manifestations and treatments.

EXTERIOR WOODWORK – WALLS/WINDOWS/DOORS/FLAG POLES

Problems

Wet rot
Where woodwork is in contact with walls or the ground or has water traps in its construction (mortices, grooves and joints that fill with water and have no means of drainage).

Sunshine

Heat causes wood to contract, and often therefore to split. Pieces then detach, and water penetrates the splits. This is frequently seen on wooden tracery windows, where the carved areas split on the short grain.

Nails/iron fixings

These corrode rapidly outside, and split the timber causing the same problems as for sunshine above.

Wear and tear

Doors often drag on floors because they have 'dropped' on their hinges. This causes significant flexing of the structure which will eventually loosen joints and so forth.

Poor maintenance

Much exterior woodwork is inaccessible (barge boards etc.) so is not maintained.

What to do

1. Try to isolate woodwork from dampness. Create air gaps wherever possible. Provide drainage holes (as large as is feasible) in the bottoms of mortices and grooves.
2. Repair split timber using wood dowels. Try to make allowance in the future for movement. Match wood carefully and use exterior glues. If you have to use reinforcement, use stainless steel.
3. Take out old iron nails and use stainless steel.
4. Keep up maintenance work. If in doubt, apply colourless woodwork preservative. Try to avoid varnishes as they all peel off, though the new PVA-based products seem to work well. If you have to use linseed oil dilute it at least 50 per cent and let each coat soak in. Never leave thick skins on the surface.
5. Make sure doors and windows don't drag. Keep their structure in good order.

INTERIOR STRUCTURAL WOODWORK –
ROOFS/SPIRES/BELLFRAMES/TOWER FLOORS

Likely problems

Wet rot
Wall plates, joists and beams buried in walls, eaves and timbers beneath valleys. These are all inaccessible spots where leaks occur without being noticed, and where timber is encased in naturally damp masonry.

Beetle infestation
Death-watch beetle and common furniture beetle.

These timbers provide ideal conditions of dampness, inaccessibility, dirt and poor quality materials (cheap previous repairs using softwoods or cheap hardwoods, or oak with a high proportion of sapwood).

As many of these problems have structural connotations no simple specification can be prescribed, and almost certainly an expert (architect/conservator) will have been called in for advice. I can only say modern techniques of preservation can save almost anything, so always insist on saving everything, and make the expert persuade you if something has to be renewed. Do examine timbers for old marks or evidence of previous use. Do make certain the structure and particularly the bits that are going to be renewed are properly photographed first.

INTERIOR FURNISHINGS ATTACHED TO
WALLS

This includes reredoses, memorials, text boards, charity boards, hatchments/Royal Arms, panelling and dado panelling, which all have one thing in common: one unseen side fixed to a wall, usually with no access to the hidden side.

Problems

Wet rot
Often rubble and dirt etc. fills the narrow gap between the wall and the woodwork. This allows damp to bridge across the gap causing the back of the woodwork to decay.

Beetle infestation
Both common furniture beetle and death-watch beetle will infest woodwork where damp builds up in this manner.

What do to

1. Clear out rubble etc.
2. Mount objects further from walls if feasible.
3. For independent objects make certain the gap between object and wall is kept clear. In the case of panelling provide ventilation and removable cover strips.
4. Treat woodworm.

FLOORS

In many cases these are laid straight onto the soil; they have therefore suffered decay continuously and have been patched frequently. Very often this was done with poor materials.

Decay can be detected by bouncing floors and tilting pews. Death-watch beetle will often be found in oak sills to platforms beneath pews and in the boarding. Common furniture beetle will also be found in softwood floor boarding. There is a greater likelihood of infestation in damp areas where the floors meet the walls.

What to do

Decay can only be treated by taking up floors and replacing decayed joists etc. As with all damp-related problems, the new joists should be relaid isolated from the subsoil, and pressure treated wood should be used. If old floorboards are involved, do take these up carefully, take out all the old nails, patch edges or knot holes, and relay them. The platform and size of old flooring will always help date its origin as well as preserving the ambience of an old building.

If woodworm infestation is present, selected boards should be lifted and the extent of the infestation properly assessed. Treatment, renewal and resiting will all be options.

FIXED FURNISHINGS

This includes screens, pews, choir stalls, and some pulpits. These all either stand directly on the old soil, or on floors. Those directly on the soil all have similar problems to floors, in that damp in the soil causes decay in the sills and lower areas of woodwork. Those on floors are protected to a certain extent, except where decay in the floors transfers straight into tenons from pews etc. located in the flooring structure.

Both death-watch beetle and common furniture beetle will be found in areas that are or have been damp, and in sap edges used throughout construction. Wall ends of pews are susceptible in the same way as panelling etc.

What to do

Isolate sills etc. from the source of damp, create air gaps and good ventilation and treat woodworm. Obviously take great care where painted and carved objects need treatment, and call in a conservator.

'LOOSE' INTERIOR FURNISHINGS

This includes altars and altar ornaments, lecterns, chairs, kneelers, chests, flower stands, banner stands, font covers, pulpits and organs. The likely problems will be woodworm infestation only. Check the bottom areas first where the wood may be damp. Sadly much modern woodwork has been bought on low budgets. Sapwood will practically always be present and can usually be detected because of its paler colour. It will always be found on the edge of boards or posts etc. These areas invariably become infested. Much of this work is also poorly jointed and falls apart easily, so it is important to check joints.

A short while ago I visited a tiny parish in South Wales where they had recently acquired a brand new clergy stall and desk as a unit. It looked fine and had been given in memory of a recently deceased parishioner. I noticed the mitres on the skirting were open and with the aid of the vicar we turned the piece over. There was no proper construction and after nine months the platform was already falling apart. Sadly it was made by a well-established company whose reputation would suggest something better should have been expected, though it was a catalogue piece and therefore built to a tight budget. Unfortunately, the continued use of sap in oak, in new furnishings, is still found.

In organs, check the case, and make certain the organ tuners report any infestation in the organ mechanism.

Old chests are often very old, and of considerable interest and importance. They are often stuffed with old hymnals etc. and the great weight and age takes a toll on the construction. Really ancient hollowed out logs will usually have split and warped; lids may no longer fit and hinges will have worn.

What to do

Treat the woodworm and repair broken joints etc. using an experienced conservation joiner.

WOOD SCULPTURE

Where this stands, or is laid straight onto damp stonework, there is likelihood of decay and infestation at the junction of wood and stone. This also often occurs on the hidden sides or backs of pieces against walls.

What to do

Where feasible isolate sculpture from damp by placing it on bearers, which also allows ventilation, but if decay or infestation is present, it must be dealt with by a conservator.

VESTRY CUPBOARDS AND OTHER FURNITURE

This group consists of the appalling collection of cheap wardrobes, tea chests, hanging cupboards and shelves, which litter most towers and vestries. They are frequently of poor construction and are infested with common furniture beetle.

Watch out for dry rot and common furniture beetle. Usually the inertia of doing nothing is normally only reversed by collapse and breakage of vast collections of old jam jars etc. I would insist, however, that rampant common furniture beetle is thoroughly treated, or better still eradicated by throwing out the affected object.

PRACTICAL MAINTENANCE

1. *Do* dust using a soft suitable sized clean paint brush or soft bristle brush and a vacuum cleaner. Always hold the nozzle an inch or two from the object, *do not* run the nozzle clattering over the surface. The idea is that you collect the dust you have dislodged with the brush in the vacuum cleaner.
2. *Wax* all unpainted woodwork with pure beeswax and turpentine. This can be made by buying pure beeswax from your local beekeeping supplier; grating the wax on a coarse cheese grater, warming this and when liquid add the same quantity of pure turpentine. When this cools into a thick paste, re-dilute with more pure turps into a thin paste like cream. Apply this thinly with a brush, leave for a day, and buff off with a shoe polishing type brush. *Do not* bash carving and projecting pieces with over enthusiastic buffing. *Do* check first that the surface has not previously been painted or specially stained or coloured. Fragments of colour are difficult to see so always err on the side of caution. *Do not* do anything to any piece more than 400 years old without first checking with your architect or a conservator.
3. *Do* apply colourless wood preservative and insecticide on limited areas of infestation *after* taking professional advice. *Do not* splash anything else with the liquid, such as fabrics, walls etc. Carefully absorb any dribbles with tissue or cottonwool. *Do* remember that you are only treating the surface, so try and get the liquid into all nooks and crannies and joints etc. *Do* carry out the treatment from April to September. *Do* remember that you may have to treat the wood again.
4. *Never* ever put linseed oil in any shape, form, or quantity anywhere near a piece of interior woodwork.
5. *Never* try and clean something without checking with a conservator first.

This may all sound a bit restrictive, but more and more history is being gleaned from previously unconsidered surfaces. Often this is fragmentary and one ill-conceived treatment now, could wipe out whatever has survived until now.

MAINTENANCE POLICY

1. Reduce dust by vacuuming.
2. Keep out birds; keep little used spaces as clean as possible.
3. Get rid of all rubbish, always.
4. Check doors and windows move easily and have stays.
5. Check for dead death-watch beetle or common furniture beetle each spring.
6. Take professional advice before carrying out work on any ornamental piece.
7. If repairs or restoration is needed or recommended, take heed on one very important point. Your professional advisers themselves are likely to be aware of only one technique for the preservation of woodwork. This is 'cut out the decayed and damaged pieces and renew'. This is self-evidently destructive, there are other conservation techniques which allow retention of the original material. If you are really concerned by proposals made by professional advisers do recommend they get in touch with the CCC and failing that, do so yourself. If your local joiner has been employed, try and recommend reinforcement rather than beautiful new joinery, and that treated timber is used and non-ferrous screws – not nails.
8. If you have to treat against woodworm remember the new laws regarding bats. Get in touch with your local Nature Conservancy Council Adviser. Also make certain your contractors acknowledge that their work will be done within the new COSHH Health and Safety at Work Regulations.
9. Do not attempt to cure wet or dry rot by applying a fungicide from a supermarket. This may mask the problem causing worse damage later.
10. Do not put nails into woodwork for your Christmas and Easter decorations.
11. Many churches have valuable genuine antique chairs, tables and pieces of carving. Do put your fragments of carving on display, but in a secure manner. As regards chairs, Elizabethan tables, ancient wooden effigies, and other easily removable items, you must make a conscious security policy dependant on all local factors.

HUGH HARRISON

Hugh Harrison founded the company Herbert Read Ltd in 1972 when the last member of the Read family died. Hugh Harrison has built on the company's past expertise in the restoration of woodwork and is now concentrating on conservation as a means of retaining as much as possible of all original material. The company is now owned by Mr and Mrs R.J. Stanley.

~ 11 ~

FLOORS

✳

Jane Fawcett

HISTORIC CHURCH FLOORS

One of the difficulties of protecting historic floors is that, until very recently, no one has thought them worthy of serious consideration. This has meant that no methods have been developed, either for recording important elements or for conserving the historical artefacts with which many are so richly endowed. They have been virtually ignored.

Even today, following a comprehensive survey, the first to be carried out, of the historic floors of forty-four cathedrals and greater churches, there still seems to be considerable prejudice amongst church authorities, architects and conservationists, who sometimes display a deep-seated conviction that floors can look after themselves, while more important structural defects are tackled without hesitation.

However, with the present dramatic and uncontrolled growth in tourism, this is exactly what they cannot do. With the grinding of grit and dust into the brasses, ledger stones and tiles of cathedrals by forty million feet a year, the historical evidence of centuries is being obliterated under our eyes, and there is very often no other available

---

11.1 Detail of mediaeval tiles (c thirteenth century) from Prior Crauden's Chapel, Ely. (Photograph by John Critchley.)

source for the information they contain. History is being destroyed at an unprecedented rate and few people are aware of the gravity of the situation.

Many inscriptions that were still legible ten years ago have now been lost; neither the position of the ledger stone nor the name of the person commemorated are known. A state of total anonymity will soon be reached, when churches, our most historic buildings, will no longer hold adequate information about the past; the feet of visitors will have destroyed it all. Surprisingly, even the NADFAS church recorders, who have done such systematic and excellent recording of many churches, including all the furnishings and monuments, have usually ignored the floors.

Fortunately, under the Care of Cathedrals Measure (1991), all cathedral authorities are required to produce within five years an inventory of contents, of which historic floors are now regarded as an essential component. It is time that churches, which also qualify for government grants, should take similar action before it is too late, and grants should be made available for the recording and treatment of floors.

Before considering what steps are necessary to conserve historic floors, we should define the elements worth conserving, and identify where they are usually to be found.

1. Ledger stones, particularly those containing heraldic devices and/or important inscriptions. Mediaeval ledgers, with marginal inscriptions in Latin or French, are valuable because of their rarity.
2. Mediaeval tiles are of particular importance where some of the original tile carpet, or overall layout, is still visible.
3. Encaustic tiled pavements, many of them laid in the nineteenth century under the influence of the Ecclesiological Society, are now showing signs of deterioration.
4. Cosmati pavements, in which the individual tiles do not carry a pattern, but where an overall design, often based on a guilloche, is created out of a variety of marbles and mosaics.
5. Monumental brasses and, where these have been removed, stone matrices on which the indents of brasses are still visible.
6. Decorative pavements, in which an overall design is created with contrasted materials, such as that designed by Lord Burlington for York Minster.

7. Archaeological pavements, which by reason of burial vaults below ground or of a variety of paving stones of different dates, reveal archaeological information about the earlier history of the church.

Many of these elements are present in our churches, and are a cause of concern. Their conservation can be considered individually.

The most serious problem, because it is so widespread and so intractable, is that of conserving ledger stones. Some church floors (Bath Abbey is an example), are completely covered in inscribed ledger stones; many others have a large proportion of the floor covered by inscribed stones, and very few churches have none at all. There are relatively few records of the inscriptions of these stones, or of the person commemorated, or of their position in the church, or even of whether there is a burial beneath. The first and most urgent requirement is therefore to initiate recording programmes of all inscriptions. The NADFAS Volunteers, who are now also working in several cathedrals, could be asked to provide a record of inscriptions before they are all erased. The Council for the Care of Churches, which holds copies of all the NADFAS church recordings, could encourage volunteers to add floor records to those already completed concerning furnishings and monuments, and should urge the church recorders to include surveys of historic floors in all future church surveys. This would go some way towards preventing the destruction of historical evidence, much of which is of considerable importance regionally, if not nationally.

The second requirement is to establish, through the advice of the Diocesan archaeologist, which ledger stones mark burials. The relationship between the inscription recording the details of the person commemorated and the mortal remains beneath, is recognized as of considerable importance by archaeologists. This also becomes significant if the decision is taken to re-order important ledgers, and to relocate them in another position in the church. Those which do not relate to burials, or to wall memorials nearby as is often the case, can be moved with less concern than the ledgers which belong in that position and no other. Many, as at Bath Abbey, have already been moved, some more than once, and cut down to fit into their new site. In such cases, the location is of less importance than the ledger itself.

Another alternative method of conservation is to recut the worn inscription. This is only feasible if the words are still legible or an accurate record of both text, siting on slab, lettering and heraldry, if it exists, are available.

In considering the conservation options, it must be remembered that ledger stones are not only of historical interest, but the text or poem, the lettering, armorials and the stone itself are all of importance, and can be very beautiful. Mediaeval ledgers with marginal black letter inscriptions are, by their rarity, rendered treasures of the first order, and should be treated as such. Many of the late seventeenth, eighteenth and nineteenth century inscriptions employ lettering that is worthy of admiration in itself. Taken as a whole, ledgers also demonstrate to a unique degree the development of monumental lettering over a period of more than one thousand years.

When thinking about methods of conserving important elements of historic floors, the possibility of limiting the wear and tear to which they are subjected should be considered, either by limiting the number of visitors, or by re-routeing them to avoid the most sensitive areas, or by controlling their footwear. Stiletto heels are notoriously damaging, as they concentrate all the weight into one small area: they are not allowed in National Trust properties. Trainers are also damaging, because grit embedded in the soles causes scratching. In all cases, large coir mats should be fixed at every entrance, and regularly cleaned; these will extract a large proportion of the dust and grit from visitors' feet before it reaches the sensitive floor areas.

The next component of historic floors of most concern, because of their rarity and extreme fragility, is mediaeval tiles. Recent studies have been carried out to establish the causes and methods of destruction of the decorative details of these tiles, and research has revealed that, once the original glazed surface has been damaged, the destruction of the patterned area takes place with alarming speed, leaving a plain red tile. This is, alas, all too common a feature in many churches. It is therefore necessary to remove wear and friction from all remaining mediaeval tiles, either by taking them up, or by cordoning them off, as at Winchester Cathedral.

Very few mediaeval tiled pavements have survived in situ, with the overall design of the original tile carpet preserved. The Chapter House at Westminster Abbey contains a rare survival, the library at Lichfield Cathedral another, and at Ely Cathedral the remarkable floor of Prior Crauden's Chapel retains its complete pattern. In these cases we have a prime responsibility to protect both the individual tiles and the overall design and layout. This can only be done by the prevention of any access by visitors except, as at Westminster, where the provision of a perimeter viewing area enables the public to gain some experience of this exceptional survival dating from the rebuilding in 1268 by Henry III.

There are particular difficulties in protecting pavements that contain some mediaeval tiles mixed with ledger stones, and that lie on the main tourist route, as in the Ambulatory at Winchester Cathedral and the Lady Chapel at Gloucester. Replicas have been made and are already showing signs of wear in the North Ambulatory at Winchester, after twenty years of use.

Another element of risk has recently arisen, the danger of theft. At Winchester, several mediaeval tiles were stolen from the Retro-choir and sold at a leading auction room. Replicas also had to be used to replace four tiles stolen from the important floor in Prior Crauden's Chapel, Ely. Protection from theft as well as from wear is therefore vital nowadays.

Although of less rarity and considerably more robust, the great encaustic pavements of the nineteenth century are also now deteriorating. Designed by leading Gothic Revival architects such as Pugin, Scott and Pearson, and manufactured by the ecclesiastical firms of Hardman and Minton among others, these pavements are of historical interest, as many of the designs were based on mediaeval prototypes. They are also an art form of considerable importance in their own right, contributing as much to the overall richness and complexity of the interiors of the great Gothic Revival churches as the stained glass, furnishings and monuments; all form integral parts of the design. Many of these pavements are now showing serious signs of wear: levels are becoming uneven, surfaces and even designs broken down and colours eroded; in some cases replacements may have to be considered. Having lost so many of these wonderful pavements at a period when their true value was not understood, we have a duty to preserve those that have survived.

Cosmati pavements, derived from Italian examples and composed not of individually designed and patterned tiles, but of contrasted materials of marble and semi-precious stones, laid in the form of an overall mosaic or guilloche design, are also of great importance and rarity. The most significant mediaeval example is the Great Pavement in the Sanctuary at Westminster Abbey, laid by the mosaicist Odericus from Rome during the rebuilding in 1268. It contains re-used antique stones from ancient Rome, including red and green porphyry and early Moorish coloured glass, and the central roundel is a vast agate, possibly from ancient Egypt. The whole elaborate design is set in a Purbeck base and, ironically, it is this, new when the pavement was constructed, that is now breaking up, rather than the antique stones.

This type of pavement, rare in Britain, was another of the mediaeval treasures taken over and adapted for their new churches by the Gothic Revival architects. Nineteenth century Cosmati pavements are therefore relatively common, usually found in the chancel, and often one of the most richly ornamented features of the church. Owing to the large number of small sections with which they are composed, they have a tendency to break up, particularly if there are problems of rising damp. However, because none of the fragments contain a design element, their repair is easier than that of encaustic tiled pavements unless, that is, they contain irreplaceable ancient stones, as with the Westminster Abbey Great Pavement.

The next category of historic floor components to be considered is monumental brasses, and the matrices in which they were laid, which still contain the indent originally made for the brass even if this itself has disappeared. The majority of monumental brasses were destroyed at or after the Reformation, and represent one of our great art losses, along with much of our mediaeval stained glass. Those that have survived have, in many cases, been moved and placed on the walls of churches where they can be seen, but are out of harm's way. However, a great many important examples of this delightful art form – selected in the Middle Ages as a cheaper way of commemorating the dead than a monument – are still on church floors and greatly at risk.

Brass, being a soft metal, is particularly subject to scratching, bending and denting and as monumental brasses were originally made in thin sections, and have over the years worn thinner, the dangers of damage are serious. There have been many cases of brasses breaking up, and sections being lost altogether. Without a record (and despite the enthusiasm of brass rubbers, many brasses are unrecorded), the repair and restoration of damaged brasses is difficult.

Their conservation in situ is also complicated. The vast majority still on the floors are covered with dirty mats which are seldom lifted or cleaned and consequently harbour grit, dust, cigarette stubs and other rubbish; being loose, they act as a kind of sandpaper, moving backwards and forwards over the brasses with an abrasive motion which over the years entirely removes the delicate incised design which is so subtle a feature of this art form. A brass worn smooth has lost most of its character.

The alternative to using a dirty mat, which is prevalent in many churches and cathedrals, is to rope off the area. This has the advantage that the brass can be seen and enjoyed, but is only practicable where it does not cause an unacceptable obstruction. In such cases, the re-routeing of the public, or the lifting of the brass and its re-positioning elsewhere are the only alternatives. It is only acceptable to consider re-siting if the brass does not mark a burial beneath, and if there are no archaeological objections, and is also dependent on finding a suitable site not too far from the original. In many churches this is difficult, as the walls are often covered in plaques and monuments, and there is no vacant site available. It is also important that the brass should be carefully mounted on a suitable base to protect it from rising damp from the walls, and to give it stability. Old brasses are very fragile, and deserve as much care in handling as any other church treasure.

It is not unknown for brasses to be covered, not only with carpets, but also with items of furniture such as prayer desks and kneeling stalls which inevitably create friction whenever they are used. Where brasses are sited in the chancel this is a common and serious problem, and one to which attention should be given.

In the case of brass indents, the difficulties of conservation are more complex. There is no doubt that the remarkable groups of indents at Lincoln Cathedral and Ely Cathedral have a beauty of their own and, although they are only a shadow of their former selves, they never-theless give one a ghostly impression of their original grandeur. The outlines of the brasses are clearly visible and create a moving reminder of what has been lost. In the case of mediaeval examples, the matrix itself is of importance, owing to its antiquity and, frequently, to the beauty of its stone. However, where these indents lie on the main route of visitors and worshippers, it is hard to envisage adequate protection for them other than to cover them with a soft mat or a false floor. No evidence has yet been produced to determine whether damage by feet is greater, in the case of stone slabs, when they are covered or uncovered; scratching takes place in either case, and gradual but irreversible damage is inflicted.

This brings us to a consideration of general principles which should be applied by all church authorities in the conservation of all historic floors. These principles apply either where wear and tear is inflicted by use, often by conflicting patterns of use, or where damage is created by the placing and moving of furniture and fittings. Maintenance of the floor surfaces should also be considered; many well-intentioned operators still use harsh abrasive cleaners, too much water, heavy duty suction machines and silicone based, non-removable polish, which can seal in the damp. Some cathedrals now limit themselves to dry sweeping with occasional wet mopping in particular problem areas, or to the use of a light wax polish.

11.2 Memorial brass to John Brook, Sergeant-at-Law, Justice of Assize, Chief Steward of the Monastery of Glastonbury, 1522, and his wife Joan.

The wear and tear patterns of use can often be mitigated by careful thought. Visitors' feet do more damage in confined spaces, or in areas where changes of direction are imposed. It is therefore important to analyse where the most sensitive floor surfaces and artefacts are placed,

11.3   The Great Pavement (1268), Westminster Abbey. Engraving by Ackerman (1812). Cosmati work by Odericus of Rome.

and to attempt, by altering the routeing and regular patterns of use, to reduce the wear on these areas. Where there are particularly rare or delicate brasses, tiles or pavements, thought should be given as to how the daily routines can be varied to take account of these, or if this is impossible, then re-ordering should be considered, but only after consultation with the Council for the Care of Churches, the consultant architect and archaeologist, and other specialist advisers where appropriate. To do nothing is to condemn such areas to eventual destruction.

Much of the damage caused by the placing and regular movement of furniture could also be avoided with thoughtful planning. A survey of each church, with an assessment of its individual features and a rationale of their relative significance, would make a good start. Since historic floors have not been given the serious consideration that they deserve, very little is known about them, and knowledge is a necessary tool for the formulation of an informed conservation policy.

Particular care should be taken when outside contractors are employed to install furniture or equipment for a special event. Without the most rigorous supervision serious and irreversible damage can be

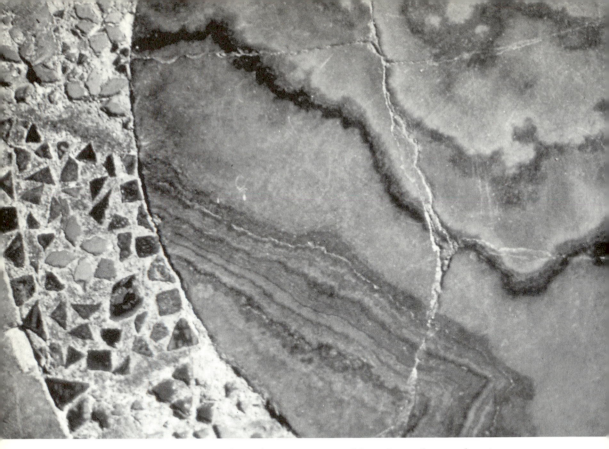

11.4 The Great Pavement (1268), Westminster Abbey. Central onyx showing signs of damage.

inflicted by scratching, scoring, chipping, staining and fracturing historic floor surfaces.

Equally, ill-judged cleaning programmes can, if too vigorously applied, do untold damage to sensitive floors and furnishings. Heavy-duty machines can chip and crack delicate surfaces; caustic and abrasive cleaners can remove the patina and destroy the surface finish of mediaeval tiles and ledger stones; too much water may damage the mortar and loosen or stain the slabs; and commercial polish may permanently discolour and deface encaustic pavements and precious stones.

The cleaning of monumental brasses must also be carefully supervised, since too much rubbing with household polish will remove the delicate surface features, and treatment with long-term polish can also have a detrimental effect on ancient metal.

All the disparate elements that go to make up a historic floor must be regarded as treasures, and must be given the sensitive treatment that they deserve. The uninformed attitude that a floor is of no consequence and can be swept, slopped out and forgotten is no longer acceptable.

11.5 Pavement (1220), Trinity Chapel, Canterbury Cathedral, showing damage.

The architects and master masons who built our great heritage of mediaeval, Tudor, seventeenth and eighteenth century, and Gothic Revival churches gave as much thought to beautifying their floors and interiors as they did to designing the parapets, pinnacles, spires and statues with which they embellished the exteriors. All of these form an essential part of a unified whole. The accretions of history, represented by the historic succession of ledger stones and monumental brasses, supply another dimension. All aspects deserve the same degree of understanding and care. This is our legacy and our responsibility. We must not fail our ancestors, who created their churches for our inspiration.

JANE FAWCETT
Jane Fawcett studied art history at London University under Sir Nikolaus Pevsner and Sir John Summerton, and architectural conservation at the Architectural Association. She was Secretary of the Victorian Society and UK Secretary of the International Council on Monuments and Sites. She is the academic tutor of the Building Conservation post-graduate course at the Architectural Association and has published extensively.

12

STAINED GLASS

✳

Keith Barley

Among forms of art the functions of stained and painted glass are unique. Three elements unite the technical and artistic functions. The mosaic of glasses close the window openings and colour the filtered light; the lead holds the glass in a flexible network to the design of the composition; and the painting depicts the subject and regulates the degree of light transmitted. This ideal union performs so well, and barring catastrophe, for so long that its durability is taken for granted.

Stained glass, however, is a fragile and sensitive medium unable to withstand extremes of stress. The glass being a man-made material, consisting basically of natural silica with a flux of potash or soda is subject to organic damage. From the time a window is installed and subjected to moisture in the form of rain, dew, condensation and relative humidity of 30 to 40 per cent the process of decay begins. The rate of deterioration is dependent on the chemical composition of the glass and the environment in which it exists.

The care and maintenance of stained glass is often neglected. Within

---

12.1 Church of St Nicholas, Stanford on Avon, Northamptonshire. Damage to the stone sills, mullions and jambs has resulted from the severe rusting of the original fourteenth century external ferramenta. Prolific growths of lichen on the window are damaging and marring the stained glass. (Photograph by Barley Studio.)

the next fifty years a wide range of technical problems, and years of deferred work, will descend upon craftsmen, few of whom will have the required knowledge and experience to deal with the conservation and renovation. Custodians are unlikely to be aware of the financial burdens to be borne, and would be daunted if they did.

The production of stained glass reached a peak in the fifteenth century. It was so highly valued that master glaziers were appointed for its maintenance in the cathedrals of mediaeval Europe. By the end of the seventeenth century in England, a decline had set in, brought about by the Reformation, which so effectively reduced the craft that understanding of the materials and techniques, traditionally passed from master to apprentice, was almost lost. The seventeenth and eighteenth centuries saw little production of stained glass. The discovery and use of enamels for applying several colours on a single pane led to new fashions and to a disregard of original techniques. The majority of the mediaeval windows were neglected, lost, sold or discarded. The nineteenth century saw a revival of stained glass rekindled by an interest in the styles and techniques of the Middle Ages. The craft flourished once again, skills were rediscovered and new technical advances made. Sadly, further losses of mediaeval glass occurred in the course of restoration. The decaying remnants of mediaeval glass were either discarded and replaced by new copies, or rearranged into a patchwork window to make way for new commissions. Occasionally the remains of an original mediaeval glazing scheme can be found in the tracery sections of restored windows.

Unfortunately this century has again seen a decline; recent interest in the craft has been predominantly non-traditional and does little to promote an understanding of past achievements. The majority of our British stained glass windows were manufactured, restored or re-leaded during the nineteenth century. The lead cames holding these mosaics of painted and coloured glass gradually deteriorate. The life expectancy of nineteenth century lead cames is 100–150 years; we are approaching this time.

During the last twenty-five years the Corpus Vitrearium Medii Avie Technical Committees in various countries have drawn up guidelines, founded on experience and experimentation, for the conservation and restoration of endangered stained glass. With the aid of these guidelines, and a few practical tips, the following points will help to encourage sound practice in the care, maintenance and conservation of our heritage of stained glass.

GROUND PLAN showing window numbering system

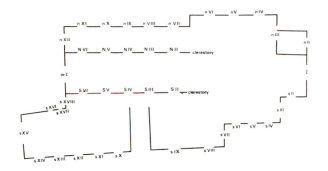

A line is drawn from (liturgical) east to west. The east window is always I, the west w.I. Lower case n(orth) and s(outh) are used for all the windows of the relevant orientation above and below the centre line. Upper case is used for all upper (clerestory) windows. Roman numerals are used to number each opening from east to west whether or not the window contains historically important glass.

WINDOW PLAN and panel numbering system

Numbering always follows the same sequence from bottom to top, left to right. In order to distinguish between main light panels and tracery lights, the number precedes the letter for main lights, the letter comes before the number for the tracery. Both follow a sequential grid pattern directly related to the panel divisions, number of tracery openings and architectural divides. Transom divisons are treated as integral with the panel numberings.

12.2   CVMA numbering system. The CVMA numbering system is mnemonic, simple to use and internationally recognized. It obviates the necessity of using lengthy worded descriptions to locate a panel precisely within a building. Although primarily designed for churches, it is based on compass orientation and can be adapted for secular structures. Should you require assistance in using the system, the CVMA Archivist at the NMR will always answer queries. In many cases a building containing historically important window glass will already have been numbered for the Archive. (Reproduced by kind permission of Jill Kerr.)

RECORDING AND SURVEY

This important first step is indispensable to the planning of a possible restoration programme, gives time to seek grants, launch appeals and draft specifications for tenders. Initially a ground plan of the church should be drawn and all windows numbered. An example of CVMA window and panel numbering system is shown in Figure 12.2. Your architect may have plans of the church. A photographic record in 35mm colour transparencies and black and white prints should be taken of the windows overall, inside and out, with detailed shots of any important, unusual or defective areas – heads, inscriptions, studio signatures, paint deterioration and impact fractures for example. Research into the history of the window should be gathered. If possible, the following details should be included: name of studio; artist or designer; date of manufacture and date of previous repairs or re-leading.

Church accounts, faculty applications, the press and parishioners may be good sources of information. Collate the details and identify with your plan and numbering system. It is advisable to make more than one copy of your records.

The structural survey of the windows should, if possible be aided by a competent craftsman and architect. The condition of the related fabric should be assessed with the glazing of the windows. For example, it is wise to combine window repairs while scaffold access is available for other structural work, as scaffolding costs are a large percentage of any high-level work.

The window survey should look to the following points as a guide to assessing condition and defects.

1. *Inspection of the lead cames.* Look for fractures around the soldered joints and lead fatigue, are the cames rare mediaeval cast or later milled flat or convex profiles? See Figure 12.3.
2. *Condition of the waterproof cement.* Inspect under the leads, is it cracked, lost or washed away? Tell-tale streaks on the glass, sills and walls should be looked for. Streaks should not be confused with those formed by excessive condensation.
3. *Stability of the panels.* Do they rattle, are they buckled, springy and weak, solid or separating, stretched and split by subsidence or settlement? Are the panels slack or tight fitting, is there a fillet glass border, are the overlapping panel joints sound and free or are they sealed between the ferramenta with putty?
4. *Ferramenta and support system.* Note the type of material used and dimensions: T bar, lug bar etc. Are they original? A through bar at the spring line is often all that remains of the original ferramenta.

   Are the supports later additions, internal or external; strong; rusting; staining glass and stone; fracturing the mullions; non-ferrous or restored with non-ferrous tips; still firm and secure

Mediaeval window lead profiles (cast)

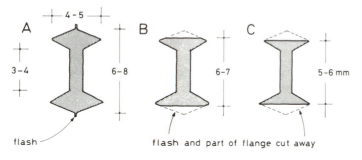

flash

flash and part of flange cut away

Cames cast in hinged two-piece moulds about 500 mm long.

Type A has thick diamond shaped flanges and a prominent casting flash along the outside edges.

Types B and C have been made from cast came (as Type 1) by scraping off the casting flash. Types 2 and 3 differ only in the amount of lead removed from the flange. Being hand-made there is considerable variation in Types A , B and C , even within the same piece.

Post-mediaeval window lead profiles (milled)

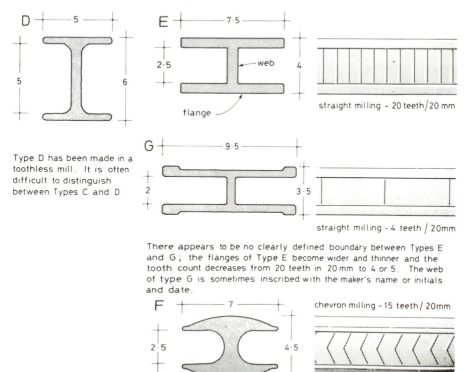

straight milling - 20 teeth/20 mm

Type D has been made in a toothless mill. It is often difficult to distinguish between Types C and D

straight milling - 4 teeth / 20mm

There appears to be no clearly defined boundary between Types E and G ; the flanges of Type E become wider and thinner and the tooth count decreases from 20 teeth in 20 mm to 4 or 5. The web of type G is sometimes inscribed with the maker's name or initials and date.

chevron milling - 15 teeth / 20mm

12.3 Window lead profiles. (Reproduced by kind permission of Dr Barry Knight.)

within the frame; are the panels wire or lead ties still attached or broken away from the panels?

Evidence of previous fixtures should be noted, and the condition of ventilator sections given.

5. *The glass.* Is it fractured, corroding, inside out, that is painted surface on the outside, damaged by acid or sand blasting, supporting growths of lichen, is the paint stable, flaking, fading with pigment loss, over painted with varnish or similar coating, damaged by previous cleaning methods, is the surface clean, or are there deposits of corrosion, loose dust, decorating paint, organisms, soot from old boilers or candles, putty, mortar, scaling from leeching stonework, crazing due to fire damage or stress or other unusual findings?

6. *Non-traditional techniques and previous repair.* Is there more than one layer of glass? If so is this for decorative reasons or for the stability of previous fractured pieces glued together. Has the plating failed? Look for signs of water penetration, organic growth and even thunder bugs. Has the adhesive broken down or discoloured? Are the original lead designs lines or artwork marred by the insertion of mending or strap leads, are repair pieces a satisfactory match in tone, texture and style with the original. Have amateurish repairs using tape, or other damaging methods been used? Occasionally, copper or tinned steel T sections were used as an alternative to lead cames, resulting rust and corrosion causing fine glass fractures. Modern techniques of appliqué glass (layers of glass or plastic shapes glued to a larger pane) and dalles de verre (1 inch thick glass set in concrete or resin) should be examined for thermal stress damage and the failure of materials employed in their manufacture.

7. *Protective glazing.* The system employed should be identified and defects noted. If wire guards are present are they galvanized steel, copper or stainless steel? Their condition, type of fixings and side effects of staining stonework should be noted. If glass, is it toughened, laminated, cast, wired, patterned or distorted? Are they plastic, perspex or polycarbonate sheets; are they scratch resistant, fire proof, discoloured, crazed or buckled due to insufficient tolerance given to fixings for expansion and contraction? Ventilation between the stained glass and protective glazing is necessary. Check that ventilation holes or gaps exist, are not blocked and are of sufficient size. The aesthetic appearance and fixing methods of all these systems should be evaluated.

It is useful to draw a diagram of the window with its overall dimensions, sizes of ferramenta, details of obstacles to access, pews, organ, screens, monuments and height from the ground.

A programme of priority work should be given and then plans for care and maintenance can begin. At present the most difficult yet important decision to make is the right choice of studio or workshop to undertake the conservation. A well-meaning but ill-informed glazier can cause more damage than all the years of neglect. The variety of problem areas in different windows will demand certain levels of competence. Mediaeval glass conservation demands techniques beyond the traditional craft skills. An accreditation scheme run by The British Society of Master Glass Painters in conjunction with the Conservation Unit of The Museums and Galleries Commission has recently been established. This will help ensure that a studio with the appropriate specialist skills is selected to treat the window competently. If required ask the advice of The Council for the Care of Churches, English Heritage, British Society of Master Glass Painters or The Conservation Unit and inspect previous similar commissions of a proposed studio. Unless the condition of the window has been properly evaluated, and solutions specified, requiring only costings, the selected specialist studios should provide a report on the condition with a full explanation of proposed remedies and methods of treatment. The studio should also provide a quotation for their suggested work. It is normal to pay a fee for these reports.

It is important to know the principles of stained glass conservation and question any proposed solution that may breach them.

Any intervention should be reversible if technically possible. As much of the original glass as possible should be retained. All additions should be harmonious and compatible with the original materials. All changes should be recorded and identifiable.

GUIDE TO RECOMMENDED METHODS AND SOLUTIONS TO PROBLEMS

Window removal

This is a time for coordination between the custodian, architect and glazier. It is essential that the custodian is informed of the length of time required to complete the work and the degree of disturbance entailed. The removal of windows from stone work is a dusty process and protective measures should be taken to safeguard the fabric and

12.4   Brough Park Chapel. This window was installed with insufficient saddle bar support, the panels buckled, the leading fractured resulting in the loss of two sections. Prior to its removal for restoration the panels are labelled and temporary tape applied externally to prevent further loss. (Photograph by Barley Studio.)

contents. The church organ is particularly sensitive to stonedust and should be well-covered if sited close to the work. Movable objects should be set aside and fixed monuments and decoration below the window, especially if delicate, be padded with some suitable material to withstand damage from falling cement chips and possible accidents. Temporary replacement glazing must be thoroughly considered. It may need to cater for specific needs of security, light, weatherproofing or any combination of these.

The removal of windows set in rock-hard cement or putty is potentially damaging, especially if the glass is thin and designed without a sacrificial fillet border. Conventional hammer and chisel techniques are inadequate and sometimes a secondary groove needs to be ground out close to the glass to relieve the stress when chiselling. This is messy and can damage the fabric, a safe alternative is the use of air-powered stone carving chisels that shave the hard material away. If the lead cames are fractured and the panels on the verge of collapse, temporary taping will be needed; this should be applied to the external surface, taking care to avoid areas of back paint, and removed at the earliest opportunity. The glass should be transported vertically in packing cases or racks in such a way that the glass surface is not rubbed or scratched. It is recommended that all iron saddle bars are replaced by an appropriate non-ferrous section. If ancient ferramenta exist they should be conserved by tipping with non-ferrous ends to avoid further damage to the stone by rust expansion.

Occasionally the ancient top horizontal bar was installed while the window opening was built. These fixed bars pass continuously through all the mullions and are barbed or hooked at each end, set into the wall jambs with lead cast around them. The aid of a stonemason may be required for the safe removal of this bar. Stonework repairs may be the reason for the removal of a window and the glaziers must ensure that the masons are aware of their limitations. Stained glass was designed and manufactured to fit the stone openings; any later replacement stone must then be made and sited to fit the glass. Too often this is overlooked, and costly mistakes are the result.

Recording of the restoration and conservation work

Continuous records are very important and supplement those made at the survey stage. Any evidence of previous glazing schemes, or discoveries while removing the window, should be noted. Photographic records of the glass before and after conservation, with details of the corrosion and deposits found on the surface of the glass and any unusual findings should be taken. Full-scale rubbings of the panels should be made, detailing the size of lead cames used. These can be photographed and reduced for record purposes.

Notes on the methods of cleaning, repair, type of materials used and dimensions should be recorded. If the window is of artistic or historic importance and therefore eligible for grant. Standardized record forms are required as a condition of any grant made. The Royal Commission on Historic Monuments for England will, if invited, also photograph the conserved glass prior to reinstatement.

The cleaning of stained glass

Cleaning is the most controversial topic with varied methods employed. Glass requires cleaning for two purposes, to improve its translucency and to remove moisture-retaining deposits. Glass will not deteriorate without the presence of water. The use of household cleaners, steel wool, scouring pads or any method that will scratch the glass surface must not be used. Hard tap water is potentially harmful!

The most acceptable and widely used cleaning method is by glass fibre brushes, available in a variety of sizes to suit specific requirements. It is essential that the stability of the paint pigment is established before cleaning begins. If sound, the removal of loose dirt by gentle brushing with soft hair brushes will reveal the extent of the hard deposits. If organic growth or soft deposits exist they may be removed by swabbing with deionized water.

If the cleaning requires more attention than can be achieved by the above methods, it must be entrusted to a specialist conservator only. The complexity of glass deterioration inevitably leads to alternative cleaning methods being suggested. However, when specialized methods are recommended it is important to remember that the conservation of stained glass is in its infancy. Considerable time and money has been spent in recent years on scientific analysis of the chemical composition and behaviour of glasses. A brief conclusion is that a greater understanding only fuels the realization that little is still known.

Any cleaning method is an intervention and some have proved to be disastrous. It must be remembered that no amount of cleaning will remove the scars and patina of age and restore the vibrancy of a new window. It is my belief that we should be cautious and conservative in our approach to cleaning. Who knows what harm may result from a small trace of chemical cleaning agent being absorbed into a deposit of

12.5 Church of St Mary, Cottingham, Yorkshire. Detailed examination of the glass must be made prior to cleaning to determine the stability of the paint pigment and differentiate between it and the deposits of dirt and corrosion. Careless and harsh cleaning would easily destroy the subtle and delicate shading seen on this angel's head by J. B. Capronnier 1875, from the East window of the church.

corrosion and not fully removed when rinsed? The skill and knowledge of the conservator must be appreciated, for the harshest of cleaning methods in the right hands can be safer than the mildest in the hands of the inexperienced.

The following alternative methods of cleaning may be suggested by skilled conservators.

Ultrasonic

With this method the glass is immersed in a diluted ammonia-based cleaning agent and ultrasonically vibrated for up to six minutes. This system would loosen any delicate paint and thorough rinsing must ensure no trace of cleaning agent remains. This method is uncontrollable. The safety of the chemical solution chosen must be established and understood before use. If this method is suggested I would prefer it to be restricted to the cleaning of unpainted glass only.

Air abrasion

This method is selected for the removal of hard or deeply pitted deposits where access with glass fibre brushes is restricted. Microns of glass bead are shot from a pen type holder with a fine nozzle by compressed air. The use of harsher media should not be necessary. The control and safe use of this tool relies totally on the skill of the operator. The choice of nozzle size, amount of media and air pressure provides a variety of control when sensitively selected.

Reagents

The fluid EDTA (ethylene diamine teracetic acid) is applied to the glass to remove both dirt and corrosion. The length of time required to achieve the desired level of cleaning varies, dependant on the type of glass. The method is controllable in experienced hands but the glass must be completely rinsed. The paint pigment is vulnerable and contact with the fluid must be avoided.

Dental descalers

Pen type tools are used, either dry or with water for the removal of deep pitted corrosion deposits. Precise control is needed by the operator to clean problem pieces safely.

As a precaution, methods of applied protection to paintwork and delicate areas may be used in conjunction with the above cleaning methods. Other methods of cleaning that may be suggested must be questioned. It is worth bearing in mind that in Austria water is rarely used for the cleaning of ancient glass.

The repair of fractures

The removal of disfiguring mending leads and restoration of fractured pieces to their original form is aesthetically rewarding. Bonding is an intervention and must be restricted to the fractured edges only. The techniques and adhesives used have advanced in recent years. Two types of adhesive are widely used today. Epoxy resins have developed to a stage when cracks can almost become invisible by using a resin having a similar refractive index to the glass itself. Colour can be added to the resin to match the glass for the infill of lost chips and gaps. Resins give excellent visible results and are reversible chemically. Caution is important, since resins may discolour in time, in daylight conditions. The bond is often stronger than the glass itself and may, if a larger piece is joined to a smaller piece, result in stress fractures due to the differing thermal expansion. Resins are safer in museum, or constant temperature, conditions. Temperature changes varying from $-10°C$ to $95°F$ may prove to be damaging.

Self-curing silicon adhesive, although not as aesthetically pleasing, provides a flexible bond that is mechanically (though not chemically) reversible. Fractures may still be visible on close inspection, but given the high position of most windows these will not be noticed. New glass may be cut, ground and painted to match the original and glued into lost sections. Silicone adhesive with an acetic acid curing agent must be allowed adequate time to cure fully before being leaded, as the acid will corrode the lead. As with the resins, various types of silicon are available. The long-term durability of adhesives is not proven and periodic inspection of bonded glass is recommended.

As a precaution against the failure of adhesives, bonded glass fragments not physically held by the lead cames are generally supported with a backing plate of thin sheet glass moulded to the undulations of the original. Back plating should be avoided if at all possible as moisture may penetrate between the two layers and accelerate corrosion. In some instances such as star fractures it is possible to insert a rivet to hold the fractures physically at the point of impact and avoid the use of a backing plate.

The repair of fractures is predominantly made to features such as heads and symbolically important pieces. Other less important fractured pieces can be aesthetically improved by either inserting a fine string lead came or joining with fine copper foil. Both are used when the fractured edges are damaged and edge bonding is impracticable.

The leading

A great deal of debate surrounds the type of lead used in a re-leading of a window. The width of cames, seen as the black line around the edges of glass plays an important role in the effect of the original design. The dimensions should never be altered unless severe structural defects have resulted. Having achieved a match with the width of the original lead the most important consideration should be in the durability of the lead. Often, if flat milled lead was previously used it is specified for the appearance from the outside only. Flat milled lead used from the sixteenth century onwards has never achieved the durability of the mediaeval cast leads that in a few instances still survive today.

The durability of lead used today is dependent on its composition, the proportion of pure lead to added alloys, its method of manufacture and design of profile. Speaking from my own observations and experience, mediaeval leads because they are cast, are not subject to the same degree of metal fatigue as milled leads, which are stretched from being two feet to six feet in length. Milled convex profile lead of the same date as flat lead is stronger, but neither have the qualities of mediaeval cames.

Modern lead cames are either milled or extruded. Because extruded lead is not subject to fatigue in stretching, regardless of the composition, it may prove to be the more durable of the techniques today, especially in a convex profile. It is essential to retain discovered mediaeval leads. They are often found to be strong, repairable and of artistic and historic importance. If reinstated with protective glazing they will survive many more years, as may nineteenth century windows if protected.

Protective glazing

Windows require external protection for two reasons: to prevent mechanical damage, either accidental or willful, and to shield them from the ravages of weather and atmospheric pollution. When choosing a protective system suitable for your specific needs, bear in mind the following points. Are the materials and fixings suggested durable and compatible with the window framework? Are they designed to be as aesthetically pleasing as possible in the given situation?

Wire guards are often used for protection against mechanical damage. The best on offer today are of stainless steel in crimped wire, manufactured to the glaziers templates and fitted within the framework of each light and tracery section. Copper guards are durable but can stain stonework green. Galvanized wire will eventually rust and stain the fabric unless regularly maintained by painting. Plastic coated wire will deteriorate especially when the coating is damaged. Weld mesh and other rolled wire products are best avoided. The fixings for wire guards must be non-ferrous and fitted in such a way as to avoid damage to the fabric. Guards protecting glass that is lightly painted will be disrupted by the shadow cast from the wires, especially on south-facing windows.

When vandalism is an acute problem, external protection may be offered using acrylic or polycarbonate sheeting. These materials will protect against stone or air gun attack but are often the object of abuse themselves. Plastics will scratch and melt easily, ideal material for graffiti and cigarette burns. Of the plastics offered, the scratch resistant, fire retardant polycarbonate sheet would be the wisest choice. As with all plastics the manufacturer's instructions must be followed. On large sheets the specified tolerance must be provided on the fixings to allow for expansion. If the sheets are tight fitting they will severely buckle and may spring from the opening and cause damage. The fixings must allow for the periodic removal to undertake cleaning and maintenance work. Sufficient gaps at the base and top of the openings must be given to allow for a circulation of air. If the circulation is restricted, moisture will be trapped and serious damage to the window will occur. Plastics will attract dust, loose their glaze being scratched by airborne grit, may discolour, craze and fracture. The sheets should be fixed within the openings of the framework, not over the complete opening. Aesthetically their appearance externally may be disturbing but internally it is good until deterioration of the plastic occurs.

A variety of sheet glass external glazings have been widely used for mechanical and environmental protection. As with plastics they must be installed correctly to avoid frost fractures and moisture problems. They clean easily, are not disruptive to the internal appearance but offer only sacrificial protection. All glasses used, be it wired, polished or cast plate, toughened, laminated, or sheet leaded to the main design lines of the stained glass will break and require replacement. Wire guards may be used in addition to the sheet glazings, providing the extra protection to valuable or vulnerable windows.

Protective backing plates of thin sheet glass moulded to the contours of the stained glass are occasionally used to protect the external surface of severely weathered glass. The plate and stained glass is sealed and re-leaded in wider heart leads. This technique is time consuming and adds weight to the window and the possibility of extra support bars may be considered. The system is used when environmental protection is required and it is felt aesthetically inappropriate to use the alternative systems.

The application of synthetic coatings has been used in some instances but is now largely rejected. The coating to the cleaned external surface of the glass has to be flawlessly applied to ensure no moisture penetrates between the coating and glass. Some of the past coatings are irreversible, others may be removed with solvents but damage is likely to occur. The coatings may discolour, craze, or have a different thermal expansion rate to that of the glass, causing fractures. The delicate painted surface of the glass is still vulnerable to condensation.

12.6 Church of The Holy Trinity, Tattershall, Lincolnshire. The corroded panel is being framed in manganese bronze for its protection and conservation by isothermal glazing. The glazier is soldering on ties for the bar supports to be attached across the frame. (Photograph by Barley Studio.)

To protect these monumental works of art from mechanical and environmental damage is difficult to achieve considering the technical functions and the architectural settings for which they were designed. Museum-type conditions, isolated from all forms of damaging moisture would be ideal. The most effective method of protection, nearing museum conditions within their original settings, has proved to be isothermal glazing. The system in use since 1950s is a form of double glazing with ventilated space that keeps a near equal air temperature over both faces of the endangered glass, hence 'isothermal'. As the glass is kept dry, especially on the delicate inner painted surface, no longer subjected to condensation, deterioration is effectively reduced. A new protective window is sited generally in the original glazing groove or rebate previously occupied by the stained glass. The stained glass is framed and suspended inside the new protective glazing with internal ventilation provided to the largest degree at the base and top of the openings. The air inside the building is drawn up in between the glazings by the chimney effect, keeping the stained glass dry. The variety of materials used to achieve the desired results are numerous, frames have been made of wood, steel, aluminium, zinc, copper and brass. The outer protective glazings are equally various resulting in a choice of materials that are acceptable for most situations.

The gap between the glazings and the ventilation slits is the most critical element. It is known that a safe distance between the glazings must not be less than two centimetres and the air flow not restricted or deflected at the base of the openings. Generally the gap is governed by the profile and design of the original openings. The stained glass is originally made to fix within a glazing groove or rebate and will not fit when framed between the flush sides of the opening without the removal of original glass. Consequently the stained glass is sited at the narrowest point permitted by the profile of the opening.

Solutions to most problems encountered by the installation of isothermal glazing have now been found. A slightly matted non-reflective glass distorted in a kiln to deflect light at random will eliminate the mirror effect of flat sheet protective glazings. The glass may be leaded to the design of the original external ferramenta or leaded to the main design lines of the stained glass. The most complicated of tracery shapes can be framed in materials that are strong, light and compatible with the fabric.

The problem of side light around the edges of the frames has been overcome by attaching fine sheet lead to the back of the frames which are then folded flush with the undulations of the openings. The problem of parallax caused by having two saddle bar supports is reduced by aligning the bars to suit the average viewing position. Isothermal glazing is particularly important as a holding process for the protection of our most endangered glass and windows suffering from pigment loss, until a time when an improved, reversible technique is discovered.

General advice for care and maintenance

Many of the problems encountered could be avoided or reduced by simple maintenance jobs and thoughtful planning. The following list of advice and guidance will prompt custodians and those responsible for the care of stained glass to look for improvements that can be made.

1. Malicious damage is a growing problem. In many instances it could be avoided by removing potential missiles from the vicinity of the windows. Clear away stones, rubble, bottles,

fallen tree branches and other loose objects that may be used as missiles. If new paths or drainage channels are being considered, try to avoid the common use of gravel that may be ideal for its application but provides endless ammunition to the vandal. Have any damage attended to promptly as the sight of holes appears to attract and lead to the appearance of further holes. Avoid the siting of such objects as oil storage tanks beneath windows, making them accessible to thieves and vandals. If vandalism is persistent seek the advice of the police.

2. Notify the police and fire service of any valuable windows. Unless informed the point of entry to extinguish a fire may be through your valued window.

3. Regularly check external wire guards. Ensure they are still firmly attached. Loose guards may be torn away by vandals or make excellent nesting places for birds. Clean away growths of ivy and creepers and any old leaves or debris. Seek professional advice if the guards are ageing and require replacement.

4. Check external sheet glazings for fractures. Clean off deposits from birds, lichen, plant growth and dirt at regular intervals. Ensure that the ventilation holes are still open and allowing the air to flow freely. Check that condensation grooves, weep holes and lead sills permit the exit of collected water.

5. If contractors are employed for other works, ensure that protection is provided where necessary for the windows. Ladders, rubble and tools should be cleared away at the end of a day's work. Stone cleaning is notorious for damage to glass. The chemical and sand blasting techniques are especially harmful and all windows must be flawlessly protected before the cleaning work begins. Allow for protection when internal decoration is to be undertaken.

6. The environment can be improved for windows by ensuring that any available ventilation systems are free and working. Overhanging branches that may cause damage and trees that shadow the windows, especially on the north side should be trimmed back. Check that fall pipes and gutters are not blocked allowing water to run down the walls and glass.

7. Ban all ball games within the vicinity of the windows.

8. Little importance has been attached to plain diamond quarry and rectangular leaded glazing in the past. Many of these windows contain hand-made, tinted historic glass and deserve the same attention as recommended for stained glass. Too

often these windows are being replaced with new modern sheet glass, inferior in character to the original glass. New hand-made glasses are available for their repair, and re-leading of these windows should be specified.

In conclusion, it is always wise to seek sound and competent advice before embarking on any plan or action that may jeopardize the windows.

KEITH BARLEY

Before establishing his own practice, Keith Barley was apprentice and glazier with the York Glaziers Trust. He pioneered the protective isothermal glazing system and undertakes glazing, conservation of historic glass and supply of glass for historic buildings. He has participated in many international conferences and symposia and was a founder member of the British Society of Master Glass Painters, Conservation Sub-committee.

13

TEXTILES

❊

Elizabeth Ingram

Churches, whatever their size, generally possess some textiles which are either directly related to the liturgy such as chasubles, stoles, altar coverings, or an enhancement of the building and its worship. By their very nature, textiles tend to have a limited life, yet some may be found to date back many centuries. Conservation needs to embrace not only the care, cleaning and repair of textiles but also their storage and the prevention of damage during use.

Many churches have only a hazy knowledge of the textiles in their care and a good written record is of paramount importance. Church legislation does call for a property inventory, but this is more often honoured in the breach than in reality. However, an inventory can form the best basis for a programme which will include general conditions within the church, everyday cleaning and repairs, storage and conservation.

THE INVENTORY

The inventory may either be in book form or constructed as a card index. Each article needs to be entered with an accurate description

13.1 Date and emblem of the Convent of St Margaret, East Grinstead, concealed in embroidery. (Photograph by Jack Allen.)

giving its correct name, size, colour and a description of any decoration. The date of acquisition and any historical information should be added when these are known. Colour photographs are a great advantage in conjunction with the written details. The NADFAS guide, *Inside Churches* is an excellent source from which to identify and describe all the contents of a church.

Dating and identification

Dating and identification of the textile is not easy, but a thorough examination of the article can be rewarding. A label sewn inside may give a maker's name, and often the date it was made will have been inked onto the label. Scrutiny of the embroidery can reveal a motif and a date (see Figure 13.1). This was found, for example, on an altar frontal designed by John David Sedding and worked by the Sisters of St Margaret's Convent, East Grinstead, whose emblem it was. The motif only measures 2.5 cm × 1.2 cm and was quite difficult to spot. Over the years many vestments, particularly chasubles, have been made up from ballgowns of the eighteenth and nineteenth centuries. Beautiful brocades, damasks and embroidered silks were rightly considered too good to be thrown away, so were re-made for use in church; some still showing signs of unpicked darts or the shadow of pleats that could not be entirely pressed out.

Working through old Parochial Church Council Minute books, which are usually to be found in county record offices, may give a clue as to when a certain item was purchased or received as a gift, and old photographs of the inside of a church are worth studying with a magnifying glass which can pick out details not apparent to the naked eye. Many vestments, rugs and carpets have been given by the family of the big house in the parish and their descendants may have recollections or records which are worth investigating. The memories of people whose parents perhaps worked for the family may turn up photographs or other snippets of information to back up hazy recollections. Old local newspapers can be checked in the Reference Library where they are usually available on microfilm which makes them easier and faster to read.

Museum textile departments should be able to help with the dating of fabrics, either by giving an opinion themselves or by suggesting other avenues of research. Designs influenced by the Art Nouveau movement, the Needlework Development Council, William Morris or the work of well-known architect-designers are obvious to the trained eye and provide clues for further study. An embroidered cope hood in York Minster was identified when it was compared with one illustrated in the *History of Ecclesiastical Dress* by Janet Mayo. The figures worked on both hoods were shown standing on identically designed and worked floors. Research confirmed that both were designed by Sir Ninian Comper and worked by the sisters of Bethany in the early twentieth century.

Every corner in a church, the backs of drawers, the bottoms of chests and even crumpled 'sacking' used to stop draughts, needs to be examined before an inventory is complete. Even then it is never finished as it must be kept up to date when new textiles are acquired or additional information comes to light. Details of cleaning, conservation or recycling should always be recorded as it would be unfortunate if future generations had the same difficulties with identification and provenance through inadequately kept records in the late twentieth century.

Based on the inventory, it should be possible to work out a plan for future action. Not everything can be done at once so a list drawn up in order of priority will make the task less onerous.

ALTAR FRONTALS AND THROW-OVER CLOTHS

Throw-over cloths are known as 'Laudian throws' because Archbishop Laud stringently enforced the Canons (regulations) of 1604 which decreed that, at the time of Divine Service, the altar must be covered with a decent carpet of silk. 'Carpet' was then a normal description of a table covering, so the throw-over altar cloth was adapted from rich table coverings.

Everyday use of frontals

This should present few problems but it is important to ensure that the frontals are hung correctly. Those mounted on stretchers are kept taut and in good shape, but the frontals which hang on rods at the top front of the altar need to be checked to see that the pockets through which the rod runs have not started to tear or pull away. When this happens, the frontal will sag, putting a strain on the fabric and forming shallow swags which trap dust; dirt lines thus formed are difficult to remove. Frontals, hung from a linen cloth passed over the top of the altar and counter-weighted at the back with a rod passing through a wide hem, need to be carefully adjusted so that they too hang straight, with the lower edge just clear of the floor. Many frontals show patches of wear at the centre top and bottom caused by the priest's body and toe contact. This is inevitable wear and tear and there is nothing that can be done to prevent it happening.

Storage

Frontals are ideally stored in specially made frontal boxes. These large boxes need to be sited away from damp walls and the type which have doors opening at the front are preferable to those which are top-loaded. Each frontal should hang on its own long bar which slots into cups at the ends of the box. If the frontals are not too long and heavy, the bars may be hinged at one end so that they can be swung out for ease of access. Top loading boxes are more difficult to use as the frontal on its bar has to be lowered in from above; the frontal may catch as it is being lowered and, if this is not noticed, permanent creases will be formed. Top loading boxes are also not easy to clean and anything which falls to the bottom may go unnoticed. It is important to have ventilation holes at the base of both types of box but they must be covered with insect-proof gauze. Ventilation prevents the formation of mould growth.

Before returning a frontal to store it is wise to check it over for loose braids, fringes, embroidery or suspension loops and for signs of insect damage which can be attended to before the damage has time to get worse.

Free-standing altars

Free-standing altars with their sharp corners can strain the fabric of throw-over cloths and a fitted under-cover with lightly padded corners will cushion these vulnerable angles and prolong the life of the cloth.

General cleaning

General cleaning of both frontals and Laudian throws need only be minimal. Brushes should never be used as they can catch in the embroidery and tend to rough up the surface of the fabric. A light cleaning with a low suction hand-held vacuum cleaner such as a dustette will remove surface dirt, but the cleaner must always be used over a piece of nylon monofilament net or with the nozzle covered with a piece of net secured with a rubber band. Provided the cleaner is passed gently over the surface of the frontal, the net will prevent any threads, beads or other vulnerable decorations from being sucked into the machine. Hard pressure should be avoided as it can damage the material. A piece of net needs to have its edges bound with tape so that the sharp fibres do not catch when in use, and it should be washed frequently.

Except during services, altar tops should be protected with dust covers so that they do not become soiled, especially from bird or bat droppings.

Redundant frontals

The moving of altars away from the east wall, necessitating the provision of new throw-over coverings, naturally render the old frontals redundant. Sometimes the old frontals can be incorporated as panels appliquéd onto colour-coordinated fabric for new covers. If old frontals are of intrinsic beauty or historical value (and this should have been investigated for the inventory) they should be preserved. The ideal solution is to keep them in the church for which they were made, or perhaps pass them on to another less well-endowed parish which might be glad of the offer. Alternative suggestions may be sought from the diocesan furnishing officer or the Council for the Care of Churches.

Display

There is so much more interest nowadays in visiting churches that it may be a good solution to conserve a fine frontal and display it in a purpose-made wall-mounted display case. The case needs to be on a south wall or in some other situation where it will be out of strong light and fixed so that there is air circulation between wall and case. Plain glass is recommended. Any special lighting needs to be operated by a time switch and intensity kept within the optimum 50 lux. Curtains give added protection against excessive daylight and they can be pulled back for viewing.

If a textile is to be displayed on a wall, care must be taken so that it is not hung over a radiator or hot pipes as the rising heat will not only dry out the textile but will cause dust and dirt to circulate upwards in the hot air. Blocks of wood or corks attached to the back of a frame or case will allow fresh air to circulate and counteract damp.

13.2 Detail of altar frontal (c 1890) displayed in the Church of St Eloy, Great Smeaton, North Yorkshire. (Photograph by Hugh Murray.)

Cleaning and conservation for display

A textile conservator will be able to give advice on cleaning a frontal and how much conservation is necessary. The minimum, for example, would require anchoring loose threads, underpatching weak areas and possibly covering other small areas with net dyed to blend with the background to prevent the fabric from falling away. This technique is especially useful for faces and hands. It cannot be stressed too strongly that conservation is a highly technical and specialized undertaking and it is far better to leave well alone until professional advice has been sought, rather than run the risk of causing irreparable damage.

Leather frontals

A number of embossed and painted or gilded leather frontals still exist and these need very special handling under the guidance of a conservator.

Professional conservation is expensive, but it is well worth considering for outstanding textiles; a detailed estimate should be sought at the outset.

13.3 Example of embroidery protected with a net. (Photograph by Jim Kershaw.)

Storage of redundant frontals

Frontals no longer in use, which cannot be displayed and for which there is a storage problem, can be fitted into a comparatively small space by rolling them up from one end to the other. A cardboard former or tube of not less than 15 cm diameter can be obtained from a carpet shop, and this can be cut down in length so that it is 20 cm longer than the depth of the frontal and makes an excellent base. Cover the former with acid-free tissue paper and interleave more tissue paper as the frontal is rolled on loosely. Always roll with the right side of the frontal to the outside as this keeps the face fabric smooth and any creases will be taken up by the lining and interlining. Wrap the rolled frontal in cotton sheeting, label it clearly and then place it either on a shelf or suspend it in a cupboard with a rod through the centre of the cardboard tube.

Frontals sometimes have to be kept in drawers. If so, keep the drawers dust free and line out with cotton sheeting. Fold the frontal with the right side out and pad the folds with crumpled-up tissue paper

13.4   Altar frontals rolled and stored in racks. (Photograph by Hugh Murray.)

or a light roll of wadding covered with cotton, which is more practical for everyday use and is long lasting. The sheeting can be turned back over the frontal and tucked in to keep out the dust.

VESTMENTS

The number of vestments owned by a church varies greatly, and so does the quality, but it is just as important to take care of those of simple form as those of greater significance.

Storage

Vestments kept in drawers should be stored in a similar way to altar frontals, the drawers kept clean and lined out with cotton sheeting. Any folds in the vestments need to be padded with tissue paper or rolls of wadding. Vestments hung on hangers do need to have properly shaped and padded hangers. An ordinary wooden coathanger can be enclosed between two pieces of hardboard cut to the shape of the shoulder seams of the vestment, and then well-padded with wadding and finally covered with a cotton cover which can be stitched on firmly. This will keep the shoulder-line nicely rounded and the vestment will hang correctly without strain.

A dust wrap is beneficial, especially for copes. They are best made of cotton and with a front opening, and, if secured with tapes, press-studs or velcro, such covers minimize surface soiling and handling, however they must be cut generously so that they do not restrict the fullness of the vestment. Care needs to be taken when hanging vestments in a cupboard so that they are not compressed when the doors close nor get nipped in the door hinges.

Cleaning

Some vestments can be cleaned commercially but it is advisable to consult the manager of the cleaning firm so that he or she may examine the piece and confirm that is is still strong enough to withstand cleaning and that the cleaning process will not cause damage. Many vestments and frontals have been ruined because sufficient care has not been taken. Weak threads couching down gold or silver threads have broken and the metallic threads have become unravelled. These metallic threads are made up from an inner silken core wound round with a very fine strip of gold or silver foil. The swirling action of the cleaner drum can unwind this foil. It cannot be repaired.

KNEELERS OR HASSOCKS

Many churches are furnished with beautifully worked kneelers or hassocks which add greatly both to the beauty and comfort of the building. Embroidered kneelers require just as much care and attention as frontals or vestments, not least because they are usually in such a vulnerable position on the floor.

General care

During the week, placing kneelers on chair seats or storing them on the back of a pew or the chair in front, keeps them out of the way of floor cleaning and prevents them from being used as foot rests by visitors. Those which are hung from a hook need to be carefully upholstered so that the suspension loops are firmly anchored. A D-shaped loop attached with very strong tape should have the tape running the full length of the kneeler as this will spread the weight more evenly and the upper end of the kneeler will not bow upwards as can happen when the ring is only attached to the top end. A lot of time, energy and expensive materials go towards the making of embroidered kneelers and they do deserve to be well upholstered. A firm packing is more comfortable to kneel on and it keeps the embroidery in good shape with well defined square corners. As an alternative to compacted foam, squabs may be made up from layers of wool carpet felt stacked on a plywood base and covered with a calico inner cover.

Cleaning

Scotchguard sprayed onto kneelers when they are new is sometimes advocated, but it is not recommended after any cleaning has been carried out as the spray tends to trap residual dust.

Light cleaning, using a dustette over monofilament net, should be sufficient if it is done on a regular basis. If embroidered kneelers have become heavily soiled, it may be worth considering more extensive treatment. It is best to take the kneelers into the open air on a fine and breezy day, where they can be beaten with an old-fashioned cane carpet beater, available from Oxfam shops. As dust is raised, it will be dispersed by the breeze. Do not use a stick for beating as this is far too violent and may damage the embroidery. Kneelers can be shampooed using a small carpet shampooing machine and Boot's Sensitive Skin washing-up liquid used in the same proportions as one would use in washing up. The surface of the kneeler should not be saturated, but just wet enough to raise the dirt which will be sucked up into the machine. Drying needs to be fairly slow, and it is best done in the open air, out of direct sunlight and where the breeze will hasten the process.

CARPETS AND RUGS

These are often neglected because a church is unaware of their importance and value, perhaps having been given them many years ago; they have probably never been professionally examined, and their condition often leaves much to be desired.

Position and general care

Church floors range from good wooden boards to tiles, flagstones, ledger stones and other worn areas which are potentially dangerous to walk on. Often it is these very areas which are covered with a rug which will consequently wear unevenly. All rugs and carpets should be provided with well-fitted hairfelt underlay, cut to reach to the edges of the rug and, if there is rising damp, special carpet paper should be laid down between the floor and the underlay. Special care needs to be taken on steps so that the underlay fits well and neither it nor the rug will slip when walked on. The edges of underlay should never be turned in as this causes a ridge and uneven wear. Rubber-backed underlay is not recommended as it has a more limited life and can wear unevenly if used over a ledger stone or other rough surface. It can press into lettering, disintegrate and is then hard to remove.

Conservation

Once carpets and rugs have been properly assessed, valued and entered in the inventory, decisions can be made as to what treatment is necessary. Providing they are laid sensibly and have been fitted with appropriate underlays, light vacuum cleaning will be sufficient for everyday care. Repairs and special cleaning should be left to professionals. An estimate of cost is of prime importance and it must be accepted that it is probably not possible to carry out all necessary work at one time, but if an order of priority is worked out, conservation can be spread over a number of years.

Druggets

Druggets, especially those of plastic are not recommended as they can raise damp from stone floors and by trapping moisture and grit within the rug, encourage the formation of mould.

Summary of care

A good underlay, sensible positioning, gentle hoovering on a regular basis and specialist repair and cleaning when funds allow should be adequate once a church is fully aware of what carpets and rugs it possesses.

BANNERS

These may include Mothers' Union, British Legion, Scouts and Guides and other special categories. The banners themselves do not sustain a great deal of wear and tear, but sometimes damage is caused through faulty positioning.

Positioning and hanging

A banner in full sun or daylight will begin to fade as the light can bleach out dyes and weaken fibres. A banner leant against a wall can rub the back and, if it is hanging at an angle, creases form which collect dust. A simple bracket on a wall or pillar, allied to a small block of wood on the floor with a hole into which a pole can be set, will make the banner hang better and it will minimize damage from wall contact.

Plastic covers

Plastic covers have sometimes been made, especially for Mothers' Union banners. These are excellent when the banner has to be taken to a service away from the church, but they should not be used other than on special occasions as they cause sweating and encourage mildew. If a cover has got wet, it needs to be very carefully dried both inside and out as moisture cannot escape through water-impervious plastic.

Cleaning

A light hoovering with a dustette over monofilament net once in a while is all that is needed.

HANGINGS AND TAPESTRIES

The same care and attention applies to hangings and tapestries as to banners.

Hanging

Care must be taken so that the banners are not in direct light and are placed against a dry wall with a gap between the wall and the article to allow air to circulate. Never hang any textile over a radiator or hot pipes as the rising heat not only takes up dust with it, but the warmth will dry out fibres and make them brittle. Velcro fastenings are ideal for all hangings as they are simple to fix and use. One half of the Velcro attached along the top edge of the hanging will interlock with the other half fastened to a wooden batten fixed to the wall. This ensures that the hanging is quite straight and it is so much better than the old method of using tacks or nails which rust and cause holes to form. Some hangings are suspended from a linen sleeve at the top edge through which a rod is passed and then hooked onto wall brackets. Both systems allow the passage of air between the wall and the fabric. All hangings benefit from a good lining as this protects them from rubbing against the wall and cuts down on dust penetration from behind.

Cleaning

A light hoovering with a dustette over monofilament net will deal with any cleaning required, but the net is especially important if the piece has been made as a collage, perhaps by children, as it will protect any loosely fixed materials.

PICTURES

Embroidering religious pictures was a popular pastime in the late nineteenth and early twentieth centuries and many of them are beautifully worked. They are usually glazed, so little needs to be done to them other than check that the glass is undamaged or it will let in dust. See that there is no sign of moth damage and look for woodworm either in the frame or in the plywood backing. Woodworm can penetrate the embroidery too, but any infestation should not be treated in situ as the fumes from the fumigating liquid can damage the embroidery. It is better to seek the advice of a textile conservator or a picture framer who may suggest that the plywood mount is replaced and the textile treated before it is re-glazed. Any damage to the frame should be treated as it is a pity to re-frame an old picture which usually looks best in its contemporary frame.

REGIMENTAL, ROYAL NAVY AND ROYAL AIR FORCE COLOURS

It is still the practice to lay up Service colours in cathedrals and churches but there are now few instances of tattered and fragmentary colours suspended in netting supports. It is at the discretion of the unit concerned, together with the church authorities, to decide when colours have become so fragile that they can no longer be displayed hanging free. They can continue to be on view either in a display case or mounted and glazed in a frame, or they can be stored away for safe-keeping.

Framing and glazing

Light-restricting glass can be fitted or a self-adhesive plastic film or varnish applied to the glass which will eliminate harmful ultraviolet radiation from the light source.

Storage

Colours should be rolled round cardboard tubes or formers of not less than 15 cm diameter, well-covered with acid-free tissue paper which should also be interleaved as the colour is rolled up loosely. An outer cover of cotton will keep out dust and the colour, correctly labelled, may be stored either in a cupboard or even underneath an altar.

FINANCIAL GRANTS

A textile of special beauty, historic interest or value which needs cleaning and restoring may qualify for some form of financial grant. Cleaning and restoration are expensive but the results make them well worth considering in special circumstances. The Council for the Care of Churches should be able to make suggestions and enquiries could also be made through museum textile departments. Churches which are members of their Area Museums Service should also explore their system of grants. Further suggestions will be found in Chapter 17, Conclusion and Sources of Advice.

CONCLUSION

The proper care of textiles owes much to common sense and an appreciation of the conditions under which they are kept. A comprehensive inventory is of the greatest importance and it must be kept up to date. Cleaning should be carried out on a regular basis but done with care and, if in any doubt, do nothing without first obtaining expert advice.

It must also be remembered that for the majority of alterations, additions or removals within a church, a Faculty or other appropriate authorization is required.

ACKNOWLEDGEMENT

I am indebted to Caroline Rendell, textile conservator, and the Reverend Richard A. Robson, Curator of the Castle Howard Costume Galleries, for their contribution to the text of this chapter.

ELIZABETH INGRAM

Elizabeth Ingram has been involved with church textiles for over twenty years through research, conservation and storage projects. An embroiderer and upholsterer, she also lectures and has written about the embroideries and textiles in York Minister.

~ 14 ~

ORGANS

❈

William Drake

HISTORY AND DEVELOPMENT

Ever since music has had a role in the worship of the church, the
organ has been the natural instrument to accompany singers and
provide a lead in congregational singing.

Until the Restoration in 1665, organs were generally sited on a west
gallery or on the screen separating the nave from the chancel. As organs
increased in size, the west gallery position gradually predominated,
until the Oxford Movement (which began in about 1833) called for a
robed choir to process to the chancel from which they sang. The
favoured site for the organ became in a position behind the choir (often
in a side chapel or 'chamber' built on the side of the chancel), thus
preventing the projection of its sound directly into the nave. This
resulted in the need for a larger and louder instrument than hitherto,
and the effects were far-reaching.

1. It became accepted the organ must be of a certain 'minimum'
    size to fulfil its role.
2. The indirect sound of the organ (in the Nave) became fashion-
    able and although adequate to accompany the choir, organs

---

14.1 The western side of the organ case showing diapered pipes, Gloucester
Cathedral. (Photograph by Gerald Pates, with kind permission of the Cathedral.)

frequently needed to be 'revoiced' and enlarged to cater for congregational singing, producing an effect quite different from the direct, clear quality of earlier instruments.

3. New, louder stops, requiring higher wind pressures, were also sometimes introduced and this, combined with the now complicated layout of the organ caused the mechanical (tracker) actions to become heavier. At first these problems were overcome through the application of pneumatically-assisted mechanisms (Barker-lever) and then with increasing ingenuity, pneumatic and electric actions were developed.

4. With the increase in elaboration, organs became more prone to the development of faults and it was no longer possible for an organist to make the simple adjustments previously possible: the time-scale between 'rebuilds' became increasingly short; and most importantly, the organist was deprived of the accurate and precise control of their instruments which all other musicians expect as the norm.

Organs of this general type continued to evolve throughout the latter part of the nineteenth century and it was not, in fact, until the early 1950s that the advantages of smaller, free-standing instruments were again realized. The models for this 'new' type of organ were greatly influenced by work being done abroad, particularly in Germany, and resulted in a very un-English type of organ, not particularly well-suited to the accompanying of church services or even to the performance of much of the classical organ repertoire. (Some of these instruments have undergone subsequent revision, producing a sort of hybrid previously unknown in the musical world.) Only during the last decade or so has there been some movement towards the re-creation of an earlier type of instrument with a distinctly English character.

It must be admitted, however, that in most of our more prestigious churches (and cathedrals), the legacy of the large, ungainly organ, incapable of sensitive control, continues to hold sway and the necessity of the frequent rebuilding and refurbishment of such instruments seems to be accepted as inevitable.

CAUSES OF FAULTS

It was usual for organs to be constructed of solid wood and their trouble-free operation is dependant on a limited range of relative humidity (see Chapter 2, Heating and Ventilation). Large changes in the relative humidity, due either to an alteration in the type or level of heating in the church or to abnormal weather conditions can cause a frequently found fault in the form of *cyphers* (the unwanted sounding of a note, or pipe when a stop is drawn), and *runnings* (additional notes sounding to those being played). When a *cypher* is caused by a part of the mechanism becoming out of regulation, organists who are conversant with the layout of the organ can often make a simple adjustment to cure this fault. *Runnings* are caused by a leakage of wind at the soundboard (the section where the wind is distributed to the pipes), and are likely to cause the organ to be out of tune.

An organ will have become acclimatized to a range of conditions and when they change, these faults are likely to occur. If they are due to a reduction in the relative humidity caused by the heating, means to control or compensate for this must be sought. (It will be noticeable that other items of the church's furnishing made of solid wood will also change their dimensions, for example, panelling.) Possibilities include a change in the way the heating is used or controlled, a different form of heating or the installation of a purpose-made humidifier for the organ.

Where a short-term change in conditions is responsible for such faults, the organ is likely to return to good working order when conditions again become normal. A prolonged change, however, will require the organ to be dismantled and repaired, or in extreme cases, parts may have become so distorted that they require replacement. General dampness in a building (other than that due to condensation caused by poor ventilation, or leaks) is usually less detrimental to an organ, but the direct ingress of water will almost certainly result in the need for extensive repair.

If an organ is found to be leaking wind, the cause can be either too low a level of relative humidity or deterioration of the leather (sheepskin) of the bellows. In the former case, the relative humidity must be raised and in the latter, the bellows will require re-leathering.

NATURE OF REPAIRS

Some of the more usual faults with organs concern their action, that is the mechanism which controls the pipes from the keyboard. Three main types of action are found, as follows.

Tracker action

The organ will often have been in service for many decades with a minimum of attention, giving an indication of its original quality and the durability of the mechanism. The most usual complaints will be of noise and heaviness of touch. Both of these are the natural consequence of wear and tear, and the heavy touch may additionally be the result of steps taken to alleviate the defects of age by, for example, increasing the tension of the pallet springs, which serve to raise the keys. As with any piece of mechanism, the cure is obvious and straightforward: the worn bearings (and pivots) require attention.

Pneumatic action

As already mentioned, large organs were increasingly built (and re-built) with pneumatic action from the middle of the nineteenth century onwards. The reliability of this action depends on the properties of leather which, in time, will become hard and brittle. There are instances where this form of action is original to the organ and the instrument itself is of sufficient artistic merit to warrant the expenditure of re-leathering or replacing the many pneumatic motors, valves and other components which such actions contain. It should be accepted, however, that this type of action deprives the organist of any nuances of control, and depending on the prevailing conditions, will be unable to continue working at its optimum level for longer than 30–40 years without further re-leathering.

Electro-pneumatic action

During the last decade or so of the nineteenth century, a combined system of electrically controlled pneumatic action was developed to help improve the poor response of pneumatic actions. Even now, some new organs are built with this form of action. As with all non-mechanical action, however, the organist is prevented from making a differentiation in the control of the pipes, allowing him to do no more than switch a note on or off in his chosen sequence and rhythm.

Where organs were originally built with this form of action, it is not usually possible to equip them with new mechanical action but where the organ originally had tracker action, the feasibility of reinstating it should be investigated. Although the initial cost is likely to be higher that repairing an electro-pneumatic action, the long-term advantages to the organist of regaining accurate control and the accepted longevity of tracker action may make this a worthwhile expenditure.

ADVICE ON REPAIRS

For many decisions concerning the advisability and nature of repairs to an organ, help from outside the parish will need to be sought. Each major denomination has its own advisory group and in the case of the Anglican church, the appropriate Diocesan Adviser must give his approval before a Faculty for the work will be granted.

Where the organ is not of recent manufacture, an organ builder will need to be located who has both the necessary experience and just as importantly, who is able to recognize and respect the original character of the particular instrument.

In Great Britain, organs of historic importance unfortunately lack the protection that is afforded to their Continental counterparts, where such instruments are listed and have the protection of the state. Although this system is by no means foolproof, it is far more difficult for uninformed decisions to be made about alterations or 'improvements'. The responsibility for making appropriate decisions relies initially, therefore, far more heavily on the awareness of the parishioners in recognizing that, as with all other work, of artistic merit, we are only custodians for future generations. Idiosyncratic whims and personal preferences should have no part in taking decisions which, unwisely made, may destroy or irretrievably alter a valuable artistic asset.

RESTORATION

Our churches contain a great variety of organs, both in age and quality. As already mentioned, many of our earlier organs have been 'improved', changing their size, sound and sometimes appearance to conform with the taste of the time. As a starting point in deciding on how to consider a particular instrument, a good approach is always to discover, as far as possible, how the organ may have been altered and how these changes affect its character. When built, each organ was designed to suit certain musical needs and any alteration will have affected, to some degree, the unity and cohesion of the whole. Organs which have been moved to a constricted chancel position to conform with the recommendations of the Oxford Movement will usually have been enlarged and revoiced but are nevertheless not as effective as the original, smaller instrument would have been in a more open position.

Depending on the date, original builder and the state of the organ, the feasibility of restoration should be considered. (In this context, the word 'restoration' is used specifically to indicate the returning of the organ as closely as possible to its original form or, if appropriate, to a later state which retains the artistic integrity of the instrument.) An organ is likely to represent the most valuable single object in the church, at least in terms of its replacement cost. Due care should be taken, therefore, when deciding on the nature of work and by whom it is to be carried out.

TUNING AND MAINTENANCE

The principal causes of organs being out of tune are changes in temperature and relative humidity, dirt or dust, and the general condition of the organ.

The metal flue pipes are most affected by changes in temperature, their pitch rising in warmer conditions and lowering with colder temperatures. They do this uniformly, however, and return to their former pitch when the temperature at which they were originally tuned is reinstated. Wooden pipes also change pitch in the same manner, but to a different degree, and are also affected by changes in relative humidity. Reed pipes are the most stable in pitch but being fewer in number and relatively easy to tune, are re-tuned to the pitch of the metal flue stops.

The frequency with which an organ should be tuned depends on the musical requirements placed on the instrument. *Small* changes in pitch of the metal flue pipes are not normally disturbing, although differences in temperature in the various parts of the organ, particularly in the heating season, can cause discrepancies in the pitch between the departments or manuals. This temporary discrepancy should not be corrected, for to do so would require the re-tuning of all of the pipes of the department for the current conditions; and when the conditions return to normal, everything which has been adjusted would again require re-tuning. Where the metal pipes are cone-tuned, frequent re-tuning to a new pitch would also create severe damage to the pipes. The tuning of the wooden pipes can be readily adjusted to that of the metal pipes of the same manual and the reed pipes can be tuned as frequently as found necessary without harm, provided that this is done by a person with a musical ear and who has been adequately instructed.

If an organ is in good condition, small, specific adjustments to the tuning made once each year should be adequate for it to remain at an acceptable level. (The need for a general re-tuning of the organ usually indicates either that the organ requires cleaning or that the conditions of relative humidity in the building have changed.) These should be made at a time when the temperature in the building is 'normal' and has been constant for several hours. Tuning during the heating season should generally be restricted to the wooden pipes and the reed stops, at the temperature at which the organ is to be used. Care must also be taken not to tune pipes which are subjected to direct sunlight.

CLEANING

Dust and dirt are another cause of the organ being out of tune. If any work likely to create dust is being carried out in the building, the whole organ must be sealed off, either by an organ builder or under his instruction, to prevent dust from entering the instrument. The natural accumulation of dust can be reduced when cleaning the church by using a vacuum cleaner, rather than a broom, or using a (damp) mop. Even so, an organ will require occasional cleaning by an organ builder. According to the location of the building, this will usually be necessary every fifteen to twenty-five years and should be regarded as a normal maintenance expense.

ACOUSTICS

Organs benefit from a reverberation time of at least one and a half seconds. Although many English churches have a shorter reverberation time than this, the voicing of the organ will have been adjusted to suit the existing acoustical environment when being installed in the church. It is important to realize, therefore, that any significant change in the reflective surfaces will have an effect on the sound of the organ.

When considering any refurbishment of the church building, it is particularly important to do nothing which will worsen the acoustics, such as covering the floor with carpet or introducing other sound-absorbent surfaces. The introduction of cushions on the pews, for example, will also have an adverse effect and if they are felt to be necessary, unused cushions should be stored in a way that does not allow them to cover sound-reflective surfaces.

CASEWORK AND FAÇADE PIPES

Until the middle of the nineteenth century, organs were generally fully encased and free-standing, at least at the front and sides. As a general rule, oak was used for the casework until the early part of the eighteenth century, after which some instruments were made with mahogany-veneered pine, often with applied panel mouldings. In the latter part of the eighteenth century, mahogany or oak-grained pine cases became more common, and from the middle of the nineteenth century, pitch-pine became a fashionable material. It was not usual for organ cases to have polychrome decoration after the Restoration, but gilded mouldings are frequently found. The wood of organ cases was usually stained, and polished with a shellac, oil or wax finish.

Until the second half of the nineteenth century, façade pipes were always made of tin/lead alloy. In a few instances, these pipes were left with their natural finish but in most cases, they were gilded or decorated (diapered). Some early examples of diapering are to be found at Framlingham (Suffolk), Stanford-on-Avon (Northamptonshire), and at Gloucester Cathedral (see Figure 14.1 at the beginning of this chapter) but these seem to have been the exception rather than the rule. During the first half of the nineteenth century, diapering again became popular, first as painted decoration (usually with some gilding) and later in the form of stencilling. Embossing was another decorative treatment of the façade pipes and examples can still be seen in the 'Milton' organ at Tewkesbury Abbey, the organ at Nettlecombe Court in Somerset, and in the organ at Old Radnor in Wales.

REDUNDANT ORGANS

With increasing numbers of churches finding it necessary to close, a number of redundant organs are available. These will, of course, vary in size and quality but a church with a poor quality of instrument in need of repair may wish to consider acquiring a suitable redundant organ.

The purchase price of these instruments is often relatively modest and, if in fair condition, could economically improve the quality of

14.2   Organ case (*c* 1570) with diapered pipes, Church of St Michael, Framlingham, Suffolk. (Photograph by Roger Yates.)

music in the church. The costs of moving the organ, together with any necessary repairs, must of course be taken into account. The British Institute of Organ Studies Redundancy Officer is a good source of information about the availability of such instruments.

14.3 Organ case and front pipes by John Loosemore (1665) with embossed pipes, in the Hall of Nettlecombe Court, Somerset. (Photograph by Roger Yates.)

14.4 Organ case (*c* 1580) with diapered and embossed pipes in main case and diapered pipes in chaire 'screen', in the Church of St Nicholas, Stanford-on-Avon, Northamptonshire. (Photograph by Roger Yates.)

CHAMBER ORGANS

A number of small village churches contain chamber organs, often built originally for a private house in the neighbourhood. Where the church is indeed small and the size of the congregation modest, such instruments can adequately provide music for services. They are, however, usually quite gentle instruments and where they are found to lack the necessary volume to lead the congregation, the temptation to have them loudened should be strenuously avoided. The pipes of such organs are designed to produce only a small sound and if forced, will lose their pleasant quality.

GRANTS

The cost of work on an organ often places a severe financial strain on the church and since this work does not have the immediacy of, for example, repairs to the roof, it can be difficult to find the means to raise the necessary money. A person with fund-raising experience, who is ideally also interested in music, can be a useful ally and it is often helpful to form a committee to help realize their suggestions. (It must be pointed out that although helpful in assisting with increasing the general awareness of the fund-raising effort, coffee mornings and jumble sales will make little impact in achieving the level of finance needed.) In special cases and where the parish can be seen to be doing their best to raise money, grants are sometimes available. A central Anglican body, the Council for the Care of Churches in London, can offer information on the procedures for applying for grants and have experience of trusts who might be interested in a particular project, usually on the grounds of the organ or its casework being of historic importance.

OTHER MUSICAL INSTRUMENTS

Other musical instruments found in churches include harmoniums (air *pressure* instruments) and American organs (*suction* instruments) and pianos. When a harmonium or American organ requires attention, an organ builder will often be able either to undertake the repair himself or to give advice to the church. Many reed organs, as they are collectively known, are undistinguished but those made in France, in particular by the firm Alexandre et Fils, are of good quality. It is usually possible readily to locate a reputable person to tune or repair a piano.

NEW ORGANS

Some churches will find themselves in a situation where the provision of a new organ is appropriate. The decision in front of them is important, since a substantial sum will be involved and if well-chosen, the new instrument will be capable of serving many future generations.

In most cases, it will be necessary to seek help from outside the parish, initially to assist in locating firms with suitable experience to undertake the project, and then to evaluate the proposals which are submitted. It is usually best to allow each builder to suggest a scheme which they feel will be appropriate to the church, since their approach will often indicate their suitability for the work. It is good practice to ask three firms to make outline proposals, based usually on a visit to the church and discussion with the organist and/or incumbent. If travel for this purpose exceeds, say, a hundred miles, it is appropriate for the church to offer to pay for travelling expenses.

The church should request the selected organ builders to submit a specification (list of stops) for the new organ, specify the type of action they propose, suggest where the organ should ideally be placed and give an indication of their approach to the casework. (It is not usually appropriate, at this stage, to request a drawing for the new organ unless this will be a major factor in the selection of the firm, in which case provision should be made to reimburse the firms who are not chosen to build the organ.)

Having received the proposals and, if appropriate sought advice, time should be taken to visit recent work by the tendering firms. These visits, together with the views of people with experience of the instruments visited, should go a long way towards making a decision on which firm to select. At this point, one or more firms might be requested to clarify or amend their proposals and finally, one firm asked to submit drawings showing the appearance and arrangement of the casework. Most firms will be keen to design the façade themselves. If their design should be unacceptable to the church, they should be requested to provide an alternative design, perhaps in collaboration with an architect. (Architects themselves, although sometimes being more aware of an appropriate style, usually lack the experience which would enable them to take into account all the requirements of a good organ. Few good designs exist where architects have been allowed to specify the detailed appearance of the organ.)

When all the major details of the organ are agreed, a contract should be drawn up by the organ builder and, if satisfactory, signed by both parties. By this time, the church will of course need to feel convinced that they have made an appropriate choice, since they must now be prepared to trust the integrity (both artistic and commercial) of the chosen firm. No amount of contractual detail will, in itself, ensure the quality of the finished instrument. Each firm will usually have its own form of contract, which should include the following:

Specification.
Material of casework and other major components.
Price, including any adjustment for wage increases, inflation, etc.
Terms of payment.
Guarantee.
Date of delivery.

It is usual for organ builders to request a deposit when the contract is signed. This will secure a place in the firm's work schedule, allow for materials (in particular timber) to be purchased in advance and this amount will be excluded from any price increases. Subsequent amounts are normally agreed on as stage payments, usually in the form of a sum paid when work on the project commences and further amounts during construction in the workshop, with final payment due within thirty days of completion and acceptance by an agreed person or authority.

The period of guarantee varies from one firm to another but should be given for a minimum of ten years. Many firms are rather over-optimistic when giving a date for delivery but unless a delay is due to subsequent commissions being 'fitted in', it should be recognized that additional time is being spent on the project and if undue pressure is applied to a firm, there can be a danger, in some cases, that it will result in short-cuts being taken. Since most organs are custom-built, it is often not possible accurately to anticipate the precise time needed. Small firms, in particular, are unable to transfer additional men to a project and are likely to be doing their best to keep any delay to the minimum.

WILLIAM DRAKE

William Drake has trained and worked abroad for over eleven years and assisted Patrick Collon with the conservation of two Italian organs in Yugoslavia. He set up his own workshop in 1974 and, as well as restoring and reconstructing historic organs, he has built a number of new organs in differing styles.

~ 15 ~

BOOKS AND
MANUSCRIPTS

✳

David Dorning

Virtually all churches have collections of books and manuscripts, ranging from small parishes with perhaps a few registers and collected papers to large cathedral libraries with extensive current and reference collections. Some may be in use, in the form of hymn books, service books, music or current registers, while others will be kept for their historical or archival interest, or as permanent exhibits. Although the differences of content and scale between collections may be considerable, the factors which lead to their degradation are often the same. All books and manuscripts (with manuscripts defined as any written, as opposed to printed, material) are to some extent at risk from a variety of degradation processes.

There are many reasons why books and manuscripts degrade. Some are caused by the environment in which they are kept or exhibited, some are caused by users, and some are natural processes. They may become damp, and so be damaged by fungi. They may be chewed or eaten by mice or insects. They may be stored in a warm dry place so that book covers distort and papers start to cockle at the edges. They may be handled, or mis-handled, to the extent that they fall apart, or they may

---

15.1 The use of book shoes. An unobtrusive form of support which protects book sides and provides a solid support for the book block, preventing it from sagging in its boards. (Photograph courtesy of Chichester Cathedral Library.)

simply degrade due to their own inherent instability. This chapter is designed to give an idea of the sources of damage to books and manuscripts in churches, how best to avoid them, what can safely be done, and what should be referred to a conservator.

THE NATURAL DEGRADATION OF MATERIALS

Apart from any physical or environmental damage which may already have occurred in books or manuscripts, the characteristics of the materials of which they are made will in most cases change over a period of time, and such change constitutes the degradation of the material. Paper, bookcloth and wood are all primarily composed of vegetable fibres, and leather and parchment are made from animal skins. All are organic materials which are susceptible to natural chemical degradation processes which will gradually alter their physical nature and make them more susceptible to damage as they are handled and used. All organic materials degrade continuously, even in the most ideal circumstances, and it is our objective to make the rate of degradation of the treasures in churches as low as possible.

Most organic materials tend to lose both strength and flexibility in the long term, leading to a much greater tendency to fold or tear when subject to stress, rather than flexing naturally. The rate at which this degradation proceeds can vary enormously from one item to another, so that collections may contain items ranging from physically near-new condition to those in the final stages of degradation. In addition to physical changes to their structural materials, the images carried by books or manuscripts can themselves degrade, either by gradual chemical action and corrosion, or physical detachment caused by the shrinkage of the substrate to which they are attached. Text and painted images can become very fragile and be damaged by the lightest touch.

Because of the natural degradation of materials, it is a good rule of thumb to regard all old books or manuscripts as potentially fragile, and to handle them accordingly. Books are composite objects, often held together by a combination of adhesive and thread, each of which can resist a certain amount of stress, but the structure overall is only as durable as its weakest part. Because these organic materials lose their physical integrity with time many books appear more mechanically sound than they really are. Although their components may still be in place, many will have lost their strength to the extent that they can no longer fulfil their physical function. However, provided the potential fragility of books and manuscripts is borne in mind it is usually possible to handle and use them without causing further damage. The following sections give advice in specific areas.

NUMBERING THE COLLECTION

In many parishes most of the historical books and manuscripts may already have been deposited at the local record office, as advised by the Parochial Registers and Records Measure of 1978, leaving only current volumes and, perhaps, displayed items in need of care within the church. Record offices are well equipped to look after such material and will often also carry out conservation work where necessary. However, there still exist larger collections kept in churches or cathedrals, and small numbers of individual items in almost all churches, which are in need of care and preservation.

In order to care for any collection of church books and papers, no matter how small, it is necessary to be aware of what that collection consists of. The Church of England Legislation on the Care of Cathedrals and Churches, respectively, requires an inventory to be made of certain property, and although this does not extend to books and manuscripts, it is nevertheless of great value to prepare an inventory of all books and manuscripts. In a few cases there may already be a numbering system which allows books to be identified but, if not, the initial exercise of numbering or preparing an inventory serves not only to identify all items in the collection but also to bring to light any obviously damaged items or other immediate problems.

If a collection is being numbered for the first time, the order in which the books or manuscripts have previously been stored, or any existing numbers or shelfmarks written on them, may be of historical or bibliographical significance. It may be possible to retain the existing order as the permanent storage arrangement, but if not, the original order should be recorded before it is changed, and any original numbers ought not to be erased. As a general principle, any decisions taken concerning the re-arrangement of material should take into account the possibility that historical evidence may be lost in such a move.

GOOD HOUSEKEEPING – CLEANING

The condition of materials can be monitored continually by good housekeeping. A good cleaning regime requires inspection and cleaning of all parts of the collection at regular intervals, and ensures that any developing problems are seen at an early stage. These may include the presence of dust, mould growth on book covers, cockled edges, brittleness, darkening or fading of exposed surfaces, the presence of insect droppings, or edges chewed by mice. Some problems will require professional advice, and it is advisable to contact a conservator in the vicinity. Keepers of registers of conservators are listed at the end of the chapter.

Inhouse cleaning should be limited to simple processes such as dusting and removal of loose dirt. If dust is allowed to build up on the surface of objects it will not only disfigure them but will also provide a local environment which can attract moisture or insects and provide conditions in which micro-organisms can develop. Simple dusting can be carried out provided items are physically sound, but should normally be confined to the outer surfaces of items. Dusting of text or coloured areas is best left to a conservator. Dusting should, if possible, be done away from the storage area in order to avoid re-depositing dust on other items. It can be a dirty job and large quantities of dust can be a considerable irritant; dust masks should be worn.

Dusting can be carried out either by brushing or vacuum. Large, soft brushes are ideal, although they can become soiled quickly, so they should be washed regularly. It is possible that some historical items may not be sufficiently strong to withstand even gentle dusting. If there is any doubt as to the ability of a book or manuscript to withstand gentle treatment it should be set on one side and the problem referred to a conservator.

Care should be taken not to push dust further into the surface of the item being cleaned. Always brush towards the edge of the item, but never towards any cracked or rough parts of the surface where dust may become lodged. Items which are damp or wet should not be cleaned, because this will tend to stick dirt to the surface rather than remove it. If an item is slightly damp it should be allowed to dry out gently, in a well-ventilated room but without any additional heating, before dusting. If anything is significantly wet, or if many items are damp, there is a possibility that micro-organisms will develop and a conservator should be consulted immediately in order to arrange controlled drying. Any damp items should be removed from the rest of the collection. Items which have previously been mouldy may carry deposits of fine powder on their surfaces. This is a particular irritant and care should be taken not to inhale it.

Vacuum cleaning is useful when tackling large numbers of dirty documents, which may have lain forgotten and untouched in the vestry for many years, gathering dust. However, it should be used with care, as it is easy to suck loose pieces into the nozzle. Items cleaned by this method should be selected carefully to ensure that no fragile or loose material is subject to strong suction. Even when working on apparently undamaged material there should always be a piece of gauze or loosely woven material stretched over the nozzle to avoid losing any pieces.

STORAGE FOR SAFE HANDLING

Some books and manuscripts kept in churches may be handled regularly, so measures must be taken to preserve them by encouraging safe handling. Handling begins with retrieval, and all items should be stored so as to be easily located and removed. Bookshelves, if used, should be packed so that books support each other, yet remain sufficiently loose that they can be removed without pulling at the top of the spine. Excessively loose packing should be avoided, however, as it may lead to sagging and distortion, particularly if books are leaned on by their neighbours. Any books with metal bosses attached to their sides or corners, such as heavy bibles, should be stored individually, preferably flat in boxes to avoid damaging themselves or their neighbours during retrieval. Most books are actually safer if stored flat, as long as they are not piled up high, although this is often not practical.

Any single sheet manuscripts or papers can be enclosed to protect them from everyday handling and sorting. Each item can be wrapped in a four-flap folder of acid-free paper which is clearly marked to identify the document it contains, and stored flat. This will reduce the amount of direct handling involved in locating it. Four-flap folders ensure that the document does not fall out when the folder is picked up. If the collection is extensive the folders can themselves be stored systematically in labelled acid-free archive boxes. Alternatively, single-sheet items can be enclosed in transparent polyester enclosures, which are robust yet allow the item to be consulted without unwrapping. Manuscripts in bundles often should not or cannot be separated for storage, due either to their provenance or space available. Bundles can be stored in archive boxes of appropriate size. In general, single sheet documents are much safer enclosed in a system which allows them to be located easily and individually, rather than kept as loose sheets in boxes or bundles. Thin, flimsy books, such as parish magazines, can be treated as if they are flat papers, rather than housed vertically with books.

Large flat items such as maps or music may be stored in drawers. In such cases it is advisable to enclose them in portfolios which can be removed bodily from the drawer. This will avoid the difficulty of removing and replacing single, floppy items from a heavy pile within the drawer, and subsequently avoid a great deal of unnecessary handling damage to all items in the group.

Some items may be stored or displayed in picture frames. Unless they have been framed recently to archival standards it is advisable to remove them from their frames, or, if the frame is of historical significance or part of a permanent display, to have them reframed to archival standards. This entails hinging the item to an acid-free mount and using a dustproof frame. A leaflet on framing is available free from the Institute of Paper Conservation, listed at the end of the chapter.

DEALING WITH DAMAGED MATERIAL

All collections will contain some items which are already damaged, and it is important to ensure that pending conservation such damage does not increase, either during retrieval or in use. Ideally any damaged item should be carefully wrapped and not consulted until it is conserved.

In the case of books it is common for the boards to become loose or detached, and in such cases the book and its boards should be tied up with a flat tape, preferably of unbleached linen or cotton. This simple preservation measure serves to keep all loose parts together. Additional protection can be given to books by the use of phase boxes (so called because their use is a phase in the overall conservation of the book). These boxes can be bought in flat format in various sizes, and folded to make a hinged box. Damaged books, and any detached parts of such books, can be enclosed in the phase box to avoid losses pending conservation.

Phase boxes are an interim measure taken to combat the problem of

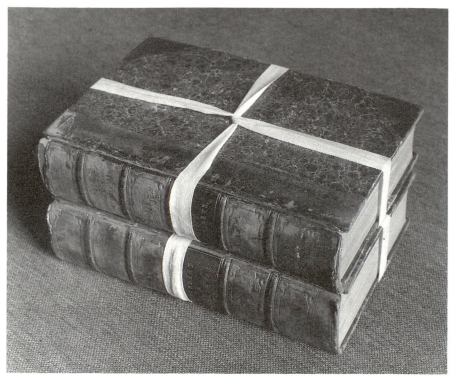

15.2   Flat linen tape used temporarily to hold together two books whose boards have become detached. (Photograph courtesy of Chichester Cathedral Library.)

damaged books. Ideally damaged items placed in phase boxes should not be consulted until they are conserved. Phase boxes have the effect of hiding a damaged book and making it look tidy and neatly stored, and it should be borne in mind that each phase box represents a problem which is only partially solved.

Books or manuscripts may have been carelessly stored for long periods under stress, becoming temporarily or even permanently distorted from their original shape. This is particularly likely if books have been leaning on a shelf for any length of time, gradually distorting under the weight of their neighbours, or otherwise carelessly packed. Distorted books may not open easily, and to force them open can be particularly damaging. In general, if any item is distorted it should not be pushed back immediately into its original shape, because this may cause permanent damage to its structure. Some distorted items may regain their original shape with gradual, gentle pressure, reversing the pressure which caused the original distortion, while others, such as rolled items which have been crushed, may need more complex treatment. Distorted items, or any other type of damaged items, should not be handled any more than is strictly necessary, and should be referred to a conservator.

All boxes and enclosures which come into contact with original material should be made of stable materials which will not adversely affect the documents they contain. Acid-free paper or polyester enclosures are recommended for enclosing papers, although polyester is not suitable for documents with loose ink or pigment particles because it develops static electricity that can lift off loose parts of the image. Phase boxes and archive boxes should be of acid-free board.

Some books and manuscripts are inherently badly designed, and unexpected handling damage while in use is always a possibility. Victorian bibles are a prime example of the kind of poorly-designed bindings which may be found in churches. The paper itself is often made of low quality fibre, perhaps loaded with china clay, giving an excessively heavy book-block sewn with very thin and relatively weak thread. The attachment of the massive bookblock to the boards is often inadequate, with the result that, in time, the sewn block of leaves is pulled away from the covers by its own weight, and falls down inside them. This can happen gradually as the book sits on the shelf, or catastrophically as it is being handled. Long-term stress on heavy books standing on shelves can be reduced by the use of book shoes. These folded card structures can be simply made of acid-free card, and will help the book to stand upright while supporting the weight of the bookblock, and preventing it from falling down inside its boards (see Figure 15.1).

HANDLING BOOKS AND MANUSCRIPTS

Many other types of book have similar inherent problems where design and function have not been satisfactorily combined, making it especially necessary to be aware of the danger, when handling any book, of damaging an already weak structure. Books can be damaged by being opened too far, particularly if they have tight leather bindings and weak joints. It is often possible to feel how far a book can comfortably be opened. If any resistance is felt the book should not be opened more than is achieved by gentle pressure. It is usually not necessary to open a book further than the angle of a hymn book in use, held naturally in the hand. If a book resists being opened completely flat, as most books do,

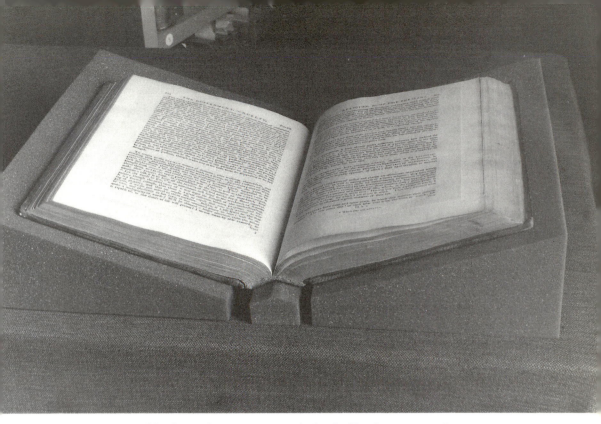

15.3 Foam blocks used to support a tight-backed book in use, avoiding excessive strain at the spine. (Photograph courtesy of Chichester Cathedral Library.)

the reader should respect this. Wedge-shaped foam blocks, designed to support books opened at a gentle angle, and can be used whenever potentially fragile books are consulted. They are particularly useful if used to avoid the stress caused by heavy bibles being opened completely flat for long periods, on a lectern for instance. Exhibited books should never be held flat for long periods, but supported on a cradle which holds them firmly at an opening angle of significantly less than 180 degrees, perhaps a maximum of 140 degrees, and preferably less.

When carrying books they should, wherever possible, be held singly, flat and supported by both hands, or held spine down and supported by one or two cupped hands. Carrying piles of books is potentially damaging, because they can slide off or abrade one another, particularly if they have metal bosses or clasps. It is always worth making several journeys to move a group of books, rather than risk dropping them. Trolleys and temporary book boxes are useful if quantities of books or manuscripts ever have to be moved about.

The same general principles apply to the handling of manuscripts. Formats are diverse, ranging from single sheets to bundles, folded or rolled items or groups of loosely attached sheets. Physically their materials may degrade in the same way as those of books, becoming weakened and inflexible. Manuscripts may have threads, cords or seals attached to themselves, or attaching several items to each other. These may be susceptible to damage and breakage, particularly if degraded threads hold together heavy paper or parchment sheets, or wax seals. Other manuscript items are difficult to handle due to their format. Many rolled nineteenth century tracings on oiled paper, such as was used for architects' plans of churches or extensions, are so brittle as to be almost impossible to unroll without damage. If such items are to be consulted they should be unrolled by a conservator. All rolled items should be supported on a firm core to avoid crushing.

Loose, brittle or partly attached items must always be carefully supported during handling, particularly if material is being unrolled or unfolded. Both paper and parchment have a remarkable tendency to spring back into their original positions, possibly causing damage to themselves as they do so. Fold-out maps attached to books always require particular care in handling. Folded items are particularly susceptible to handling damage if they have already become brittle or been damaged by mould, because the outer folds are often the parts which have been most badly degraded. These folds can lose virtually all their strength and flexibility, and be easily split if stressed. It is not unreasonable for two pairs of hands to be required to handle large manuscript items safely. Various sized weights are essential if large folded or rolled items such as maps are to be opened out and consulted.

ENVIRONMENTAL CONDITIONS

In addition to good housekeeping, storage and handling, it is important that books and manuscripts are stored in suitable conditions. Providing a safe environment for books and manuscripts can be a significant problem in churches because the atmosphere in stone buildings is often rather humid.

Although humidity is the environmental factor most likely to be damaging, temperature and light can also cause problems. Environmental factors often act in combination, causing more than one type of damage at the same time. They can alter the physical dimensions of an object, increase the likelihood of biological degradation by micro-organisms, or promote chemical change in the materials of which it is made. However, if conditions are monitored and controlled, environmental damage can be minimized.

Humidity

Books and manuscripts are particularly at risk in conditions where humidity is excessively high or low. Damage is also likely where humidity fluctuates, because cycling of humidity levels can cause long-term stress and distortion of objects. It is therefore important to promote stable humidity levels in areas where collections are stored or used. The amount of humidity in a given volume of air is known as the Relative Humidity (RH); and safe storage therefore requires a stable RH. RH is defined as the quantity of water present in the air relative to the amount the air could hold if it were saturated. Therefore air at 50 per cent RH holds half the amount of water that it would hold if it were saturated.

This is complicated by the fact that RH is affected by temperature. Warm air can hold more water than cool air, and therefore if the temperature changes, then so will the RH; even if the actual water content of the air does not. In a sample of air with a constant moisture content RH will decrease as the air gets warmer and increase as it gets cooler. Therefore in order to promote a stable RH, temperature must also be stable. Fortunately this is the case in many churches, where the stone structure buffers the atmosphere from any sudden humidity changes which may occur outside. Recommended storage conditions for mixed collections of books and manuscripts are 55–65 per cent RH at 13–18°C (approximately 55–65°F). Although it is very difficult to achieve these conditions exactly without full air conditioning, adherence to a few general principles can provide an acceptably stable storage environment inside church buildings which is reasonably close to these recommendations.

Problems caused by humidity
All organic materials such as paper, leather and parchment, are capable of absorbing moisture from a damp atmosphere, and in so doing, expanding. By the same token they can lose moisture to a dry atmosphere and shrink. Fluctuating humidity conditions can bring about continual dimensional changes in organic materials. Because most books and many manuscripts are compound objects made of more than one organic material, their constituent parts will almost inevitably expand and contract at different rates as humidity changes. Often

their components are laminated together, as for instance in the case of the boards of a book. Fluctuating humidity can promote warping of laminated items, and cause surfaces such as pigments or burnished gold on parchment to flake off.

Organic materials are also susceptible to the growth of micro-organisms, which is promoted in humid conditions. Mould spores are present in the air in enormous numbers, and will start to develop in the presence of a suitably humid environment and food source. Many micro-organisms use the materials of books and manuscripts as a food source, and can leave the material at best weakened, if not destroyed and disfigured. Most micro-organisms also leave materials acidic. Micro-organisms must be among the most significant causes of the degradation of large amounts of books and written material, particularly in church buildings, and it is extremely important that the humid conditions in which they thrive are eliminated from storage areas. Humidity encourages insects such as silverfish, booklice and woodworm, which may be present in other materials in churches anyway, and which can also cause considerable damage to books and manuscripts.

Monitoring and controlling atmospheric conditions

Temperature and its fluctuation can he monitored on a regular basis using max–min thermometers, and RH can be estimated using test strips which change colour according to RH. These methods are simple to use, inexpensive, and reasonably accurate, although they do not give a continuous record. Because stable conditions are required at all times, particularly overnight when heating systems may be turned off and readings are difficult to take, a more informative record can be kept by the use of a recording thermohygrograph, which provides a trace of both temperature and RH continuously. The recordings made by these instruments can be used to monitor conditions in storage areas and identify times when they may fluctuate more than is desirable; and therefore to identify the source of such fluctuations. A conservator can advise on appropriate methods of monitoring environmental conditions.

Practical problems in storing books and manuscripts arise because many churches are damp and poorly ventilated, and humidity can build up behind bookshelves, or in any containers used for storage. This could be a particular problem in smaller rooms or cupboards in churches where books and manuscripts may be housed. Humid, stagnant air provides an ideal environment for mould growth, particularly in warm conditions. Material kept for long periods in closed cases, boxes or drawers with poor ventilation, or in slightly damp conditions overall, is at risk. If books and manuscripts stored in this type of environment smell musty it is because micro-organisms have started to grow. Air movement will help to remove excessive moisture from storage areas, and inhibit the formation of small pockets of stagnant air in which this type of degradation is promoted. Bookshelves, archive boxes and other enclosures must always be well ventilated.

Although excessive humidity is the most obvious problem in storage areas, lack of moisture can also be a problem. Storage in a low-humidity atmosphere can dry out organic materials to the extent that they lose their flexibility and become brittle and warped, and therefore difficult to handle. Just as furniture can be damaged by dryness, so can books and manuscripts.

In order to stabilize RH all potential sources of moisture should be checked and made safe. These include pipes, sinks, drains, gutters and downpipes. Stone walls are often unavoidably damp, particularly in summer, and books and manuscripts should not be stored against walls, or in boxes in direct contact with walls. Ventilation holes should be drilled to allow air movement behind bookshelves attached to walls. Sources of fluctuating temperature or excessive local dryness, such as solar gain or portable heaters, should be insulated or switched off as appropriate and ventilation should be ensured. Smaller rooms which are excessively dry can be adjusted by using a room humidifier, and damp rooms by a dehumidifier. Again, a local conservator will advise you if necessary.

Light

Light is a potential source of considerable damage to books and manuscripts, because it is a source of energy. Light sources are many and various, and differ considerably in their potency. In churches one may encounter natural light, light bulbs, spotlights or fluorescent tubes. Light damage is evident in the form of faded book spines, faded pigments on exhibited items, or sometimes overall yellowing of items which have been exposed to light for long periods. Light not only causes fading or discolouration, but can also weaken materials.

Some light sources, such as sunlight and fluorescent lamps, are rich in ultra-violet (UV) radiation, a type of energy which characteristically promotes photochemical degradation. Others, such as tungsten lamps (incandescent light bulbs), emit much smaller quantities of UV and are relatively harmless to books and manuscripts. Therefore light sources should be understood and controlled where necessary.

Ultra-violet light can be eliminated effectively using filters. Fluorescent lamps, which may be used for local illumination of displayed items, can be filtered using transparent sleeves which fit neatly around the tubes themselves. Alternatively, in the case of exhibited items, showcases can be glazed with UV filtering materials. Sunlight should be prevented from falling directly onto books and manuscripts. Spotlights can cause heat build up, particularly in enclosed material, and filters are available to control this type of exposure.

Although UV light is the most damaging, visible light can also degrade sensitive materials. It is always advisable to reduce the overall exposure to light of all materials, by storing books and manuscripts in a dark place, preferably in boxes, and drawing blinds when a storage or exhibition area is not in use.

Atmospheric pollutants

Many materials are degraded by atmospheric pollutants. The presence in the atmosphere of substances such as sulphur dioxide, nitrogen oxides, and oxidizing agents such as ozone, constitutes a risk to both the physical strength of objects and the preservation of their surface character. The action of these acidic and oxidizing chemicals even in small quantities can cause loss of strength, changes in flexibility, and discolouration.

It is difficult to keep pollutants out of storage environments, because in urban and even rural atmospheres pollutants are present in significant amounts in the air anyway. There are some local sources which can be avoided, such as new wood, new paint or varnish, and composite boards such as fibreboard, which are all localized sources of polluting vapours. However, the most practical way of protecting from atmospheric pollution is to enclose items in archival quality material, in the form of boxes or folders which will themselves absorb polluting materials and thereby protect their contents.

It is often possible to provide acceptable conditions in churches for the long-term storage of books and manuscripts provided the collection remains in the same place. However, care should be taken, particularly if providing stable conditions in the storage area, not to remove items regularly into very different environments. Occasional use which

15.4 Instruments used to monitor environmental conditions: UV monitor (left), thermohygrograph (back), Luxmeter (front).

brings items into a significantly different RH or temperature from that to which they are used, with little or no equilibration time, can lead to stress, warping, and distortion. Any regularly used collection should be stored in conditions not too different from those in which it is consulted. These factors become particularly relevant when items are exhibited, because this can involve removal from their long-term environment for a period of weeks or even months.

AVOIDING DISASTERS

Flooding is a constant danger with collections of books and manuscripts. Where possible, material should always be stored higher than the ground floor, and the lowest shelves should be clear of the floor. Books and manuscripts are flammable, and basic fire safety is important in the vicinity of such material. Disasters may be averted by the prompt use of fire extinguishers, provided the correct type is used. Most fire safety manuals will recommend water extinguishers for use on paper and the type of material of which collections are made, but soaking books and manuscripts with water will cause untold damage, and turn one type of disaster into another. Carbon dioxide extinguishers are recommended for use in areas where important books or manuscripts are housed or used. Local fire brigades will give advice on the most appropriate extinguisher according to the requirements of the material in your collection.

IF THE WORST HAPPENS

No matter how carefully any collection is stored and used, accidents may happen. If a collection is flooded or involved in a fire it is essential to act quickly. Ideally one should have a disaster plan ready for such circumstances, with a list of useful contacts and telephone numbers, including the emergency services, a conservator, key holders, local plumber, and so on; and also specialist services such as freeze or vacuum drying facilities. Most local record offices have conservators on their staff who can help with advice on disaster planning, or who may even include your church on their own disaster plan, so that it may not necessarily be essential to know what to do, so long as you know whom to contact. All collections should be seen by a conservator and advice taken on how to act in the case of an emergency.

To summarize, it is necessary to protect books and manuscripts from several factors. Storage and retrieval methods, handling, and the storage or exhibition environment, can all be damaging to material kept in churches. Although all treasures will inevitably deteriorate, by anticipating potential sources of damage their rate of deterioration can be reduced as far as possible.

DAVID DORNING

David Dorning has worked in Warwickshire County Archives, which holds many parish collections, and has been involved with small collections within churches and repositories. He is currently working at West Dean College on the conservation and preservation of books and manuscripts.

~ 16 ~

LIGHTING

※

Graham Phoenix

Atmosphere is vital to a church's primary role as a place of worship, creating a feeling of comfort, wonder and anticipation. Lighting must be capable of encouraging this in private prayer and devotion, or in enlivening a large, joyous service. Architecture is an essential part of a church's existence. Architects throughout the ages have sought to worship God with their buildings; lighting must seek to underline this without taking over. Churches are used by young and old who are, increasingly nowadays, expected to take an active role in worship, singing, praying and reading the Bible. Lighting must enable the congregation, choir and clergy to see.

Lighting is a crucial element in the relationship of people to their churches. It affects the atmosphere in the church, it influences people's appreciation of the architecture and it controls their ability to see. In the past, light was provided almost entirely by daylight with a small contribution from artificial sources such as candles. Churches were built to take maximum advantage of natural light and consequently often had a feeling of space or 'Mysterium Tremendum' (St Augustine). They are frequently left in this state in the mistaken belief that they are as they were intended to be. Lighting is an area which has benefited

---

16.1 Vault uplighting in Christ Church, Oxford, purely as a means of highlighting the architecture. Note the over-dominant chandeliers in the arches.

from advances in technology and so is able to contribute to a church in a way which was not possible when many were built. This technology should be harnessed in order to improve people's appreciation of churches, without harming the original intent of the builders, not only during daylight but also in periods of darkness when churches are at their most gloomy and forbidding.

This chapter will discuss the elements which create good and appropriate interior and exterior lighting and will indicate the equipment and techniques required by these elements.

INTERIOR LIGHTING

The solution chosen to unite the three factors of atmosphere, architecture and visibility should be physically appropriate to the building and should combine in a seamless fashion. The following elements can be used in building the solutions.

Lighting levels

The choice of solutions should start with a consideration of the lighting levels required throughout the building. There are two methods of quantifying lighting, one purely practical and one which attempts to quantify aesthetics.

The practical method identifies recommended illuminances with specific areas of a church. Illuminance is the measure, in lux, of the amount of light received on a surface. The level specified is usually the average level over the life of the installation, thereby incorporating losses due to the accumulation of dirt and reduction of lamp output over life. The Chartered Institution of Building Services Engineers (CIBSE) *Code for Interior Lighting*, in its current (1984) edition, recommends illuminances of 150 lux for the nave, chancel and vestries, and 300 lux for the pulpit, choir and organ.

Discretion can be used in the application of these levels, 100 lux may be acceptable for the body of a small country parish church while 300 lux may be more appropriate for a large pentecostal church; the decisions will be informed by the type of atmosphere required.

The alternative method of design, the 'apparent brightness method', permits an orderly calculation of the lighting needed to produce any proposed visual effect, this effect being specified by allotting relative

16.2 Decorative lighting in King's College Chapel, Aberdeen, integrated with the seating as the major interior lighting element.

brightness values to each surface in the interior, in arbitrary units. Using apparent brightness scales, the reflectances of the surfaces, and inter-reflection calculations, it is possible to determine the relative direct illuminance needed on each major surface. Used fully this is a complex process which is most appropriate for large cathedrals, but in a restricted form it can be convenient as a method of specifying requirements.

Decorative lighting

Decorative lighting has historically been the major form of interior lighting (Figure 16.2). Since the advent of candles, through gas lighting to early electric lighting, the only source of light was a flame, or its equivalent, a bulb. This source needed disguising, especially in a building such as a church, to make it visually acceptable. In each period the design of decorative fittings was related to its architecture, but the essential function of the lamp has commonly been subordinated to the ornament and decoration of the fashions of the day. Decorative lighting remains one of the major elements today but it is increasingly being discredited due to the unfashionable appearance of many existing fittings and the difficulties of finding acceptable modern replacements.

Many churches are listed buildings or historical monuments in everyday use as a church. This means the lighting must fit the everyday use while being acceptable within an historic building. Much modern decorative lighting will not fit into this context; and it is necessary to incorporate modern lamp technology and lighting techniques into a decorative exterior appropriate to the period of the building and also to modern design. It can be difficult and expensive to achieve but is well worth the trouble.

Existing decorative lighting should not be removed without careful consideration. In the case of nineteenth and twentieth century churches the light fittings may well form part of the original decorative scheme of the building; moreover, interiors can become lifeless when the focus is removed. The eye and brain respond to an apparent source of lighting enabling additional effects, described below, to be added without them being apparent.

Decorative fittings usually take the form of suspended luminaires, such as chandeliers, which can be designed to incorporate uplighting and downlighting as well as the normal ambient lighting. Care should be taken in the positioning of these luminaires to avoid blocking vistas, or views of specific objects, such as screens or stained glass windows. Wall brackets are less frequently used but can be useful, depending on the architectural period of the building. Consideration should be given to other forms of decorative lighting, such as the small luminaires commonly mounted on choir stalls or floor-mounted post luminaires which can be located in relation to seated areas or particular points of access.

Uplighting

Uplighting is increasingly used in churches both to provide illumination and to reveal the architecture. If used sensitively it can transform the interior by opening it out and creating a feeling of space, but if used badly it can unbalance the interior by creating a false focus on the roof (see Figure 16.1 at the beginning of this chapter). In commercial buildings uplighting is used as an indirect means of illumination; all the light is reflected off the ceiling, giving a soft lighting effect similar to daylight. To achieve this the ceiling necessarily becomes the brightest surface in view. While this can be successful in offices, it is frequently disastrous in churches. The illuminance levels needed on the pews require very high illuminance levels on the roof. This can make the roof dominant in a way which is neither intended by the architect nor created by daylight.

When the illumination needed in the pews is provided by another source, uplighting can be used to reveal and accent the roof. The form and colour of the roof should be considered in choosing the source and position of the luminaire. Frequently the uplighting will be more successful if the luminaire is mounted high up, creating modelling on ribs and beams. Care should be taken to conceal the luminaires as much as possible or, if this is not possible, to ensure their location has a logic in terms of the building structure. Luminaires can look out of place if located in an apparently random fashion on the side walls of the nave. The aisles can also benefit from uplighting although their secondary importance in the architecture hierarchy should be respected.

Uplighting can benefit greatly from dimming, as discussed below, because as darkness falls the amount of lighting needed on the roof will be reduced. Depending on the window layout of the building it may be that bright uplighting will be beneficial in daylight, but that same level will be too bright at night.

Downlighting

Downlighting is vital in achieving the illumination levels needed in some parts of a church. It can be difficult, particularly in the nave, to obtain levels of 150 lux with just decorative and uplighting. Recessing the luminaires into the ceiling can be the most satisfactory solution, but this can usually only be done in modern buildings. It is important that the sources are well recessed in an optically-designed luminaire to avoid glare. One of the most successful installations of this type is in Sir Basil Spence's Coventry Cathedral.

Where such a solution is not possible, typically in most old churches, the downlighting must be concealed within clerestory or triforium galleries (Figure 16.3), concealed within decorative luminaires or mounted visibly on side walls or column capitals. If the fittings are mounted on side walls it can be useful to combine the downlight with an uplight, possibly using the same source, thereby lessening clutter on the walls. In choosing or designing the luminaires care must be taken

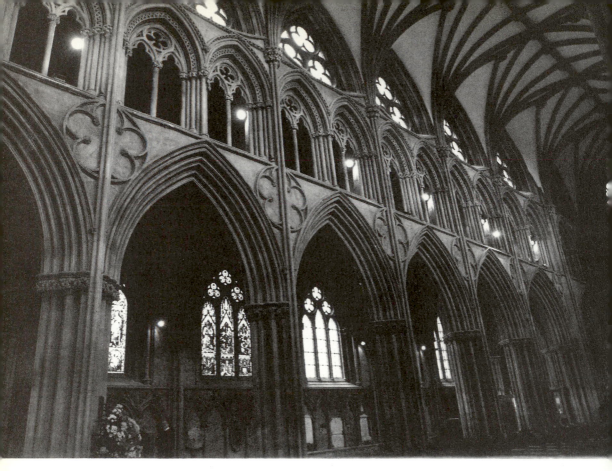

16.3 Downlighting in Lichfield Cathedral, concealed in the triforium gallery and angled to face eastwards.

with louvring of the source to avoid glare to the congregation. This problem can often be alleviated by directing the light slightly towards the east end in the general direction of view towards the chancel or other major focus.

Downlighting on its own should be avoided because it creates disagreeable shadows on the faces of the congregation and clergy.

Architectural highlighting

Church lighting does not always take the architecture into consideration. Sometimes this is justified because the building does not warrant it, but this oversight can be to the detriment of the atmosphere. It was suggested in the introduction to this chapter that a church is not just a building where people gather to worship but also a building where people feel God's presence in the atmosphere. This feeling can be accented and reaffirmed by revealing the architecture in a subtle way and by emphasizing at night the accents created in daytime by daylight and sunlight.

The sources for this lighting should be concealed and the lighting levels will be critical in avoiding the danger of emphasizing the building to the extent that it becomes the object of attention. Dimming can assist the creation of the optimum balance over different surfaces. The combinations of light and shade are the essential ingredients of this element. The form of the structure and the texture of the surfaces can be brought out by careful positioning of luminaires.

Spotlighting

Spotlighting is important for adding focus and attention on top of the basic lighting. There are areas which will always benefit from additional spotlighting, for example the pulpit and lectern, the altar or communion table, a prominent crucifix or screen, important statues or wall plaques, noticeboard areas. In many churches a more modern form of worship has evolved which involves the building of stages at the east end for drama and dance. Where this happens lighting of a theatrical form can be added, possibly with a separate control to enable it to be varied during services as appropriate. Even where the services do not use such theatrical techniques some spotlighting of the east end can be useful. It is important for the congregation to see the clergy, choir and others officiating at services. This lighting should be from the side and from the direction of the congregation; even though this will cause some glare for the clergy it will be of great benefit to the congregation.

EXTERIOR LIGHTING

Exterior lighting should reveal the architecture by night within the context of its surroundings. By day this happens naturally under daylight and sunlight but by night the building can die. It can be important for a church to look active as well as prominent and visible. Exterior lighting can do all this in a subtle manner without appearing garish or without being too dominant (Figure 16.4).

Lighting levels

The lighting levels to be aimed for are not as easy to quantify as for interior lighting. The CIBSE *Guide to the Outdoor Environment*

16.4 Exterior lighting at St Magnus Cathedral, Kirkwall, with gentle rendering of walls and clear focus on the spire.

recommends a series of average illuminances for floodlighting buildings. These range from 15 lux to 450 lux, depending on the ambient lighting conditions and the reflectance of the building surfaces, and have the objective of producing an acceptable level of overall building brightness.

The greatest mistake is to put too much light onto the building, thus washing it out. This commonly happens with discharge sources, where the lamps cannot be dimmed to achieve the desired levels. Site tests should be carried out to see exactly how the building will look within its surroundings.

Floodlighting

Floodlighting has always been the common term for exterior lighting, suggesting that this is all that is involved. Much bad lighting has been created because the building has been flooded with light without any regard to its form and shape, with a result which may appear flat and shapeless. Floodlighting has its place and cannot be ignored, but it should be soft and subtle and, where appropriate, should underscore any building highlighting. If the luminaires are positioned carefully in relation to the building then structural details can be highlighted. Great care should be taken with floodlighting to avoid glare to passers-by.

Highlighting

Most churches are historic buildings with a wealth of detail. The lighting should always seek to emphasize this detail in all its variety. Modelling the building gives the opportunity to create a pattern of light and shade which should leave in obscurity the less prominent elements of the building. This highlighting should be achieved by the use of luminaires with specific optical control giving beams of light geared to the area of building to be covered.

Window lighting

Many churches have particularly fine examples of stained glass windows which give great enjoyment when viewed from the inside against the sun. They can be equally attractive from the outside at night, if backlit from the inside. This backlighting can give life to a building and can add attractive and appropriate colour to the exterior view. Care will need to be taken to ensure that the effect of such lighting is not disturbing to those inside using the church, and to ensure that the luminaires are positioned in a manner sympathetic to the interior architecture.

LUMINAIRES

The choice of luminaires is crucial to the success of the finished scheme; a good lighting design can be ruined by inappropriate luminaires.

The choice of purely decorative luminaires has been discussed and will be very much governed by personal taste. The choice, however, of functional luminaires, whether floodlights or spotlights, can be very difficult. Once a lamp source and a desired beam spread has been chosen, consideration should be given to the form and bulk of the luminaire. It need not be of the period of the building, and usually cannot be, but it must sit sympathetically with the size, form and detail of the interior. Large industrial floodlights do not sit happily in a small mediaeval parish church, even if the light they give is exactly what is required. The finish and detailing should then be chosen to match or complement the material and style of the interior; for example, in old buildings with rough stone finishes a plain, natural metal finish can be very successful.

There is a large choice of luminaires from many different manufacturers, British, European and American and they are easy to obtain. If a luminaire of the ideal type and finish is not immediately obvious, keep looking; it is usually there. If the search continues to be fruitless then it is worth enquiring as to whether a manufacturer is willing to adapt or vary a standard luminaire; this is commonly done, and most manufacturers are only too happy to oblige. If this does not produce the desired result then recourse may be made to the design of special luminaires. Again this is very common in the lighting industry and is frequently necessary for special buildings, such as churches. A reputable manufacturer should be sought and a clear agreement should be made at the beginning on what is required and to what standard the luminaires will be built.

LIGHTING AND CONSERVATION

It should always be borne in mind that light can have a detrimental effect on certain materials and objects displayed in churches. All organic material is at risk under light and it must be remembered that light can cause not only colour change but also deterioration in strength.

Damage is caused by both visible and ultra-violet (UV) radiation. The likelihood of damage varies considerably according to the material concerned and increases the longer an object is exposed, and the more light to which it is exposed. Most damage caused both by visible and UV radiation comes from daylight, but artificial light can continue and aggravate the damage. It is rarely possible to treat the inside of a church like a museum and restrict light to the low level (around 50 lux) required by some fugitive materials so thought should be given to removing sensitive materials to a room where light can be strictly controlled. Care, however, should be taken to avoid unnecessary light on materials at risk.

SOURCES

The choice of the appropriate light source is vital to the proper creation of atmosphere. Unfortunately this is complicated by the fact that the question of finances comes into play. Few churches have spare resources, so the conservation of those resources is vital. Any lamp choice is a compromise between aesthetics and resources, a compromise which should be carefully made to avoid long-lasting errors.

The following notes on lamp sources attempt to set out the pros and cons in relation to both aesthetics and resources.

Tungsten and tungsten halogen

This is mainly the ordinary bulb for domestic use, but includes various types of candle lamps and linear halogen lamps with a colder, brighter light. It gives a warm soft quality of light in very localized situations. It is important to shield the lamp except where clear candle lamps are being used for specific decorative effects. The halogen lamps can be too stark without dimming. They are cheap to buy but do not have a long life, unless extended by dimming, so frequent replacement can be necessary. They consume a great deal of energy in relation to their light output, making it an expensive form of light but an attractive one.

Mains and low voltage reflector

These are sealed beam lamps with a diameter from 35 mm to over 200 mm with a large range of beam angles and wattages. They give controlled white light in a form which is very useful in a church. These lamps can do many of the lighting jobs required from downlighting to spotlighting particular objects. They are more expensive to buy than straightforward tungsten or tungsten halogen but can be used in cheaper luminaires. They are more energy efficient and longer lasting than tungsten.

Mercury and metal halide discharge

These are discharge sources which give a white and blue/white light. They can be useful if used in well-designed fittings which control the light, but they cannot be dimmed and can have a harsh effect. The luminaires and lamps are expensive to buy but are energy efficient particularly for long running uses such as exterior lighting.

Tubular and compact fluorescent

These are fluorescent lamps of the standard tubular variety and of the more modern compact type which can substitute for ordinary bulbs. They can be valuable for specialized uses and concealed lighting, but the colour can be distorting if high colour rendering tubes are not used. The compact lamps should be used as substitutes with care due to their ugly shape and low light output. They are relatively cheap and energy efficient.

High pressure sodium discharge

This is a discharge lamp which gives a golden white or orange colour. It is not recommended although some people find its warmth very inviting. It is more appropriate to exterior lighting although even here the bad colour rendering can distort the appearance of stonework. The luminaires and lamps are expensive but are very energy efficient, the most efficient of the lamps described, and long lasting.

LIGHTING CONTROL

Consideration of the luminaires is only part of the process when considering both aesthetics and resources. Aesthetically, individual luminaires are simply components in an overall picture created by the lighting. This overall picture, or lighting scene (a term used in lighting control to describe a combination of luminaires set at different levels), may only be one of several created to support different functions and activities in the church. There should be a method by which these lighting scenes can be reproduced accurately and easily. Frequently this is done by using a variety of switches. When the system is simple it will work well enough, but when many complex circuits are involved, as in a large Cathedral, it may not prove satisfactory.

The ideal solution to this problem is the installation of a central control system, using contactors for discharge sources and dimmers for filament sources, with control points located at strategic points in the building. There are many systems available, both large and small, which enable the programming of different scenes to be recalled at the press of a button. The selection of a scene will switch on the required discharge sources and fade the filament sources to the desired level. The dimming of filament sources is, perhaps, the most important tool in the creation of atmosphere by lighting. It allows the creation of a bright, happy atmosphere as well as a dim, solemn one. It allows the movement between different atmospheres in a subtle and imperceptible way. One of its more common uses is during a candelit carol service, where change from darkness to bright lighting, via candle lighting, is required at different times during the service.

Financially, a central control system can be of enormous benefit, enabling a tight control to be kept on running costs. With the addition of a time-clock and a photocell, to read daylight, automatic scenes can be programmed to bring up or take out the lighting at set times or particular daylight levels. This is most useful for exterior lighting but may also have uses in interior lighting. When the system is mainly a dimming system for filament lighting large cost savings can be made. The act of dimming reduces the amount of energy used and can dramatically increase the life of the lamps. Filament lamp life may be extended to that of discharge lamps, showing savings in maintenance costs, due to the cheapness of filament lamps: this can offset the increased energy costs of the more aesthetically pleasing filament source lighting schemes.

INSTALLATION AND WIRING

Electrical installation work, whether permanent or temporary, must be executed by competent electricians in accordance with the *Regulations for the Electrical Equipment of Buildings*, as published by the Institution of Electrical Engineers (currently in its sixteenth edition, 1991). These regulations are designed to ensure safety, especially from fire and electric shock. It is also important to ensure that the electricians are familiar with the types of equipment involved and with the problems of working with, and in, church buildings. In addition the booklet *Lighting and Wiring of Churches*, published by the Church of England Council for the Care of Churches, should be consulted, particularly with regard to types of wiring, as well as other matters discussed in this chapter.

All luminaires and other equipment added to an existing building should be as unobtrusive as possible. Finishes and methods of fixing should be appropriate and sensitive to the building and great care should be taken to ensure that no fixings physically damage the structure. Wiring should be concealed or at least camouflaged and control equipment should be neatly housed, if possible in existing enclosures.

There follow notes on common types of wiring installation with comments as to their suitability.

Flexible cords

These are not recommended for any part of the permanent installation, and should be used only with fused 13 amp plugs or final connections to the luminaires.

Sheathed twin and earth

This is not recommended for any part of the permanent installation other than in areas which are totally concealed and protected; even in this situation its use should be avoided if possible, as it is too prone to damage.

Mineral insulated cable

This is the ideal method of installation, particularly in old churches where much of the installation needs to be surface run. It has excellent protection against physical and fire damage.

Steel wire armoured

This is bulkier than mineral insulated cable and is thus less suitable for visible installations, but where the cable is not open to public view it is a good method of installation which has cost advantages over mineral insulated cable.

Plastic conduit

This is not recommended for aesthetic and safety reasons.

Metal conduit and trunking

This is a good method of installation where the installation cannot be seen and therefore aesthetics are not involved.

MAINTENANCE

Lighting installations should be properly maintained so that they continue to be as effective as when they were first installed. Regular servicing will achieve this and will ensure long life for the equipment. Servicing should be planned and should ideally be carried out by a professional contractor, commonly an electrical contractor. If servicing is carried out by members of the staff or congregation it is important to ensure that they know what they are doing. The following servicing must be carried out.

Cleaning

Luminaires, windows and rooflights must be cleaned at appropriate intervals: depending on how clean the atmosphere is, exterior luminaires will need to be cleaned more frequently than interior.

Lamp changing

Lamps should be changed at regular, planned intervals, ideally after a period of use somewhat less than their rated life. If replacement is only carried out when lamps fail then labour costs will be higher and there is a greater chance of incorrect lamps being inserted because the correct ones were not available.

Electrical

The installation should be regularly inspected by an electrical contractor and any alterations or additions should be carried out using the same methods as the original installation.

Concept

A regular assessment of the suitability of the installation should be carried out to ensure that old and inefficient equipment or methods are not being unnecessarily perpetuated. Lighting technology makes substantial advances year by year, and advantage should be taken of them where they result in a more efficient or more effective lighting scheme.

DESIGN

It is unrealistic to expect that people not versed in the art and technology of lighting can take the information laid out in this chapter and use it to design successful lighting schemes. The information is intended to be a general guide to good practice in the field as well as a more specific guide to the assessment of existing schemes and the formulation of briefs for new schemes. It is important that both the laity and the clergy with a responsibility for looking after churches appreciate what is involved in lighting and what is or is not possible. They may then brief and work confidently with people who will actually design the lighting schemes, knowing that they will obtain the most appropriate result for their needs.

The difficulty for many churches is in choosing who will actually design the scheme. There are different ways this may be achieved but they are essentially split into two types, free and paid design.

Free design work is carried out by lighting manufacturers and suppliers, electrical contractors and members of the congregation. The manufacturers and suppliers design lighting schemes with the specific and understandable intention of selling their own equipment. The scheme may or may not be competent, or even good, but is unlikely to be the best solution due to the limited range of equipment which that designer may have available. Contractors will design schemes in order to obtain the wiring contract but often they do not have detailed lighting skills. A member of the congregation must be judged on his merits, but it is a common mistake to allow an untrained person loose on a building because it is difficult to say no.

Paid design work puts the control in the hands of the church and the responsibility in the hands of the professional. Although at first sight it may seem an unnecessary expense, the benefits, in terms of quality and engineering, can more than repay this expenditure. Paid design work is carried out by lighting designers and consultants, architects and consulting electrical engineers. They all work professionally in their field and should have appropriate training and experience. It is important that before engaging a professional their previous work in the specialized field of church lighting is discussed. Architects and consulting engineers are more numerous and more frequently practice locally to a church but do not generally have the specialized skills of a lighting designer.

GRAHAM PHOENIX

Graham Phoenix is with Lighting Design Partnership, where he has been responsible for much ecclesiastical work, including the interior re-lighting of Durham Cathedral. He has always worked in lighting with early experience as a lighting designer in the theatre.

~ 17 ~

CONCLUSION AND
SOURCES OF ADVICE

✳

Peter Burman

This book has two main objectives. One is to serve as a 'pointer', to direct enquirers, who wish to know how best to look after their church, chapel or cathedral, towards the most fruitful and skilful course of action. The other objective is to provide a measure of *encouragement*. There are few problems or questions, especially relating to buildings constructed of traditional materials in traditional ways, which have not arisen before. There is therefore a large reservoir of knowledge and experience on which to draw.

But there are at least three cautions to bear in mind. One is that circumstances vary enormously from place to place and from time to time. So problems of rising damp, for instance, are not susceptible to the same panacea when the differing circumstances of a remote church on a windy hillside are compared with a land-locked city church standing in a paved churchyard. One church may be rich in financial resources, another struggling simply to pay its insurance and electricity bills. Then again, repair problems are often not reducible to standard answers or solutions – and this applies as much to twentieth century buildings as to mediaeval or post-mediaeval ones. And a third point is that the best answers often arise out of *dialogue*, out of interaction.

It cannot be stressed too strongly, therefore, that every church, chapel or cathedral needs to have good professional advice on a regular basis, something akin — as has been said before — to a family doctor

relationship. The principal adviser may be an architect or a building
surveyor (or 'a qualified person or persons', as it is stated in the Church
of England's *Care of Churches and Ecclesiastical Jurisdiction Measure
1992*). Others – a structural engineer, a heating or lighting consultant, a
conservator, an archaeologist, a landscape architect, an architectural
historian, a craftsman or an artist – may be needed from time to time.
There should be a sense of working in a team, involving both local
volunteer energies and the exercise of more distant professionals.

There is also much to be said for knowing where to turn for advice in
terms of organizations with specialist knowledge and experience.

In the Church of England context the principal sources are as follows.

1. The Council for the Care of Churches, 83 London Wall, London
    EC2M 5NA. Established in the 1920s, to be a focus for all the
    local Diocesan Advisory Committees for the Care of Churches,
    the CCC is a splendid example of a relatively small body doing
    an enormous good. Its publications are referred to in the
    Bibliography but it may be worthwhile saying here that a
    complete list and order form is available from its Publications
    Department, at the same address, and two very useful Advice
    Notes are available, in addition, entitled *Possible Sources of
    Grant Aid for Churches of Architectural or Historic Interest
    and Their Contents* and *Suggestions on Fund Raising for
    Church Repairs*, respectively. These two Advice Notes should
    be studied carefully by anyone considering organizing fund
    raising for church repairs, in any context. They are enormously
    helpful, and positive.

2. The local Diocesan Advisory Committee for the Care of
    Churches. Again, every diocese had established such a com-
    mittee by the early 1920s and the Secretary is now in many
    cases a full-time diocesan official and, in effect, a conservation
    officer for the diocese with a particular knowledge of and
    sympathy for churches, and their particular problems and
    opportunities. The addresses of the various DAC Secretaries
    may be found in the Diocesan Handbook or in the Church of
    England Yearbook.

3. In twenty-eight counties there now exists a local county trust
    for churches. Again the address of the correspondent may be
    obtained from the Diocesan Handbook, or from the Council for
    the Care of Churches or from the Historic Churches Preserva-
    tion Trust at Fulham Palace, London SW6 6EA. The great

advantage of the county trusts is that, being local, they have immense funds of local knowledge and expertise on which to draw; this is coupled with tremendous positive enthusiasm for preserving and caring for the churches and chapels of their respective counties. Generally speaking they take an interest in churches of all denominations, and their achievements have in recent years been quite outstanding. Very many county trusts run an annual sponsored bicycle ride which, on a particular Saturday in September, raises remarkably large sums of money for the repair of churches and chapels. They are very well worth supporting in every possible way.

In Scotland useful sources of advice are The Architectural Heritage Society of Scotland, The Glasite Meeting House, 33 Barony Street, Edinburgh EH3 6NX; Historic Scotland's Conservation Bureau at 3 Stenhouse Mill Lane, Edinburgh EH11 3LR; The Scottish Churches Architectural Heritage Trust (care of The Scottish Civic Trust, 24 George Square, Glasgow G2 1EF); and the Council for Scottish Archaeology, whose Director may be contacted care of Royal Museum of Scotland, York Buildings, 1 Queen Street, Edinburgh EH2 1JD.

In Wales, the conservation architects of Cadw are prepared to advise on choice of architects as well as on conservators and specialist contractors and the grants available from the Historic Buildings Council for Wales – through Cadw – are usually the most generous available. A handout is available from Cadw giving other sources, and the address to write to is: Cadw, Welsh Historic Monuments, Brunel House, 2 Fitzalan Road, Cardiff CF2 1UY (Cadw Ty Brunel, 2 Ffordd Fitzalan, Caerdydd CF2 1UY). A useful contact for chapels in Wales is the society called CAPEL whose secretary is currently Miss Susan Beckely, West Glamorgan Area Record Office, County Hall, Oystermouth Road, Swansea SA1 3SN.

For churches and chapels other than those belonging to the Church of England the publications of the Council for the Care of Churches will, nevertheless, be found almost equally helpful and relevant. Some denominations have their own sources of advice, like the Methodist Chapels Department.

Since December 1992 there has been a redefinition of the so-called 'Ecclesiastical Exemption' in England and Wales. All ecclesiastical buildings are subject to planning control, but the situation with regard to listed building control is much more complicated. Summing it up in a sentence, however, it will be found that the Church of England's

Faculty control system is regarded as being the equivalent of listed building control. Other denominations have been given the opportunity, by the Secretary of State for the National Heritage and by the Secretary of State for Wales, to establish equivalent systems of their own; or, if not, to be subject to listed building control in exactly the same way as listed secular buildings.

Perhaps it may be helpful to explain here briefly what is meant by 'listing' or by 'listed buildings'. In order to explain the context it is also worth saying that virtually all countries now have a way of identifying buildings, sites or structures which have a definable cultural value which, in the interests of the whole community, it seems desirable to preserve. In Great Britain we distinguish between 'ancient monuments' (which are placed on a schedule, and scheduled monument consent is required for alterations, demolition or repair) and 'listed buildings' (which are placed on a list of buildings having special architectural or historic merit – a chapel where Charles Wesley frequently preached, for instance, would be considered as having 'historic' value as well as, perhaps, architectural value). The majority of Church of England churches and cathedrals are listed, and a substantial proportion of them are listed Grade I or Grade II*. Many buildings belonging to other denominations, or indeed to other faiths, are also listed. So the question of listing, and whether a particular building is or is not subject to listed building control, is a very important one overall.

In England and Wales the exemption from listed building control, previously enjoyed across the board by ecclesiastical buildings in ecclesiastical use for worship, is retained now only for those bodies 'which subscribe to a Code of Practice, and agree to bring their internal arrangements for control of works to listed ecclesiastical buildings into conformity with the Code'. The Code of Practice provides that a church body's internal system of control over works to its listed buildings and to its unlisted buildings in conservation areas should embody the following principles.

1. All proposals for: (a) internal and external works for the demolition, alteration or extension of a listed church building which would affect its character as a building of special architectural or historic interest; and (b) works of demolition affecting the exterior of an unlisted church building in a conservation area, should be submitted for approval to a body which is independent of the local congregation or community proposing the works in question.

2. The decision-making body when considering proposals for works should be under a specific duty to take into account, along with other factors, the desirability of preserving historic church buildings, and the importance of protecting features of architectural merit and historic interest.

3. The decision-making body should either include, or have arrangements for obtaining advice from, persons with expert knowledge of historic church buildings.

4. The decision-making process should make provision for: (*a*) consultation with the local planning authority, English Heritage/Cadw and national amenity societies, allowing them (except in cases of emergency) twenty-eight working days in which to comment on the proposed works; (*b*) a notice describing the proposed works and inviting comments from any interested persons, to be displayed for the same twenty-eight-day period outside the building in a prominent position visible to the general public, and a similar notice to be published in a local newspaper circulating in the locality; (*c*) in cases of demolition, notification of the Royal Commission on the Historical Monuments of England/the Royal Commission on Ancient and Historical Monuments in Wales; and any representations made by these bodies or any other person in relation to such proposals should be taken into account before the decision is made.

5. There should be a clear and fair procedure for settling all disputes between the local congregation or community and the decision-making body as to whether proposals shall proceed.

6. The procedure of the church body should include arrangements for dealing with any breach of the control system, including provision for reinstatement of works to historic church buildings carried out without consent.

7. To permit effective monitoring, the church body should make arrangements for recording in the case of each proposal for works how the above procedures were implemented and the nature of the decision taken.

Where a church or religious body has chosen not to subscribe to the Code of Practice then the exemption will no longer obtain, and listed building consent will need to be sought (as well as, perhaps, planning permission) from the local planning authority, just as with a secular listed building. The local planning authority will bear in mind the desirability of giving 'due weight' to liturgical requirements. At the same time the Department of National Heritage (which is now responsible for listing in England, and for issues relating to the preservation of historic buildings) has made it clear that it is prepared to take appropriate action 'to bring within normal control any individual ecclesiastical building where a denomination subscribing to the Code proposes to authorize potentially damaging alterations for which wider scrutiny seems appropriate'.

The purpose of all this 'control', both ecclesiastical and secular, is to ensure adequate protection for buildings which constitute our architectural and cultural heritage.

In England, churches (and other buildings) listed Grade I or II* are eligible in principle for grant aid from English Heritage. In Wales the position is similar, in Scotland it is comparable; but for churches in Wales and Scotland advice with a more local flavour should be obtained from the sources indicated above. It is also worth bearing in mind that grants or loans for repairs or maintenance work may be obtained from the local authority under the *Local Authority (Historic Buildings) Act 1962.*

All churches, chapels and cathedrals should regard their English Heritage, Historic Scotland or Cadw officers and the Conservation Officers of local planning authorities as potential allies and friends. The officers of English Heritage, Historic Scotland and Cadw, and the Conservation Officers of local planning authorities, can provide immensely knowledgeable advice and enthusiastic support; and good counsel may lead to more successful applications for grant aid. But grant aid is not as important as correct action, and the most experienced and helpful advice is always worth having.

This is not an appropriate place to deal at length with the special situation regarding cathedrals, as it is well known to cathedral authorities. Suffice it to say that the *Care of Cathedrals Measure 1990* provides for a comprehensive system of care and control over the fabric, furnishings and works of art of all Church of England cathedrals. Every Church of England cathedral has a Cathedral Architect or Surveyor to the Fabric ('Surveyor' was the title Sir Christopher Wren himself was proud to bear at St Paul's Cathedral), and every Church of England cathedral also has a Fabric Advisory Committee of high calibre. In addition, there is a Cathedrals' Fabric Commission for England, at the national level whose address is the same as the Council for the Care of Churches.

BIBLIOGRAPHY

❋

Pride of place should go to those publications, thoroughly practical in content and helpful in tone, produced by the Council for the Care of Churches, English Heritage, Historic Scotland, Cadw and the Society for the Protection of Ancient Buildings (37 Spital Square, London E1 6DY) dealing with the care of old buildings in general, or with churches in particular. A selection is given below.

COUNCIL FOR THE CARE OF CHURCHES

The two key publications for the care of fabric are *How to Look After Your Church*, (1991 edition) and *A Guide to Church Inspection and Repair* (1986, amended reprint, with a particularly useful bibliography); the *Churchyards Handbook* (1988, fully revised edition) also incorporates a good Bibliography and a Directory of Useful Organizations. These publications and a list of all publications available may be obtained from the Publications Department of the Council for the Care of Churches at 83 London Wall, London EC2M 5NA.

ENGLISH HERITAGE

Ashurst, John and Ashurst, Nicola (1988) *Practical Building Conservation*, Gower Technical Press, in five volumes covering stone masonry; brick, terracotta and earth; mortars, plasters and renders; metals; and wood, glass, and resin. These are authoritative publications, expensive but immensely worthwhile.

Brereton, Christopher (1991) *The Repair of Historic Buildings: Advice on Principles and Methods*, English Heritage.

Michell, Eleanor (1988) *Emergency Repairs for Historic Buildings*, English Heritage.

In 1993 English Heritage published a comprehensive Catalogue of its own publications, and of publications available from elsewhere, which will be updated from time to time.

SOCIETY FOR THE PROTECTION OF ANCIENT BUILDINGS (SPAB)
The SPAB produces a whole series of technical pamphlets on topics such as *Outward-leaning walls, Cleaning stone and brick, Pointing of stone and brick walling, Control of damp in old buildings, Electrical wiring in old buildings,* and *Repair of timber frames and roofs;* and basic information sheets, such as *How to make limewash, The need for old buildings to breathe,* and *Tuck pointing in practice.*

ADDITIONAL WORKS
Ashurst, John (1983) *Mortars, Plasters and Renders in Conservation*, Ecclesiastical Architects' and Surveyors' Association.
Ashurst, John, and Dimes, Francis G. (1977) *Stone in Building: Its use and potential today*, Architectural Press.
Bidwell, T.G. (1977) *The Conservation of Brick Buildings: The repair, alteration and restoration of old brickwork*, Brick Development Association.
Binney, Marcus, and Burman, Peter (1977) *Change and Decay: The future of our churches*, Studio Vista.
Binney, Marcus, and Burman, Peter (1977) *Chapels and Churches: Who cares?* A report commissioned by the British Tourist Authority.
Brunskill, Ronald W., and Clifton-Taylor, Alec (1977) *English Brickwork*, Ward Lock.
Brunskill, Ronald W. (1985) *Timber Building in Britain*, Gollanz.
Brunskill, Ronald W. (1990) *Brick Building in Britain*, Gollanz.
Caroe, A.D.R. (1949) *Old Churches and Modern Craftsmanship**, Oxford University Press.
Castle, R.W. (1964) *Damp Walls: The causes and methods of treatment of dampness in structures*, Technical Press.
Charles, F.W.B. (1984) *Conservation of Timber Buildings*, Hutchinson.
Clifton-Taylor, Alec (1972) *The Pattern of English Building**, Faber and Faber.
Crafts Advisory Committee (Crafts Council) (1979) *Conservation Sourcebook: For conservators, craftsmen and those who have historic objects in their care*, Crafts Advisory Committee.
Feilden, Sir Bernard M. (1982) *Conservation of Historic Buildings**, Butterworth.
Insall, Donald W. (1972) *The Care of Old Buildings Today*, Architectural Press.
Powys A.R. (1929) *Repair of Ancient Buildings**, reprinted by SPAB in 1981.
Richardson, Barry A. (1978) *Remedial Treatment of Buildings*, Construction Press.
Thompson, Garry (1978) *The Museum Environment*, Butterworth.

CHURCHYARDS
Bailey, Brian (1987) *Churchyards of England and Wales*, Robert Hale.
Burgess, Frederick (1969) *English Churchyard Memorials*, SPCK paperback edition published in 1979.

* Notable classics, well worth reading and pondering.

Burgess, Pamela (1980) *Churchyards*, SPCK.

Burman, Peter and Stapleton, Henry (1988) *Churchyards Handbook*, CIO Publishing.

Child, Mark (1985) *Discovering Churchyards*, Shire Books.

Enright, D.J. (1987) *The Oxford Book of Death*, Oxford University Press.

Frazer, Harriet (1993 edition) *Memorials by Artists*, Harriet Frazer.

Greenoak, Francesca (1985) *God's Acre: The flowers and animals of the parish churchyard*, WI Books.

Harte, J.D.S. (1985) *Landscape, Land Use, and the Law*, E. & F.N. Spon.

Harvey, Michael (1987) *Carving Letters in Stone and Wood*, Bodley Head.

Kindersley, David, and Cardozo, Lida Lopes (1981) *Letters Slate Cut*, Lund Humphries.

Meller, Hugh (1985, second edition) *London Cemeteries: An illustrated guide and gazeteer*, Gregg International.

Morris, Richard (1983) *The Church in British Archaeology*, Council for British Archaeology Research Report, 47, Council for British Archaeology.

Russell Davies, M.R. (1982, fifth edition) *The Law of Burial, Cremation and Exhumation*, Shaw.

Stebbings, R.E., and Jeffries, D.J. (1982) *Focus on Bats, Their Conservation and the Law*, Nature Conservancy Council.

FURNISHINGS AND WORKS OF ART – GENERAL

Haslam, Richard *From Decay to Splendour: The repair of church treasures*, Council for the Care of Churches.

Sandwith, Hermione, and Stainton, Sheila (1992, second edition) *The National Trust Manual of Housekeeping*, Allen Lane/The National Trust.

Thomson, Garry (1986, second edition) *The Museum Environment*, Butterworth.

MURAL PAINTINGS

Burman, Peter (ed.) (1986) *Conservation of Wall Paintings – The International Scene*, CIO Publishing.

Case Studies in the Conservation of Stone and Wall Paintings (1986) Preprints of the Contributions to the Bologna Congress, 21–26 September 1986, International Institute for Conservation.

Mora, Paulo; Mora, Laura, and Philippot, Paul (1986) *Conservation of Wall Paintings*, Butterworth Series in Conservation and Museology.

Rodwell, Warwick (1990) *The Fishermen's Chapel, Saint Brelade, Jersey: Its archaeology, architecture, wall paintings and conservation*, Société Jersiaise and the Rector and Church Wardens of St Brelade.

Scott, Judith (1959) *The Conservation of English Wall Paintings* (being a Report of a Committee set up by the Central Council for the Care of Churches and the Society for the Protection of Ancient Buildings), Church Information Office.

HEATING

Arendt, C. (1976) *Heating Churches and the Protection of Monuments* (in German), Heiz. Luft. Haustsech **27** (2) pp. 435–441.

Becque, C.D. (1984) *Church Heating (Kerkverwarming)* (in Dutch), Verwarm. Vent., **41** (12) pp. 836–847.

Bordass, W. (1981) *The Role of Heating in Existing Churches*, Ecclesiastical Architects' and Surveyors' Association.
Bordass, W. (1984) *Heating Your Church*, CIO Publishing.

LIGHTING
CIBSE (1975) *Guide to the Outdoor Environment*, Chartered Institute of Building Services Engineers.
CIBSE (1984) *Code for Interior Lighting*, Chartered Institute of Building Services Engineers.
IEE (1991) *Regulations for the Electrical Equipment of Buildings* (sixteenth edition) Institute of Electrical Engineers.
Lighting and Wiring of Churches (1981), CIO Publishing.

SCULPTURE
Brodrick, A. and Darrah, J. (1986) *The fifteenth century polychromed limestone effigies of William Fitzalan, 9th Earl of Arundel, and his wife Joan Nevill, in the Fitzalan Chapel, Arundel*, Church Monuments, Volume 1, Part 2.
Clifton Taylor, A. (1972) *The Pattern of English Building*, Faber and Faber.
Davey N. (1976) *Building Stones of England and Wales*, Bedford Square Press.
Esdaile, K.A. (1946) *English Church Monuments 1510–1840*, Batsford.
Schaffer, R.J. (1972) *The Weathering of Natural Building Stones*, BRE.
Thompson, D.V. (1956) *The Materials and Techniques of Medieval Painting*, Dover.

STAINED GLASS
Ashurst, John (1988) *Practical Building Conservation (English Heritage Technical Handbook)* Vol. 5: Wood, Glass and Resins and Technical Bibliography. Gower Technical Press.
Bacher, Ernst (1977) *Medieval Stained Glass – Restoration and Conservation* Craft Advisory Committee Conservation Paper 5.
Conservation and Restoration of Stained Glass: An Owner's Guide (1988) The Census of Stained Glass Windows in America.
Kerr, Jill (1991) *The Repair and Maintenance of Glass in Churches*, Council for the Care of Churches.
Newton, Roy and Davison, Sandra (1989) *Conservation of Glass*, Butterworth.

TEXTILES
Finch, Karen and Putnam, Greta (1985) *The Care and Preservation of Textiles*, Batsford.
Gwynneth Mary, Sister CSPH, *Church Textiles – The making and care of altar linen and the care and repair of vestments*. Available from St Peter's Convent, Dovecote Lane, Horbury, Wakefield WF4 6BB.
NADFAS, *Inside Churches: a guide to church furnishings*, Capability Publishing Co.
Sandwith, Hermione and Stainton, Sheila (1992, second edition). *The National Trust Manual of Housekeeping*, Allen Lane/The National Trust.

METALWORK
Plowden, Anna and Hallahan, Frances (1987) *Looking After Antiques*, Pan Books.

FLOORS
Fawcett, Jane (1991) *Cathedral Floor Damage Survey*, ICOMOS UK.
Fowler, Daryl (1992) *Church Floors and Floor Coverings*, CIO Publishing.

PAINTINGS ON CANVAS AND WOOD
Ayres, James (1985) *The Artist's Craft*, Phaidon.
Bond, Francis (1908) *Screens and Galleries*, Oxford University Press.
Bond and Camm (1909) *Rood Screens and Rood Lofts* (2 vols), Pitman.
Cautley, H. Munro (1934) *Royal Arms and Commandments in our Churches*, Norman Adlard and Co.
Constable, W.G. (1963) *The Painter's Workshop*, Beacon Paperback, Oxford University Press.
Dirsztay, Patricia (1978) *Church Furnishings*, NADFAS Guide, Routledge and Kegan Paul.
Gettens and Stout (1966) *Painting Materials*, Dover.
Keck, Caroline K. (1965) *A Handbook on the Care of Paintings*, American Association for State and Local History.
Mayer, Ralph (1951) *The Artist's Handbook of Materials and Techniques*, Faber and Faber.
Mayer, Ralph (1976, third edition) *The Painter's Craft*, Nelson.
Sandwith, Hermione and Stainton, Sheila (1992, second edition) *The National Trust Manual of Housekeeping*, Allen Lane/National Trust.
Stephenson, Jonathan (1989) *The Materials and Techniques of Painting*, Thames and Hudson.
Stout, George L. (1975) *The Care of Pictures*, Dover.
Summers, Peter (ed.) (1976) *Hatchments in Britain*, Series volume for Norfolk and Suffolk, Phillimore.
The History and Techniques of the Great Masters (1988/9) Tiger Books International.
The Techniques of the World's Great Painters (1987) Tiger Books International.
Thompson, D.V. (1958) *The Materials and Techniques of Medieval Painting*, Dover (first edition).
Vallance, Aymer (1936) *English Church Screens*, Batsford.
Wehlte, Kurt (1987) *The Materials and Techniques of Painting*, Prentice Hall.
Winsor and Newton (1982) *Paint and Painting*, Tate Gallery.

PAINTED CEILINGS AND SCREENS
Binski, P. (1991) *Mediaeval Craftsmen: Painters*, British Museum Press.
Bond, F. (1908) *Fonts and Font Covers*, Oxford University Press.
Bond, F. (1908) *Screens and Galleries in English Churches*, Oxford University Press.
Bond, F. (1916) *The Chancel of English Churches*, Oxford University Press.
Bond, F.B. and Camm, D.B. (1909) *Rood Screens and Rood Lofts* (2 vols) Sir Isaac Pitman and Sons Ltd.
Cotton, S. (1987) Mediaeval rood-screens in Norfolk, their construction and painting dates, *Norfolk Archaeology*, Vol. 40, part 1, 44–54.
Cox, J.C. and Harvey, A. (1907) *English Church Furniture*, Methuen.
Cox, J.C. (1915) *Pulpits, Lecterns and Organs in English Churches*, Oxford University Press.

Hall, M. (1992) Magnify the Lord, *Country Life*, Vol. CLXXXVI, No. 20, 14 May.

Harrison, H.M.J. (1986) A Hidden Gem, *Church Building*, Summer, 23–24.

Harvey, J. (1975) *Mediaeval Craftsmen*, Batsford.

Haslam. R. (1985) *From Decay to Splendour: the Repair of Church Treasures*, Council for the Care of Churches.

Howard, F.E. and Crossley, F.H. (1927, second edition) *English Church Woodwork. A Study in Craftsmanship during the Mediaeval Period AD 1250–1550*, Batsford.

Hulbert, A.C. (1986) Right Royal Restoration, *Church Building*, 21–22.

Hulbert, A.C. (1987) Notes on Techniques of English Mediaeval Polychromy on Church Furnishings. *Recent Advances in the Conservation and Analysis of Artifacts*, ed. J. Black, Institute of Archaeology Press, University of London, pp. 277–279, plus long erratum slip.

Hulbert, A.C. (1991) Mediaeval Paintings and Polychromy, *Exeter Cathedral: A Celebration*, ed. M.J. Swanton, Southgate Publishers for the Dean and Chapter, pp. 90–97.

Keyser, C.E. (1883, third edition) *A List of Buildings in Great Britain and Ireland having Mural and Other Painted Decorations, of Dates Prior to the Latter Part of the Sixteenth Century, with Historical Introduction and Alphabetical Index of Subjects*, Eyre and Spottiswoode for HMSO.

Lasko, P. and Morgan, N.J. (eds) (1973) *Medieval Art in East Anglia 1300–1530*, Jarrold and Sons Ltd.

Plummer, P. (1959) Restoration of a retable in Norwich Cathedral, *Studies in Conservation*, 4, pp. 106–115.

Plummer, P. (1965) Restoration of a fifteenth century English pulpit, *Studies in Conservation*, 10, pp. 168–175.

Plummer, P. (1980) The Ranworth Rood Screen *Archaeological Journal*, 137, pp. 292–295.

Plummer, P. and Hulbert, A.C. (1990) English polychromed church screens and the problems of their conservation in situ, *Cleaning, Retouching and Coatings: Technology and Practice for Easel Paintings and Polychrome Sculpture*, edited by Mills, J.S., and Smith, P. (Preprints of the contributions to the Brussels Congress 3–7 September 1990) London, International Institute for Conservation of Historic and Artistic Works, pp. 47–51.

Rouse, E.C. (1939) Painting in Penn Church, *Records of Bucks*, vol. XIII, part 5, pp. 362–363.

Rouse, E.C. (1953) Painting on the Walls and Timber Ceiling of the Central Tower of St Albans Cathedral, *St Albans Architectural and Archaeological Society Transactions*, pp. 98–102.

Rouse, E.C. (1973) North Crawley: cleaning and conservation of the screen, *Records of Bucks*, Vol. XIX, part 3, p. 352.

Thompson, D.V. (1936, reprinted 1956) *Materials and Techniques of Mediaeval Painting*, Dover.

Vallance, A. (1936) *Greater English Church Screens, being Great Roods. Screen-work and Roof-Lofts of Parish Churches in England and Wales*, Batsford.

Vallance, A. (1947) *Greater English Church Screens, being Great Roods, Screen-work and Roof-Lofts in Cathedral, Monastic and Collegiate Churches in England and Wales*, Batsford.

Williamson, W.W. (1956) Saints on Norfolk rood-screens and pulpits, *Norfolk Archaeology*, vol. 31, part 31, part 3, pp. 299–346.

BOOKS AND MANUSCRIPTS
Thomson, Garry (1986, second edition) *The Museum Environment*, Butterworth.

WOODEN FURNITURE
Cesinsky, Herbert and Gribble, Ernest (1922) *Early English Furniture and Woodwork*, Waverly.
Cesinsky, Herbert, *English Furniture of the Eighteenth Century*, Waverly.
Hayward, Charles H. (1971) *English Period Furniture*, Evans Bros.
Richardson, Barry A. (1978) *Wood Preservation*, The Construction Press.
Rogers, John C. (1973) *English Furniture*, Spring Books.

See also listings above, especially works by John and Nicola Ashurst, Garry Thomson, Hermione Sandwith and Sheila Stainton.

Publications of the British Wood Preserving Association and the Building Research Establishment may be found helpful, but they are, generally speaking, more concerned with the conservation problems of structural timber.

ORGANS AND OTHER MUSICAL INSTRUMENTS
Dickson, W.E. (1983) *Practical Organ-Building*, Oxford University Press.
Praet, W. (1989) *Organ Dictionary*, Zwijndrecht.
Sumner, W.L. (1973) *The Organ*.
Thistlethwaite, N. (1990) *The Making of the Victorian Organ*, Cambridge University Press.
Wickens, D.C. (1987) *The Instruments of Samuel Green*.
William, P. and Owen, B. (1980) *The Organ*.

BELLS AND BELFRIES
Council for the Care of Churches (1993) *The Conservation and Repair of Bells and Bellframes*, Church House Publishing, for the Council for the Care of Churches.
Elphick, George (1970) *Sussex Bells and Belfries*, Phillimore.
Elphick, George (1988) *The Craft of the Bellfounder*, Phillimore.
Frost, A.J. (ed.) (1990) *Towers and Bells: A Handbook*, Central Council of Church Bellringers.
Jennings, Trevor (1991) *The Development of British Bell Fittings*, Jennings.
Pickford, Chris (1993) *Bellframes: A practical guide to inspection and recording*, Pickford.
Walters, H.B. (1912, reprinted 1977) *Church Bells of England*, Oxford University Press, EP Publishing respectively.

CHURCH CLOCKS
Beeson, C.F.C. (1971) *English Church Clocks 1280–1850*, Phillimore.

DECORATIVE PLASTERWORK
Ashurst, John (1982) *Mortars, Plasters and Renders in Conservation*, Ecclesiastical Architects & Surveyors Association.

Bankart, George (1908) *The Art of the Plasterer*, Batsford.
Beacham, Peter (ed.) (1990) *Devon Building* (especially Chapter 7 by John Thorp, Wallpainting and Lime Plaster Decoration), Devon Books.
Beard, Geoffrey (1975) *Decorative Plasterwork in Great Britain*, Phaidon.
Jourdain, Margaret (1926) *English Decorative Plasterwork of the Renaissance*, Batsford.

FURTHER USEFUL
ADDRESSES

❊

PAINTINGS ON CANVAS AND WOOD

Artists' Materials
L. Cornelissen & Son, 105 Great Russell Street, London WC1 3RY. Tel. 071-636
    1045.
Daler Rowney, 12 Percy Street, London W1A 2BP. Tel. 071-636 8241.
A.P. Fitzpatrick, also conservation materials, 1 Barnabas Studios, 10–22 Barnabas
    Road, London E9 5SB. Tel. 081-985 7865.
E.Ploton (Sundries) Ltd, 273 Archway Road, London N6 5AA. Tel. 081-348 0315.
Winsor and Newton Ltd, 51 Rathbone Place, London W1P 1AB. Tel. 071-636 4231.

Brass strips, screws, picture hooks, chain, wire
J. Shiner and Sons Ltd, 8, Windmill Street, London W1 1HF. Tel. 071-580 0740.

Brushes
Local art shop, decorators', local hardware stores.
Canvas – natural and synthetic
Russell and Chapple, 23 Monmouth Street Shaftesbury Avenue, London WC2H
    9DE. Tel. 071-836 7521.
Bird and Davis Ltd, 45, Holmes Road, Kentish Town, London NW1 3AN. Tel. 071-
    485 3797.

Conservation quality boards
Order from local framing shop, or Atlantis, 146 Brick Lane, London E1 6RU. Tel.
    071-377 8855.

Goggles, gloves (Solvent proof)
Local health and safety suppliers.

Hardboard, Correx
Builders suppliers.

Hypodermic syringes
Local chemist, veterinary suppliers, or John Bell and Croydon, Wigmore Street, London.

Insecticide
Wykamol, Rentokill, local hardware store, builders' suppliers.

Masks (dust and fume)
Local hardware store, or Health and Safety suppliers.

Plastic sheeting, bubble wrap
Local hardware store, builders suppliers, garden centres.

Tapes (sellotape, packaging tape, gummed paper tape)
Stationery suppliers.

Tools
Buck and Ryan Ltd, 101 Tottenham Court Road, London W1P 0DY. Tel. 071-636 7475.

Various conservation materials
Arcesso, 194 Blue House Lane, Oxted, Surrey RH8 0DE. Tel. 0883 730304.
Atlantis, 146 Brick Lane, London E1 6RU. Tel. 071-377 8855.
Conservation Resources (UK) Ltd, Unit 1, 2, 4 Pony Road, Horspath Industrial Estate, Cowley, Oxfordshire OX4 2RD. Tel. 0865 747755.
Picreator Enterprises Ltd, 44 Park View Gardens, Hendon, London NW4 2PN. Tel. 081-202 8972.
Preservation Equipment Ltd, Shelfanger, Diss, Norfolk IP2 2DG. Tel. 0379 651527.

METALWORK
Conservation Unit, Museums and Galleries Commission, 16 Queen Anne's Gate, London SW1H 9AA. Tel. 071-233 3683.
Council For the Care of Churches, 83 London Wall, London EC2N 5NA. Tel. 071-638 0971.
Monumental Brass Society, c/o Society of Antiquaries, Burlington House, London W1V 0HS.
United Kingdom Institute for Conservation, 6 Whitehouse Mews, London SE1 7QD. Tel. 071-620 3371.

Acid free tissue
Atlantis Fine Art Suppliers, 2 St Andrew's Way, Bow, London E3 3PA. Tel. 071-537 2727.
Faulkner Fine Papers Ltd, 76 Southampton Row, London WC1B 4AR. Tel. 071-831 1151.

Synperonic NDB
Conservation Resources (UK), Units 1, 2, 4, Pony Road, Horspath Industrial Estate, Cowley, Oxfordshire OX4 2RD. Tel. 0865-747755.

Tarnprufe
Tarnprufe Co. Ltd, 68 Nether Edge Road, Sheffield S7 1RY. Tel. 0742 553652.

BOOKS AND MANUSCRIPTS

Atlantis Paper Company Ltd, 2 St Andrews Way, London E3 3PA. (Supplier of acid-free paper for four-flap folders, polyester enclosures.)

The Institute of Paper Conservation, Leigh Lodge, Leigh, Worcestershire WR6 5LB. (General advice, Register of Conservators, framing leaflet.)

The Conservation Unit, Museums and Galleries Commission, 16 Queen Anne's Gate, London SW1H 3AA 9AA. (Register of Conservators.)

C.A. Coutts Ltd, Violet Road, London E3 3QL. (Phase boxes.)

Conservation Resources (UK) Ltd, Unit 1, Pony Road, Horspath Industrial Estate, Cowley, Oxfordshire OX4 2RD. (RH test strips, polyester enclosures.)

Secol Ltd, Howlett Way, Thetford, Norfolk IP24 1HZ. (Polyester enclosures.)

Casella London Ltd, Regent Hoouse, Wolseley Road, Kempston, Bedford MK42 7JY. (Thermohygrographs, max–min thermometers, UV filters for fluorescent tubes.)

CLE Design Ltd, 69–71 Haydons Road, Wimbledon, London SW19 1HQ. (Room humidifier.)

Commonwealth Mycological Institute, Ferry Lane, Kew, Surrey TW9 3AF. (Advice on micro-organisms.)

Drying Restoration Service, Building 488T6, Harwell Laboratory, Oxfordshire OX11 0RA. (Vacuum drying and emergency hotline.)

Polyformes Ltd, Cherrycourt Way, Stanbridge Road, Leighton Buzzard, Bedfordshire LU7 8UH. (Foam block book supports.)

J. Chamberlain, 88 Wensley Road, Woodthorpe, Nottingham NG5 4JU. (UV filters for windows.)

INDEX

❋